D0821927

Performance-Based Evaluation

Jon,

Hope you find the ideas useful.

Judy

Performance-Based Evaluation

Tools and Techniques to Measure the Impact of Training

Judith Hale

JOSSEY-BASS/PFEIFFER
A Wiley Company
www.pfeiffer.com

Published by

JOSSEY-BASS/PFEIFFER

A Wiley Company
989 Market Street
San Francisco, CA 94103-1741
415.433.1740; Fax 415.433.0499
800.274.4434; Fax 800.569.0443

www.pfeiffer.com

Library of Congress Cataloging-in-Publication Data
Hale, Judith A.
    Performance-based evaluation: tools and techniques to measure
        the impact of training / Judith Hale.
            p. cm.
    Includes bibliographical references and index.
    ISBN 0-7879-6035-7 (alk. paper)
    1. Employees—Training of—Evaluation. I. Title.
    HF5549.4.T7 H35 2002
    658.3'124—dc21
                                                    2002003255

Printing 10 9 8 7 6 5 4 3 2 1

Cover Design: Laurie Anderson

Dedication

To Pearl for her unwavering emphasis on being practical and to Ron for his unrelenting optimism. They were both class acts.

Contents

List of Exhibits, Tables, and Figures

CD-ROM Contents

Preface

This book is based on twenty-five years of experience working with individuals and organizations to come up with better ways to evaluate programs and people's performance. One of the paradoxes that happens too frequently is that organizations have an overabundance of available information, yet believe they lack the data they require and the funds and time to obtain it. It is my hope this book provides the reader with the courage to question what is available and to balance the need for the important information against the desire for precision and perfection.

AUDIENCE FOR THE BOOK

The primary audience for this book is human resource and training professionals whose organizations invest significant resources in programs to improve individual, team, and organizational performance. The tips, guidelines, and tools are designed to be easy, friendly, and practical, yet garner the information required to support better decisions about what is and is not working, why, and what to do about it.

ACKNOWLEDGMENTS

Some very special people played a major role in helping make this book possible. They painstakingly read the first draft of every chapter and added insights, examples, and guidance. They are Ann Berasley, MBA, Revenue Analyst Comptroller's Office, State of Texas; Mike Brogan, Manager of Organizational Development, Metropolitan Washington Airports Authority; Ruth Clark, Principal, Clark Training and Consulting; Skip Douglas, Training Team Leader, Lucent; France Gagnon, Contractor, Instructional Designer; Barbara Gough, Contractor, Instructional Designer; Cordell Hauglie, Organizational Advisor Delivery Systems Consulting & Training, Certification and Training,

Boeing; David R. Haskett, Manager, Learning Design & Development, Johnson Controls, Inc.; Karen G. Kroczek, Technical Skills Development, Plant Facilities and Services Division, Argonne National Laboratory; Miki Lane, Senior Partner, MVM Communications; Dean R. Larson, Ph.D. CSP CEM CPEA, Department Manager, Safety & Industrial Hygiene, U.S. Steel—Gary Works; Annemarie Laures, Corporate Manager in Performance Development, Walgreen Co.; Jim Momsen, Contractor, Instructional Designer; Karen Preston, Corporate Manager of Performance Development, Walgreen Co.; George Pollard, Assistant Professor of Education and Director of Advance Programs, Crichton College; Annette Rolls, Learning Development Consultant, Hewitt, Inc.; Tim Scudder, CEO, Personal Strengths Publishing, Inc.; Kenneth Silber, Ph.D., Associate Professor, Educational Technology, Research and Assessment, Northern Illinois University; Brenda Sugrue, Principal, Elearnia; Ray Svenson, President, Ray Svenson Consulting; Guy Wallace, Partner, CADDI.

I was fortunate to have the confidence of Kathleen Dolan Davies and Matt Davis of Jossey-Bass/Pfeiffer, whose support made this book possible. Special thanks goes to my friend Sue Simons, who continues to encourage me to be true to my style of simplicity and directness.

Introduction

I have given a lot of speeches about evaluation over the last twenty-six years. What continues to amaze me is the amount of expressed interest people have in evaluation compared to the amount of effort they put into it. If evaluation is so important, why aren't more people doing it and doing it well? I'm sure there are a lot of reasons, and the ones that I hear about are that people don't know why they should evaluate, how to do it cost-effectively, and what they would change or do differently based on the results. Some people feel guilty, others are just curious, and still others are afraid.

There are a number of reasons to evaluate. The main one is to get better at what we do. Evaluating helps us improve the quality of our work, better predict future costs, and prove that what we do makes a difference. This means we have to get better at finding out why performance does or does not happen, what our work is expected to change, and then measuring the impact of our work. We also have to get better at evaluating organizations' readiness to support the behaviors and results they say they want. Otherwise, too much of our work will be transient. If we do this, we will be respected and our efforts will be taken seriously.

This book was written specifically to help you:

- Prove that what you do matters and
- Show that you are a good steward of the organization's resources

It explains why you should evaluate, what to evaluate, when to do it, how to do it cost-effectively, and how to use the results wisely. Throughout the book, references are made to the overall process of measurement shown in Exhibit I.1.

Exhibit I.1. Basic Process for Measurement

1. Decide why you want to measure, what the outcome is that you want, and what questions you want answered as a result of measuring.
2. Determine what you want to measure.
3. Determine whether the subject you are interested in is currently measured. If it is, determine whether the measures are still adequate.
4. Set up new measures or revise the current measures, if necessary.
5. Estimate what effect the act of measuring might have on performance.
6. Decide how precise and certain you need to be.
7. Decide methods you will use to obtain the data you want.
8. Implement the measurement plan.
9. Analyze the results.
10. Determine whether action is required based on the results of the analysis.
11. Take action to improve performance.
12. Start over.

EVALUATION VERSUS MEASUREMENT

In the book, I make a distinction between two concepts: (1) evaluation and (2) measurement. *Evaluation* is about making judgments or placing value. *Measurement* is about gathering data, comparing what you learn to some expectation or standard, and then using what you learn to make changes. The irony is that evaluation is happening all of the time. For example, companies send people to training, which says they value it. Organizations' collective annual investment is estimated to be in the billions of dollars. The important point is that a lot of resources are consumed in the creation, delivery, maintenance, and participation of training. There are reasons why organizations choose training as a solution, for example, it seems valid on the face of it, as people cannot perform if they lack skills and knowledge. It can seem the right thing to do because we believe that training can make things better, or, in the worst case, training is evidence of doing something when no one wants to address the real problem. The organization and the people have already done an evaluation. What isn't happening is measurement. The power of measurement is that it helps you confirm why training is thought to be the best solution and whether, when implemented, it fulfilled the need. Measurement can and should happen:

- *In the beginning*—called *assessment and analysis* or discovery and used to find out whether action is required and what type of action is more likely to produce meaningful results. When done in advance of an intervention, it helps focus management's attention on results and training and HR's attention on performance.

- *During the process*—called *formative evaluation* and used to find out whether you are on track and should continue as planned or take corrective action.

- *At the end*—called *summative evaluation* and used to find out whether or not what you did met a need or actualized an opportunity and why.

The challenge is deciding what to measure. You can measure what and how much you produce, how you go about producing it, the client's readiness to make use of what you produce, and the consequences of the client using your work. Once you know what you want to measure, you can decide how to do it in a way that the benefits gained from what you learn outweigh the cost of obtaining the information.

TWO PREMISES

There are two underlying premises in this book.

1. Programs designed to improve human performance are *not* equal in intent or structure. For example, training is done for different reasons and not all programs—even though they are called training—actually train. Similarly, performance appraisal processes are done for different reasons and not all of them result in people getting an accurate assessment of their performance or timely constructive feedback. Therefore, what measures and measurement methods you use depend on the program's intent and structure.

2. The effectiveness of a performance support technology depends on the adequacy of performance management systems and the capability and capacity of the organization's infrastructure. Understanding this premise will help you select the appropriate measures and methods to evaluate:

   - The efficiency and effectiveness of your *performance support technologies,* such as training, job aids, mentoring, help desks, and electronic support systems, and their delivery mechanisms.

   - The adequacy of the *performance management system* (hiring criteria, performance goals and measures, incentive programs, and performance feedback systems) to reinforce the skills and behaviors the performance support technology is expected to instill.

   - The capability and capacity of the *organization's infrastructure* (the information and communication systems, the design of jobs and processes, and the adequacy of equipment and facilities) to enable the desired performance.

KEY DEFINITIONS

In the area of evaluation, a lot of words are used, such as assessment, analysis, measurement, metrics, measures, criteria, and so forth. These words add richness to our conversations and help us make fine distinctions when presenting an argument about why something should be done or done differently. At the same time, these words can add confusion without agreement on some core distinctions. Here are the key words and their definitions.

- *Evaluation* is placing judgment or valuing the adequacy of something. You judge things as good, bad, important, worthy, or insignificant, and so on.

- *Measures* are the features or attributes on which your judgments are based. They are frequently very personal and may not be fully expressed so that others can understand or discuss them. They can be facts and feelings. Many of the tools in this book are designed to make the measures explicit so they can be understood and questioned as to their appropriateness.

- *Metrics* are units of measurement. They are frequently expressed as time, dollars, weight, frequency, quantity, and the like. They help you to be precise in your measurements.

- *Criteria* can be a synonym for measures and metrics, depending on how specific you are in your language. For example, if you are going to evaluate a program's effectiveness based on its return on investment (ROI), ROI is a measure. If you specify an ROI greater than 5 percent, the expected minimum percentage is a metric. Therefore, criteria are the features or attributes you consider when judging the adequacy of something. When the term is used in conjunction with weights, percentages, and so forth, it is about metrics.

- *Measurement* and *measuring* are the act of gathering data and making comparisons so you can judge whether and how well something meets your needs. Measurement at the beginning is usually called assessment. Measurement at the end is called evaluation.

- *Assessment* is a synonym for measurement. It is the act of finding out, discovering what is or is not true or present so you can decide whether further inquiry or action is required. Sometimes it is used in relation to people, that is, assessing skills and knowledge. In this case it is still measurement because your goal is to gather information about people, compare what you learn to some expectation, and then decide whether or not further action is necessary.

- *Analysis* can mean both the act of diagnosis and the manipulation and interpretation of data. It usually involves some type of calculation and the application of mathematical concepts to reach conclusions based on more than intuition or one's personal perspective.

ORGANIZATION OF THE BOOK

The book is divided into twelve chapters. The first two chapters are about why you should measure. Chapters Three through Eight are about what you measure. Chapters Nine through Twelve are about how to collect and analyze data. Every chapter has examples, tools with guidelines on how to use them, common missteps, tips, and suggestions on where to learn more. The stories, tips, and tools illustrate how the ideas in the book can be applied to training and non-training solutions.

Chapter One, "Evaluation as a Strategy." This chapter is about using evaluation as a strategy for identifying, using, and measuring the effectiveness of programs and resources. It has guidelines on how to incorporate evaluation as a "way of doing business" instead of as an add-on activity. The tools in this chapter include:

- Tool 1.1: Understand Your Business Model
- Tool 1.2A: Customer Profile
- Tool 1.2B: Sample Customer Survey
- Tool 1.3A: Steps for Evaluating Your Product Portfolio
- Tool 1.3B: Product Portfolio Worksheet 1
- Tool 1.3C: Product Portfolio Worksheet 2
- Tool 1.3D: Product Portfolio Worksheet 3
- Tool 1.4A: How to Evaluate Vendors, Contractors, and Consultants
- Tool 1.4B: How to Evaluate Off-the-Shelf Programs

Chapter Two, "Why Measure Effectiveness and Efficiency." This chapter presents the idea that there is much to be gained from looking at evaluation from different perspectives. It describes the importance of measuring both effectiveness and efficiency. The chapter includes the following tools:

- Tool 2.1: Identifying What to Measure
- Tool 2.2: Sample Measures, Metrics, and Desired Results

Chapter Three, "How to Measure Effectiveness." This chapter includes tools and tips for when and how to apply effectiveness measures (the results of what you do in terms of learning, acceptance, adoption, change, improvement, and so on). It contains numerous examples of measures. The chapter includes the following guidelines and tools:

- Tool 3.1: Guidelines for Measuring Reactions
- Tool 3.2: Guidelines for Measuring Learning

- Tool 3.3: Guidelines for Measuring the Transfer of Learning
- Tool 3.4A: Guidelines for Measuring Results
- Tool 3.4B: Guidelines for Measuring Financial Impact

Chapter Four, "How to Measure Efficiency." This chapter includes tools and tips for when and how to apply efficiency measures (how you operate in terms of speed, cost, resource consumption, and so on). It contains numerous examples of measures. The chapter includes the following guidelines and tools:

- Tool 4.1: How to Measure Inputs
- Tool 4.2: How to Evaluate Processes
- Tool 4.3: How to Do Formative Evaluations

Chapter Five, "How to Measure Hard and Soft Skills." Here you will learn how to measure programs designed to increase easily observable skills compared to skills that do not lend themselves to direct observation but require you to infer their presence or absence through indirect evidence. The chapter includes the following guidelines and tools:

- Tool 5.1: Questions to Identify Behaviors, Choices, or Outputs Expected as a Result of Training
- Tool 5.2A: Action Verbs for the Cognitive Domain
- Tool 5.2B: Action Verbs for the Affective Domain
- Tool 5.2C: Action Verbs for the Psychomotor Domain
- Tool 5.3: How to Measure the Probability That Training Will Increase Cognitive and Psychomotor Skills
- Tool 5.4: How to Measure the Probability That Training Will Increase Affective Skills

Chapter Six, "How to Measure Required and Mandated Programs." This chapter explains how to evaluate programs designed to prepare people to do specific jobs and those done in response to regulatory requirements. It explains how to evaluate programs that are designed only to convey information. The chapter includes the following guidelines and tools:

- Tool 6.1: How to Determine the Driver
- Tool 6.2: How to Evaluate a Job/Task Analysis
- Tool 6.3: How to Evaluate Required Training
- Tool 6.4: How to Evaluate Mandated Training

Chapter Seven, "How to Measure Elective Training and Employee Relations Programs." Here you will learn how to evaluate programs done on the assumption they will impact retention, increase employee satisfaction, or improve performance. I explain how to evaluate programs that are designed only to convey information. The chapter includes the following guidelines and tools:

- Tool 7.1: How to Evaluate Elective Training and Employee Relations Programs
- Tool 7.2A: Measuring Probability
- Tool 7.2B: Discussion Guide 1
- Tool 7.2C: Discussion Guide 2
- Tool 7.2D: Alternative Futures Worksheet
- Tool 7.2E: Sample Comparisons Worksheet
- Tool 7.2F: Payoff Table Worksheet
- Tool 7.2G: Sample Payoff Table
- Tool 7.3A: How to Evaluate Programs That Just Inform
- Tool 7.3B: How to Determine the Reading Level of a Message

Chapter Eight, "How to Evaluate Delivery Alternatives." This chapter contains guidelines for comparing different delivery systems, including e-learning, and self-paced and group-paced methods. It considers instructional integrity, instructional requirements, and direct and indirect costs. This chapter will present guidelines on how to select an effective combination of delivery methods. The tools in this chapter include:

- Tool 8.1A: Deciding on the Criteria
- Tool 8.1B: Rating and Ranking Criteria
- Tool 8.1C: Comparison of Systems to Requirements
- Tool 8.2: Cost/Cost Comparisons
- Tool 8.3: Cost/Benefit Valuing Alternatives

Chapter Nine, "How to Sample People and Documents." This chapter contains an explanation of the importance of polling the right quantity from the right sources to assure that your finding and recommendations are solid. The chapter includes the following guidelines and tools:

- Tool 9.1: How to Define a Population
- Tool 9.2A: Sample Sizes for Small Populations
- Tool 9.2B: Sample Sizes for Small to Medium Size Populations

Chapter Ten, "How to Collect Data." This chapter contains a description of eight different methods for obtaining data. It explains what methods are best suited for assessment, evaluation, or both; how to use checklists; and how to qualify reviewers. The chapter includes the following guidelines and tools:

- Tool 10.1A: Description of Commonly Used Data-Gathering Methods
- Tool 10.1B: Best Use of Different Data-Collection Methods
- Tool 10.2A: Rules for Designing and Conducting an Open Interview
- Tool 10.2B: Planning the Open Interview
- Tool 10.3A: Rules for Designing and Conducting Structured Interviews
- Tool 10.3B: Sample Structured Interview Form
- Tool 10.4: Rules for Designing and Using the Critical-Incident Interview Technique
- Tool 10.5: Rules for Designing and Using Surveys and Questionnaires
- Tool 10.6: Rules for Designing and Conducting Focus Groups
- Tool 10.7: Rules for Designing and Using the Nominal Group Technique
- Tool 10.8A: Rules for Designing and Using the Sociogram Technique
- Tool 10.8B: Sample Sociogram Worksheet
- Tool 10.9: Rules for Designing and Using a Flanders Interaction Analysis
- Tool 10.10: Rules for Designing Checklists to Support Observations and Document Reviews
- Tool 10.11: Guidelines for Qualifying Reviewers

Chapter Eleven, "How to Analyze Data Using Descriptive Statistics." This chapter has rules for interpreting qualitative and quantitative data and how to determine whether or not a result is significant. The guidelines and tools in this chapter include:

- Tool 11.1: How to Analyze Qualitative Data
- Tool 11.2: Rules for Analyzing Counts
- Tool 11.3: Rules for Analyzing Data Derived from Surveys and Question-naires
- Tool 11.4: Analyzing Nominal Group Data
- Tool 11.5: Analyzing Critical-Incident Data
- Tool 11.6: How to Analyze Flanders Interaction Analysis Data

Chapter Twelve, "How to Analyze Data Using Inferential Statistics." Here you will find rules and guidelines for comparing actual results against expected results and determining whether or not a correlation exists. The tips and techniques are designed to make you a smart user of measurement tools, not a statistician. The guidelines and tools in this chapter include:

- Tool 12.1: If/Then Table for Deciding Which Type of Analysis to Use
- Tool 12.2A: Rules for Calculating a Rank Order Correlation Coefficient (Spearman Rho)
- Tool 12.2B: Formula for Rho
- Tool 12.2C: Worksheet for Calculating Rho
- Tool 12.3A: Rules for Applying Chi-Square Goodness of Fit
- Tool 12.3B: Worksheet for Calculating Chi-Square
- Tool 12.3C: Distribution of Chi-Square Values
- Tool 12.4A: Rules for Analyzing Data Derived from Structured Interviews Using Chi-Square or Rho
- Tool 12.4B: Sample Structured Interview Form
- Tool 12.5A: Rules for Using the Two-Tailed *t* Test
- Tool 12.5B: *t* Test Worksheet
- Tool 12.5C: Formula for Calculating *t* Scores
- Tool 12.5D: Distribution of *t* Probability Table

WHY THE EMPHASIS ON TOOLS

The tools and techniques throughout the book serve a number of purposes. They are job aids. You can use them:

- To help you make decisions, be consistent in your approach to evaluation, and avoid rework
- To engage clients and co-workers in meaningful discussions about why, what, when, and how to evaluate
- To support presentations that focus discussions on facts and processes, not conjecture or wishful thinking

Chapter 1

Evaluation as a Strategy

The training manager saw yet another rollout of one more program.
Why? How was this different from what had been done in the past?
There were too many programs now, no one was managing them,
and no one could say for sure that any problem had ever been solved
by training.

*T*his chapter is about why evaluation should be one of your strategies for managing the function of people's performance. A strategy is an overall game plan for how to use resources to achieve some larger goal. When evaluation is a strategy, validating what is required, what is in place, and what should be improved are no longer add-on activities, but a fundamental way of operating.

THE BUSINESS MODEL

Every training, human resource development (HRD), and performance improvement function operates on a business model. The model may not be well described or formulated; however, it still exists. A business model encompasses the assumptions on which a function operates. Specifically it is about how you are funded, who your clients are and what your relationship is with them, what products and services you offer, and the criteria used to judge your value. There are four common business models used by training (this includes HRD and performance improvement). They are

1. As overhead or a staff function, similar to legal, accounting, and public affairs
2. As an independent business unit with its own profit and loss (P&L) responsibilities
3. As a strategic partner to product development and sales on projects and key initiatives
4. As some combination of the above.

The factors that distinguish these models are how the training function is funded, the nature of its relationship with other departments, and what is measured.

1. Overhead. Staff functions obtain their operating budgets from allocations made by the other departments. The other functions allocate some percentage of their budgets to fund the training operation, based on headcount or a pre-defined number of training days. There are a couple of significant consequences of this model.

- The solution, that is training, is predefined. Training is expected to deliver training days. The focus of attention is on training not on improving performance.
- Funds are dedicated to delivering training. The model rarely funds needs assessments, the development and delivery of non-training solutions, change management, implementation, or evaluating results.
- Training is in a subservient position, because it is dependent on the funding benevolence of the other functions. Since the solution is predefined and considered a downstream activity, training is rarely involved in the planning stages of new products or initiatives.
- Training is rewarded for the quantity of what it does (its outputs), not necessarily for the rightness of what it does. So what is counted is quantity, not results.
- The measures of effectiveness are the number of people trained, the number of hours or days of training, and the number of programs offered, not the results or outcomes of having trained people. Measures like time to proficiency, reduced operating costs, retention of customers or employees, and the like are not considered.

- It fails to recognize the interdependence of and, therefore, the need to align the elements required for individual and organizational performance, that is, the organization's infrastructure and its performance management and performance support systems.

- It contributes to absolving management of responsibility for performance, that is, it is training's job to make people effective.

2. Independent Business Unit with P&L Responsibility. In this model, training is run as an independent business unit that must fund its own activities. Some of the consequences of this model can be that:

- The solution may or may not be predefined, depending on how training frames its business. If it only offers training as a product line, then the solution is limited. However, if it expands its product line to encompass assessment, consultation, documentation, job or process redesign, change management, and the like, then the solutions are limited only by the market demand for them.

- Funding comes from different sources. Training may still receive a basic allocation from the other functions, but it also is allowed to charge back to those functions for actual services rendered, and perhaps even to sell its services to customers and third-party partners (distributors, suppliers, and so forth). In this case, the training department might not deliver programs "at cost" but "mark up" its products enough to enable it to do need assessments, invest in new development or delivery technology, and measure results.

- The relationship can still be subservient, as training is a supplier of services to customers. However, training has to be competitive since internal and external customers can choose their service providers; therefore, training may overly focus on "pleasing" the customer.

- Depending on how much is allocated and on how charge-backs are calculated, training may or may not have a clear picture of its true costs. Depending on how the larger organization calculates headcount and overhead, training may find its costs inflated, making it hard to compete on cost.

- Training is rewarded for being responsive, innovative, and competitive in terms of cost. But there is little incentive or even a means to measure the outcome of its services.

3. Strategic Partner. In this model, training is recognized as a significant player in the other functions' ability to meet their goals. The consequences of this model can be

- The other functions are open to solutions that help them achieve their goals. Those solutions may range from alternative delivery methods to discussions about job designs, hiring criteria, performance support tools, and so forth.

- Funding may be a combination of a base allocation, as with traditional overhead departments, plus project and product budgets. Business cases are developed that address the need for specific services and the risk associated with not using those services. The business case recognizes the importance of people having the tools, direction, and skills to support new products, processes, and services.

- The relationship is one of partners. Both training and the other functions share the risk of missed deadlines, shifts in management's priorities, obsolescence of technology or products, funding new delivery alternatives or a particular solution, and so on.

- What is measured are variances in timelines, resource usage (internal measures), and results (external).

- What is rewarded is collaboration that results in success.

4. Combination.   This model includes all or some of the other models; it is often used in very large conglomerates and performance-oriented organizations independent of size.

Overhead and Self-Funding

The training department of a major retailer operates as a combination corporate overhead and a self-funding business unit. The training department offers a full array of services, including the design of jobs, work methods, and processes; documentation; and training. The corporation gave training the mandate that it must prove that 75 percent to 80 percent of its services contribute to the profitability of the business. Because of this mandate, training begins almost all programs with a needs assessment and a cause analysis study. It identifies solutions and pilots them to see if they produce the desired results. Most projects are funded when the annual budget is developed. The process includes going through an executive budget committee review process. Needs assessments, development, pilots, and deployment are budget items and are estimated based on the scope of the request. Training also operates as a vendor for the information services (IS) department. It provides on-line training at discounted prices and charges back the actual training costs to the requesting department. What is measured are

- Number of projects budgeted and not budgeted
- Actual costs compared to budget
- The amount charged back to specific functions
- The correlation of services provided to profit

Overhead and Product Towers

A manufacturer operated its training function as overhead, but that led to problems as individual, lower level departments were not able to control costs as everything was spread across the board. This model also led to irrational cost cutting by percentages rather than by design of product or by service value. The business came up with a new model whereby training only charges a few people to overhead and charges the rest to product towers. A "tower" encompasses several organizations that are aligned to a particular business function (desktop computing, enterprise servers, networking, and so on). This allows training to charge its time for analysis, evaluation, and consulting services to a tower even when the recommendation is outside the area of skill development. Any budget considerations or constraints are at the customer's end. The result is that training can no longer just spread its costs across the board, but has to deliver services of value to stay alive. They measure the number of customer requests for services, the value produced as a result of those services, and customer satisfaction.

Overhead and Strategic Partner

The training department at an international firm operates as a combination overhead function, a business unit, and a strategic partner with sales. Its products and services include internal training (technical, sales, and management development), certification of technical and professional staff, and customer training. Its internal programs are funded by headcount allocations by the other departments. It publishes a schedule of these courses that are offered for free (this cost was covered by the headcount allocation) except for any travel-associated costs. On occasion a business partner may totally fund a program; in this case the costs are directly allocated to that business partner, whether the services were used or not. What is measured are

- Training days
- The cost of the training
- Cost comparisons of different delivery methods

- How many people are trained and certified
- The correlation of certifications with business success measures, such as customer retention, profits, costs, and so on

Training also operates as a strategic partner with sales and service with a separate P&L for its customer training. Field trainers are compensated with a base salary plus a bonus on revenue and profitability for training they sell to customers. The net profit generated is returned to the local sales and service regional office. Corporate training publishes a catalogue that field trainers give to customers. Customer training is about the technology and science on which products are based and how to operate or maintain products. Customers can buy training as part of a service contract or as a discrete event. What is measured are

- How many customers participated in the programs and the revenue generated
- How much product those customers buy as a consequence of taking the training in dollars and how soon after the training they buy
- How much training is sold, the cost to deliver it, and the profit generated
- How much money is returned to the local sales and service organization
- The average profit by delivery method (customer training can be instructor-led, CD-ROM, or Web-based)

Tool 1.1 has guidelines on how to better understand your business model.

PLANNING AND STRATEGY

A *plan* is a detailed program of actions for achieving an end. Plans require resources to make them reality. A *strategy* is a scheme for how you will employ resources to carry out the plan. Training should have an annual plan detailing what it wants to accomplish, the resources required, and strategies for how to use those resources. When evaluation is one of the strategies, you legitimize asking questions and gathering data about who you service, what you offer, and why, because everything you do requires and consumes resources.

Evaluating helps you obtain data about what resources you have, how they are currently used, and what they produce. The strategy will focus your and the organization's attention on being fact-based and on being purposeful in how you use resources. The strategy can be applied to measuring your department's operations, image, market position, and customers' satisfaction so you are in a better position to know if more or different resources are

TOOL 1.1. UNDERSTAND YOUR BUSINESS MODEL

Meet with a representative of management, accounting, or finance and

- Ask on what basis your function is funded.
- Ask whether any costs are charged back to a particular unit and, if so, on what basis.
- Ask whether the funds are specifically allocated to training or whether some percentage can be applied to assessment and evaluation.
- Ask how the costs associated with your function's support for projects or products is treated and find out whether it is charged back to the project or product.
- Share the four models described in this chapter and ask which best reflects your situation; if none of the models do, then ask for an explanation and create a new model.
- Try discussing the possible consequences of each model and check whether any of those consequences are true for you.

Share what you learn with other members of your function.

- Discuss with them what each of you see are the benefits and drawbacks of how you operate.
- Discuss how you might add evaluation as a strategy and what the implications might be on your relationship with management, clients, vendors, and contractors.
- If you believe the model you operate under is unnecessarily limiting, ask what would have to happen for the organization to entertain another model.

required. You can measure the effectiveness of some or all of your programs, processes, people, equipment, capital assets, media, and materials. In the end, you should have better information to make decisions about what you do, why, what it takes, and how to improve. Making evaluation a strategy will help you:

- Identify what *customers* to service and how
- Decide what the *relationship* should be with customers
- Manage your *product portfolio*
- Select and make better use of *vendors*, contractors, and consultants

CUSTOMERS AND CUSTOMER RELATIONSHIPS

Not all customer requirements are the same. Some only require off-the-shelf programs, others require custom programs, and still others require specialized expertise. When you make evaluation a strategy, it is easier to question who your customers are, what they require of you, and what type of relationship is best for you and them. You start by asking questions and then validating:

- Who you provide services to now
- What is unique or similar about the services you provide them
- How many resources customers consume, what it costs to service them, and what they perceive as the value of what you contribute
- Who you compete with in serving those customers
- What customers expect of you, how satisfied they are with you, and if they are open to discussions about how you might structure an even more effective relationship with them

HIGH TECH

After an economic downturn, the training department was reduced to four people. The manager brought the team together to develop a plan for how they would service the other business units in the future. To help everyone get a better understanding of the customers, they decided to capture what they believed to be true about what they did and for whom. Using whiteboards, they built a map of what they do for each customer base. Part of what they put together is shown in Table 1.1.

Table 1.1. Customer Profile

Customer	Services	Driver	Projections
Sales			
Residential	Product training	Growth	Slower growth
Business	Sales training	Product development	Same # of new products
Installers	Technical training	Growth, new hires	Flat, layoffs
R&D	Facilitation	Proliferation of cross-functional teams	More tense, higher level of skills
Customer service	Product Phone Account management	Growth New products New sales terms	Slower growth Same amount of change.

Approximately 96 percent of the training the department developed was job related. This represented about 210,000 hours of technical training, 55 percent was via e-learning (mostly CD-ROM at about 75 percent and Web-based at about 25 percent). The remainder of training was in soft skills. The team divided the technical training into generic topics and topics that were unique to the company's products and business operations. They decided to purchase or lease off-the-shelf programs for the generic topics and hire contractors to develop any remaining custom courses. They set a goal to move 75 percent of the programs to the Web to reduce costs. They also wanted the contractors to join product development teams so the training was developed in parallel with the product. Other contractors would be hired to deliver courses.

The team members' jobs would be to do needs assessments, hire the contractors, and manage the projects. Some would be asked to manage client relations. They decided to broker soft skill training. One team member was to begin negotiations with a few vendors of off-the-shelf programs and update the preferred vendor list to identify contractors to do development, delivery, or soft skill training. They also decided to confirm their understanding of the business model. They understood that the remaining team members were funded through allocations (as overhead) but all contractors would be part of product development costs. Department managers could ask for soft skill training, which training would broker, but the cost would have to come out of the requesting department's budget.

Tool 1.2 is in two parts. Part A is meant for you to use with your team to gain a better understanding of who your customers are, why they are customers, and why they stay with you. Part B is a survey you can modify to confirm what customers expect of you and how they judge your effectiveness.

PRODUCT PORTFOLIO

Some programs are inherited. Others were created out of a genuine need that may no longer exist. Evaluation as a strategy looks at your products and services as a portfolio so you can understand where products are in their life cycles and identify those that add value or are profitable and those that consume an excessive amount of resources. You start by asking questions and then validating:

- What you know and don't know about your products and services
- Why you offer the programs you do, that is, what the driver (the need) was and who the customer is
- If the need is still there

TOOL 1.2A. CUSTOMER PROFILE

Purpose

This tool is designed to give you a more comprehensive picture of who your customers are, what they require of you, and how you might structure a relationship with them that is effective for both of you. As you go through the questions, change the examples so they reflect your world. Add factors that are meaningful to you. The tool is to help you start.

Steps

1. Do your homework. Preferably with other members of the training function, get together and

    a. List the departments that use your services, for example:
    - Operations
    - Manufacturing
    - Distribution
    - Sales
    - Field service
    - Customer service
    - Call centers
    - Human resources
    - Other

    b. Describe the types of services you provide them, such as:
    - Design
      Work methods
      Implementation plans
      Training
      Performance support
    - Delivery
      Technical training
      New hire training
      Mandated training
      Elective training
      Customer training
      Testing
    - Development
      Training
      Performance support tools
      Media
      Documentation
    - Team support
      Project management

Vendor management
Coordinator of implementation
Negotiate with colleges and third party providers
- Administrative services
Maintain training records
Tuition reimbursement
On-line scheduling
- Consultation
- Certification
- Other

c. Describe what causes them to use your services
- Hiring, turnover
- Reorganizations
- Product launches
- Implementation of new technology
- Compliance with regulations
- Mergers or acquisitions
- Other

d. Estimate how many resources it takes to service them
- Instructors (#, % of time)
- Developers (#, % of time)
- Coordinators (#, % of time)
- Consultants (#, % of time)
- Facilitators (#, % of time)
- Contractors (#, % of time)
- Account managers (#, % of time)

e. Describe your relationship with them
- Order taker
- Vendor
- Advisor
- Partner

2. Poll your customers
a. Ask what why they use your services.
b. Consider a survey similar to Tool 1.2B, Sample Customer Survey. (Modify it to meet your requirements.)

3. Meet with the team and discuss what you learned from your clients. Identify those clients if you want to.
a. Sustain the relationship you have with them.
b. Change the relationship to something else.

4. Develop a plan for change.

TOOL 1.2B. SAMPLE CUSTOMER SURVEY

Purpose

To obtain an overall picture of how your customers experience your department and the services you offer.

Steps

1. Interview or survey your customers. You can modify the instructions and questions in the sample so they better suit your requirements. You may want to distribute the survey by e-mail or the Web. If you do, there are software programs that will analyze the results for you.
2. Analyze the results using the tools in Chapters Eleven and Twelve.

Part A

What services have you received over the previous year from the Training Department? Circle all that apply.

1. Help with the design of
   - Work methods
   - Implementation plans
   - Training courses
   - Performance support
2. Other services:
   - On-line registration
   - Tuition reimbursement
   - Testing
   - Certification
   - Training

What services do think you will use in the coming twelve months? Check all that apply.

3. Help with the design of
   - Work methods
   - Implementation plans
   - Training courses
   - Performance support
4. Other services:
   - On-line registration

- Tuition reimbursement
- Testing
- Certification
- Training

5. What training courses have you or your staff taken in the past twelve months?
   - For new hires
   - Specific job
   - Regulatory updates
   - Professional development
   - Management development
   - Personal development
   - Other

6. If you took training, how was it delivered?
   - Classroom
   - On the job
   - Web
   - Computer
   - Video
   - Audio
   - Community college course
   - Workshop by a professional society

7. Do you use the training department in any of the following ways?
   - To facilitate meetings
   - To participate on product development teams
   - To do needs assessments
   - To participate on process redesign teams
   - To find or recommend vendors
   - To screen off-the-shelf programs or workshops offered by vendors

8. How many times have you or your staff used the services of the training department in the past year?

9. How many programs have you or your staff completed in the past year?

10. Do you use the services of contractors or consultants other than those from the training department?   ☐ yes   ☐ no

11. If the training department could do one thing to better meet your needs, what might that be?

Part B

Please give us your feedback on how well we service your needs.

1. How satisfied are you with how timely the training department responds to your training requests?

Very satisfied	Satisfied	No opinion	Dissatisfied	Very dissatisfied
5	4	3	2	1

Comments:

2. How satisfied are you with how training is delivered?

Very satisfied	Satisfied	No opinion	Dissatisfied	Very dissatisfied
5	4	3	2	1

Comments:

3. How satisfied are you with the quality of instructors?

Very satisfied	Satisfied	No opinion	Dissatisfied	Very dissatisfied
5	4	3	2	1

Comments:

4. How satisfied are you with the selection of topics offered?

Very satisfied	Satisfied	No opinion	Dissatisfied	Very dissatisfied
5	4	3	2	1

Comments:

5. How satisfied are you with the content covered in the training?

Very satisfied	Satisfied	No opinion	Dissatisfied	Very dissatisfied
5	4	3	2	1

Comments:

6. How cost competitive do you feel that the training department's services are?

Very competitive	Competitive	No opinion	Somewhat not competitive	Not at all competitive
5	4	3	2	1

Comments:

7. How easy is it to use the training department services?

Very easy	Easy	No opinion	Difficult	Very difficult
5	4	3	2	1

Comments:

8. Think about all of the training services you buy over the course of a year. About how much is provided by internal training instead of doing it yourself or using other vendors?

About all by T&D	Most by T&D	About half by T&D	Less than 25% by T&D	Very little by T&D
5	4	3	2	1

Comments:

9. If you wanted training in a technical subject for your staff, how likely is it you would choose in-house training's program over another vendor's?

Very likely	Likely	No opinion	Maybe	Very unlikely
5	4	3	2	1

Comments:

10. If you wanted training in a non-technical subject for your staff, how likely is it you would choose our training department's program over another vendor's?

Very likely	Likely	No opinion	Maybe	Very unlikely
5	4	3	2	1

Comments:

- If the programs add value to the organization
- If any programs consume an excessive amount of energy
- If any programs need to be updated
- If any programs have peaked in terms of market demand
- If any programs excessively drain resources, putting other programs at risk
- If you should continue to offer the programs you do, and if so, how frequently
- If you should promote the programs differently
- What it costs to administer and deliver each of these programs
- What it costs to market them
- If you should explore a different delivery medium, marketing method, administrative system, and so on

Based on your answers, describe your portfolio in ways that help you evaluate it. You, in collaboration with colleagues and clients, then determine what to continue doing and what to change so you better leverage your resources.

WORLDWIDE RETAILER

Training was told it had to reduce the cost of training. The company had eight hundred retail outlets and three distribution centers. The corporate office consisted of purchasing, merchandising, marketing, information technology, HR, legal, and finance. The six-person training team got together after they discovered each had a different account of what they did, for whom, and how frequently. Prior to the meeting, the training manager created a few templates and had them enlarged to make wall-sized charts. She wanted the team to capture as much data about what they did as possible to identify opportunities to change the way they did business in the future. She asked the team to come up with descriptors or factors that might be useful. The group suggested classifying training by the curriculum it falls under, who owns it (V for vendor and C for the company), how it is delivered (C is classroom, O is on-the-job, V is video, and PC is computer-based), and the purpose (S is build skills, I is inform). They included training done in the stores, the distribution centers, and at corporate headquarters. Table 1.2 is an excerpt of one of the wall charts.

When they had completed their work, they realized a significant amount of their training was actually sharing information, sending out updates about products, merchandising rules, labor laws, and so forth.

They also realized they were using vendors whose programs were computer-based. They began to question whether or not the same programs could be distributed on the Web and what the cost implications might be. Next, they identified how changing the delivery might affect costs, but also discussed any challenges or conditions that might limit the delivery alternatives.

Table 1.2. Description of Training Programs

Course #	Owner	Delivery	Purpose S or I
Clerk (stores)	C	O	S&I
Labor law (stores, centers)	V	PC	I
Merchandising (stores)	V	PC	I
Distribution/Logistics (centers)	V&C	PC	S&I
Systems (corporate)	V&C	C	S&I
Mgmt development	V	C	S&I

Tool 1.3 is designed to help you evaluate your product portfolio. It is in four parts. Part A explains the process for evaluating your products. Parts B, C, and D are worksheets that you can adapt to meet your needs.

VENDORS, CONTRACTORS, AND OFF-THE-SHELF PROGRAMS

Training organizations purchase products already on the market instead of developing their own, outsource some of the work, and periodically hire experts. Measurement can drive questions about why, what selection criteria you use, and how to best use their services. It can also help you identify over the course of the relationship whether your needs are being met and at what cost. Start by asking questions and then validating:

- What do you hope to accomplish by using outside talent or products?
- If you are considering buying or leasing off-the-shelf programs, what must those programs include, to what degree will they accomplish the goal, and will you have to add resources to fulfill the objective?
- What project and contractor management abilities must you supply to optimize the capabilities of the vendor, contractor, or consultant?
- What does it cost in time and dollars to orient the vendor or contractor to the task?
- What do you and the vendor or contractor expect of the relationship?
- What will you and the vendor or contractor use to measure the success of the engagement?

TOOL 1.3A: STEPS FOR EVALUATING YOUR PRODUCT PORTFOLIO

Purpose

This strategy looks at training from the perspective of managing a series of products. It helps you understand where products are in their life cycle. It helps you distinguish products that are profitable from those that cost too much. It is best used when you want answers to questions such as these:

- Which programs need our energy (dollars, time)?
- Which programs should be updated?
- Which programs have peaked in terms of saturating the defined market?
- Which programs are draining our resources?
- Should we continue offering a program, and if so at what level of frequency?
- Is it time to explore a different delivery medium?
- Should we promote the program in a different way?

Process

1. With the people who help you administer, schedule, deliver, and market your program, create worksheets like the ones that follow. Across the top, list the variables you want to consider.

2. List the programs you currently offer (those in your course catalogue) and fill in as much information as you have for each one. Based on what you learn from completing the worksheet, you will be in a better position to decide which programs to concentrate on.

3. Decide what factors you want to consider and create a tool that includes those factors (see Sample Worksheets A, B, and C and modify them for your situation).

4. Put together enough descriptive information about your product portfolio to give you the big picture (how many programs, how often offered, how frequently filled, what each costs to deliver, delivery mode, use internal/external instructors, and so forth).

5. Where you can, record the original driver behind the program (why was it offered in the first place, what problem was it solving, why was this delivery mode selected, who was the originally intended audience, who was the original sponsor). It is possible the need was satisfied.

6. You can create a similar worksheet for all of your services. The goal is to understand the resources they consume and why.

7. Use the results of your evaluation to identify your next steps, such as stop offering, offer in a different way, improve, or better promote.

TOOL 1.3B: PRODUCT PORTFOLIO WORKSHEET 1

Course #	Date 1st Offered	Last Update	Average # Scheduled	Average Enrollment	% Filled/ Canceled	Type S/I/R	Driver	V/C

1. Somehow label the program by title or number.
2. If relevancy and market penetration are important, record when it was first offered and perhaps last updated. This might indicate the need to dedicate resources to making a program current.
3. Track how often it is made available and what the average enrollment is. Compare that with the number of "no shows" or cancellations. Ask what the consequences are on your resources.
4. Pay attention to the purpose of the program, for example, is the purpose to build skills (S), just inform (I) and keep people current on changes, or to reinforce (R) a skill or a rule?
5. Who owns the course, the vendor (V) or you the company (C)?

TOOL 1.3C: PRODUCT PORTFOLIO WORKSHEET 2

Course #	Size of Market	% Reached	# of Resources	Cost to Deliver	Cost to Maintain	Cost to Purchase	Cost to Create

1. What was the original or current size of the market, and how much have you reached?
2. How many resources are consumed in delivery, maintenance, administration?
3. What did or does it cost to deliver, maintain?
4. What did or will it cost to purchase or create?

TOOL 1.3D: PRODUCT PORTFOLIO WORKSHEET 3

Delivery Mode	Evaluation Level/Method	Rating						Comments
		q	ic	dc	e	l	o	

1. Delivery mode refers to how the course is offered, for example, I means instructor-led, EA means electronic with an administrator, ES means electronic without an administrator, C means offered at a college or university, and S means booklet and self-study. Add other classifications that have meaning to you.

2. Evaluation level refers to what type of evaluation is used now, that is, end-of-course reactions, testing of learning, application on the job, or correlation with business measures.

3. Rating. You and the people who help you administer, schedule, deliver, and market the course should individually and then together rate each course on a scale from 5 (best/most positive) to 1 (worst/least positive) for each of these factors: q refers to quality, ic (indirect costs), and dc (direct costs). Together they tell you what it costs to deliver; e is how easy it is to set up; l is how well it is linked to business drivers; and o is the overall participant response.

   Note: A rating of 2 or below means you should seriously consider giving the program attention.

4. Comments is a way for everyone involved in scheduling, delivering, marketing the course to say whatever they want about it. Comments can give you a richer picture of what people think about a program and why it should or should not be offered in the same way.

5. Use what you learn when planning what resources you will require and how you might use them.

VENDOR MANAGEMENT

The training department had always used its own employees to develop and deliver training. However, it was becoming increasingly difficult to hire trainers or to take people off their jobs to help develop and deliver programs. The training manager decided it was time to consider outsourcing some of these services. Before asking contractors to present proposals, he met with members of his department. He focused the discussion on three areas:

- What exactly they wanted contractors to do
- How they saw the relationship, both sides working together
- On what basis they would select the contractors

The discussion rapidly surfaced the group's assumptions about what it would do and what the contractor would do. This led to the realizations that contractors could be in direct contact with clients and would be seen as an extension of training. The group decided it was important that contractors understand the business and its culture. Another realization was that the team didn't have any standards or agreed-on templates for its training. The team came up with a list of what it would do, such as orient the contractor to the business, help manage the project, create a set of design standards, facilitate client introductions, frequently check with clients to confirm that deadlines were met and that the product met the client's expectations, and so on. It also came up with a set of expectations for the contractors, such as debriefing training's management regularly, not using time on site to sell other services, staying current on events affecting the business or the specific work group they were assigned to, following the design standards or recommending standards, doing the work expected, not something else, and so forth. The next step was for the training team to come up with criteria it would use to compare and finally select the contractors. The criteria included:

- Having done work for the business in the past that met expectations
- Having evidence of being able (having the cash flow or lack of competing assignments) to commit the time necessary to complete the project (not leave at mid-point)
- Committing to do the work themselves, not bring in substitutes, except in the case of an emergency and with the approval of the training department

- Having the capability (instructional design, delivery, computer skills, et cetera) to do the job
- Having evidence of working effectively as part of a team

The training manager and his team agreed to meet monthly to see how well their ideas were working and to make changes as necessary.

TIME MANAGEMENT

A large consulting firm purchased a course called "time management" as part of its required curriculum for new account executives. Time management is usually thought of as an elective program; however, the firm depended on account executives capturing and allocating their time so the firm could accurately bill clients. The training program focused on (a) why time tracking was important and (b) how to use the time tracking tools provided by the firm. Account executives had to turn in their time allocations at the end of every Friday to accounting. Abuses were reported to the supervisor.

The program had been licensed from a large training vendor for the last five years. The vendor supplied all of the materials and qualified the firm's trainers. The program seemed to be meeting the firm's expectations. A new training manager was hired to manage the curriculum for account managers. His mandate was to evaluate all of the programs in the curriculum and identify those that had exhausted their market, those that were in need of replacement or updating, and those whose costs seemed exceptional in light of the benefit gained. The training manager compared the cost of the current time management program with other programs on the market. He found other programs covered the same concepts at significantly less cost. He replaced the program with another vendor's course on time management.

Tool 1.4 is in two parts. Part A walks you through a process for comparing vendors, contractors, products, and consultants. Part B starts you on the process of evaluating off-the-shelf programs.

TOOL 1.4A. HOW TO EVALUATE VENDORS, CONTRACTORS, AND CONSULTANTS

Purpose

To identify the criteria you will use to evaluate and compare vendors, contractors, and consultants. The examples are meant to help you start. Modify and add what is needed to reflect your situation.

Steps

1. Begin by defining what you want done or have the vendor do.

   - Facilitate group sessions (focus groups, process redesign teams, and so forth)
   - Develop documentation
   - Deliver a program that already exists
   - Implement the program in your organization
   - Modify the program so it better reflects your requirements
   - Develop a custom program just for you
   - Develop the media, materials, and so on
   - Convert a program to a different medium
   - Conduct a needs assessment
   - Whatever else is required

2. Decide how much direction, supervision, or involvement you can contribute. The less supervision, the more skilled at the particular task and at client management the vendor must be.

3. How long is the engagement? For how long do you want the person to make a commitment?

4. Check with your purchasing, procurement, or legal department to see whether they have any standard contracts or requirements and see whether they are relevant and useful. They probably have language concerning:

   - Ownership of materials
   - Employee status
   - Termination clauses
   - Confidentiality agreement
   - Conflict of interest clauses
   - Payment of travel and out-of-pocket expenses

5. Meet with your team to come up with a list of requirements such as, but not limited to:

- Honesty, integrity
- Knowledge of the industry, your organization, the topic, and so forth
- The ability and willingness to stay through the duration of the assignment
- Not sending in any substitutes without approval and only in the case of an emergency
- Not pursuing other contracts within the company without your approval
- Not using subcontractors without your approval
- Ownership of materials developed especially for you
- Debriefing you on a frequent basis on what happened, and making sure to tell you anything in particular that you should know
- Staying current on events that affect the business or the group they will be working with, such as layoffs or celebrations
- What to do if they run into any difficulty obtaining the information or cooperation they require
- That you will poll the client to collect feedback on their performance and ability to work effectively with the team
- That they can be terminated without cause
- On what basis time is calculated, such as whether you pay for travel time at a flat daily fee, by the hour, or however

6. Ask candidates to speak directly to the requirements.

7. Develop a set of interview questions and identify what must be in their responses for you to consider them as viable candidates. See the examples in Chapter Ten on gathering data, specifically the performance check sheets.

8. Have selected members of your team conduct the interviews.

9. After the interviews, have each person rate the candidate. Ask yourself: Is this someone I could work with and would want to work with?

One of the decisions you may have to make is whether or not to purchase or lease an off-the-shelf program or develop one instead. Development is perhaps the most costly process in terms of time and money. Part B of Tool 1.4 has suggestions on how to evaluate off-the-shelf programs.

TOOL 1.4B. HOW TO EVALUATE OFF-THE-SHELF PROGRAMS

If you currently use or plan to use off-the-shelf programs, here are some suggestions on what you might consider.

1. Decide what problem you are trying to solve.
2. Based on the problem you are trying to solve, identify the attributes the product must possess to accomplish your goal. Include:

   - The objectives of the product
   - The integrity of the content
   - The ratio of practice to explanation
   - The ability to give feedback

3. Also consider factors such as what else you will have to provide or how you might have to supplement the program to fully realize your goals.
4. Identify any constraints or limitations the product must satisfy to work in your environment, such as having the time, incentives, and equipment to make use of it.
5. Identify the direct and indirect costs associated with buying or leasing the product.
6. Make sure there is an exit clause, a way for you to end the relationship when the need is met or another solution becomes available.

MISSTEPS

Here are some of the more common mistakes trainers and training managers make.

1. They don't stop to reflect on how their business model influences what they do, how they do it, and for whom.
2. They don't initiate conversations with key clients and management about other models and how they might be beneficial.
3. They accept that evaluation is an add-on, after the fact activity.
4. They fail to integrate measurement in everything they do.
5. They see measurement as formal surveys rather than asking questions, documenting the answers, periodically reminding clients of what was learned, and using the information to compare results with goals and expectations.
6. They don't initiate discussions with clients about the working relationship and use that opportunity to pose other possibilities.

TIPS AND TECHNIQUES

Here are some suggestions about how to make evaluation a business strategy:

1. Create tools similar to the ones in the tool section to drive meaningful discussions about responsibilities, relationships, and roles.

2. Create posters or wall charts so you can direct and sustain people's attention on topics like evaluation, what data to gather, what might change, and so on.

3. Practice asking questions about assumptions, what if things were different, what is really known, and what is assumed.

4. Integrate measurement into your day-to-day activities and decisions. Worry less about being right or precise in your decision; instead instill the habit of validating as best you can given the opportunities you have to get good information.

SUMMARY

There is an old adage that says, "What you measure is what you get." This holds true for training as well. When evaluation becomes a strategy, not just a by-product of how the function is funded, then measurement results in data that leads to better business decisions. When measurement is a strategy, it forces you to validate that what you do and how you do it actually add value. It changes the nature of the conversation you have with colleagues, clients, and contractors.

WHERE TO LEARN MORE

Kaufman, R. *Strategic Thinking* (Silver Spring, MD: ISPI, 1998). You should check out all of Roger's writings about the micro, macro, and mega aspects of planning.

Schwartz, P. *The Art of the Long View: Planning for the Future in an Uncertain World* (New York: Doubleday, 1991).

Wallace, G. *Lean-ISD,* the chapter on Performance Analysis (2, 21–27), and *T&D Systems View,* the chapters on Governance & Advisory Systems and Strategic Planning.

Watzlawick, P. *Change* (1974) and *Ultra-Solutions: How to Fail Successfully* (New York: W.W. Norton, 1988). These books brilliantly integrate mathematical axioms with theories of human behavior.

Chapter 2

Why Measure Effectiveness and Efficiency

The training department was told that two-thirds of its staff was to be laid off. It didn't matter that they delivered hundreds of hours of classroom training or produced hundreds of hours of Web-based training. It didn't matter that the organization had been growing at 1,800 new hires a month and training was able to bring them on board and up to speed within weeks. What mattered was that the priority of the organization had changed. It went from building its market share to maintaining it. The focus shifted from growth to reducing costs while improving the performance of the people already on board. The department had become efficient at producing training, but now the job was different.

*T*his chapter is about why you should measure your effectiveness (the value you bring to clients) and your efficiency (how you operate). If you only measure to find out whether or not your programs made a difference, you may provide effective but costly solutions. If you only measure to be more efficient, you may get faster in what you do or produce programs more cheaply, but not necessarily add value. Therefore, it is important to understand and appreciate the benefits of doing both. There are four major reasons for evaluating.

1. To become better at what you do in terms of speed and cost

2. To obtain the data required for future planning and cost- and time-estimations

3. To improve the quality of what you do

4. To be able to prove that what you do makes a difference, that you contribute to your client's success

All of these reasons depend on your willingness to obtain facts about how effective and efficient you are and to be open to the possibility that solutions other than training may be best for the organization.

EFFECTIVENESS AND EFFICIENCY

Effectiveness and efficiency are analogous to the information on a financial sheet. The top line (effectiveness) is the revenue generated by the business. The next line is the cost of doing business (efficiency). The difference between the two, the bottom line or the result, is the profit margin. If you focus on the top line you are revenue based or, in the case of a training department, output based. You focus on how many people you train, how many training days you offer, how many modules you produce, and so on. If you focus only on costs, you are cost based. Yet, the bottom line, the difference between the two, is what matters. If you just focus on increasing revenue or outputs, your costs may go up proportionally, resulting in no change in profits or added value. If you just focus on controlling or reducing costs, it is harder to justify money to invest for growth or to make improvements in how you operate. Some training organizations are production houses; others are cost centers. Those with staying power are both. They manage their costs by being efficient in their operations so they can afford to do up-front analyses and invest in development, and they make sure that what they do contributes to their clients' effectiveness.

Another analogy for why it is important to measure your efficiency and effectiveness comes from human performance technology. Worthy human performance is the consequence of efficiently executing those activities that lead to results clients value. If you overly focus on activities, that is, how much you do and how fast it gets done, without considering whether what is done actually contributes to the desired results, performance suffers. If you overly focus on end results and fail to consider how you went about achieving them, long-term performance may be compromised or unnecessarily costly.

Figure 2.1 shows one way of thinking about efficiency and effectiveness. You find out what triggers a need for your services (drivers), what you have

Figure 2.1. Process Model

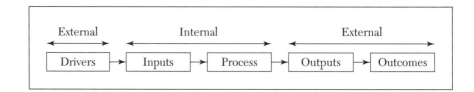

to work with (inputs), what you do with it (processes), how much you produce as a result (outputs), and what the consequences (outcomes) are of what you do.

When you evaluate how effective you are you find the information to answer questions such as:

- What drives our customers' decisions about products, services, delivery methods, and deployment of human capital?
- How will those drivers affect our department's products, services, and way of operating?
- What might our clients require from us now and in the future? What are their constraints, goals, cost drivers, and so on?
- What is the best way to satisfy that need? What services other than training might we provide?
- How did our training and performance support tools improve people's ability to do the job?
- How did people's behavior change as a result of our programs?
- How did our work contribute to the organization meeting its goals?

By measuring you will find out the facts so you can say with confidence that performance improved, behavior changed (one hopes in a positive manner), and that the organization benefited.

When you look externally, you can measure what drives your work, how much you do, and the value to the organization. You are in a better position to anticipate changes that might affect what and how much you do when you understand what drives your work and the need for your services. When you look internally, you can measure how efficiently you identify drivers, manage the inputs, and carry out your processes. The important part of measuring is being clear about what you want to do with the information you gain. Which brings me back to knowing what questions you want to answer for yourself or for others.

Measuring lets you find out what your speed, time, rate of access, and so forth are now and compare that to what is required. You measure the efficiency of all of your processes, as shown in Figure 2.2.

Figure 2.2. Training and HRD Processes

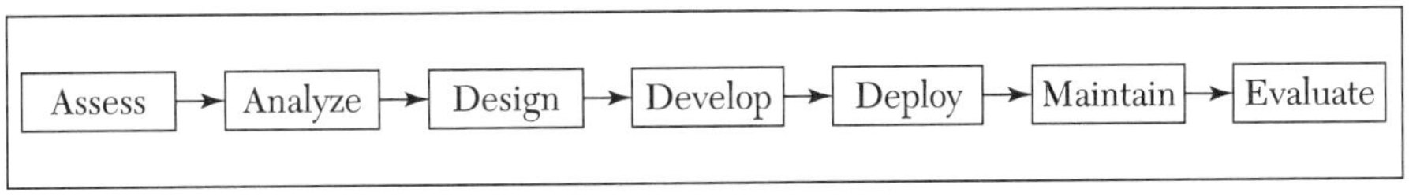

Assess → Analyze → Design → Develop → Deploy → Maintain → Evaluate

When you evaluate how you operate you get the information to answer questions such as:

- How can we best deliver training and other support services?

- How can we reach more people faster, allow for greater access, and stay within budget?

- Is it better to invest in Web-based training or to use contract trainers, and if we do what will we gain?

- What is the better delivery method, CBT, Web, self-paced, classroom, or some combination? What are the tradeoffs?

- Should we have a strategic alliance with the local college? Will it reduce our fixed costs? Will it slow us down?

- Should we outsource training? If we do, how do we re-deploy our trainers? What is the best use of our capabilities?

CUSTOMER MANAGEMENT SOFTWARE

A company decided to update its DOS-based billing and customer management software to a Windows-compatible system. The company had over three hundred retail outlets located in twenty-five states. The new system would integrate point-of-sale transactions, customer purchase profiles, customer service, and inventory management. Retail clerks would use the system to create and update customer profiles, handle cash and credit card purchases, and receive payments by phone and from walk-in customers. The data would be fed to corporate accounting so it could generate purchase orders for inventory replenishment, invoice customers, pay bills, and produce reports for management on the rate of inventory depletion, actual revenue, and expenses compared to budget. The firm expected the migration to the new system to take about four years at a cost of $30 million. The rollout was staged according to geographical regions, which would allow the company to introduce system upgrades as each region was brought on-line. Training for store personnel who knew the old DOS system and those trained on earlier versions of the Windows software was to be done on-line.

Training of new hires on the Windows system was designed as a two-phase process. During the first phase, clerks would attend a four-day instructor-led class at a regional training center that would be delivered by company personnel. The centers would be equipped with computers connected to a simulated database, allowing clerks to practice all of the functions they were expected to do in the store. Phase two would be one week of on-the-job training at the store on the live system.

Anywhere from fifteen to thirty contract trainers would be hired per region to conduct the in-store training. Contract trainers were required to have previous experience doing on-the-job training in computer software applications. Contractors were to go through a three-week train-the-trainer session that included on-the-job training in the stores.

Measurement played a major role in all aspects of the project. The ultimate measure was for clerks to execute transactions with minimum errors and attain a level of transaction speed similar to what it was with the DOS system. Clerk performance after the training was measured by the frequency of data errors, the frequency of calls to the help desk, and the type of errors. The error rate and the number and type of calls were turned over to the training department to improve the classroom and on-the-job training. The training manager then correlated the number of trainers with the average store transactions and the error rate. This information helped her in the following ways:

- To identify the optimum number of trainers per store
- To manage the contractors
- To assure trainers were available to the stores when the system went live
- To coordinate the development of the on-line training so clerks familiar with the old system or previous versions of the new system could be kept current
- To continually improve the classroom segment and simulation

She could then better plan and coordinate the logistics for the other regions. Her questions were

- Are trainers in the stores in time to support bringing the system on-line? If so, why? If not, why?
- How many trainers should be assigned to each store? What was too many or what was not enough and why?
- How were the store managers and clerks reacting to the trainers? Did their reactions interfere with learning the new system, and if so why or how?
- Was the on-line training available when required?
- Did clerks who were used to the older DOS system know how to use the on-line training? Were they using it?
- What is their error rate or frequency of calls to the help desk? What do they need help on?

She tracked the information given to her from the help desk to identify the need to change the training or its delivery; however, only those changes were made that were not too costly or would not interfere with the roll-out schedule. The training manager had set the measures in advance, and this helped her and management stay focused on an efficient implementation.

REPAIR, INC.

Repair, Inc., employed about two thousand people and manufactured over one hundred pieces of equipment used by trucking firms. The trucking firms used the equipment to service and repair their vehicles. Repair, Inc., prided itself on continually improving its product line, which drove the creation of new products and modifications of old products.

The training department also prided itself on providing "just-in-time" training, and had five full-time instructional and media developers and twenty field trainers to train the trucking firms in how to use and service the equipment. As a result, the training department had become very efficient at developing instructor-led modules on new products and product updates.

When the company experienced an economic downturn, two of the instructional and media developers and twelve of the field trainers were laid off. The remaining instructional designers and media developers were assigned to develop job aids and Web-based classes the trucking firms could access directly. The trainers' jobs changed, too. Four trainers were assigned to train field technicians in how to train, instead of delivering the courses themselves. The other four trainers were used to advise management on performance improvement initiatives, strategic planning, and process improvement initiatives.

An outcome of the layoffs was that the training manager now tracks what he does, how much he does, how he is a good steward of corporate assets, and how his department helps the company be more profitable. The lack of measurement had made training vulnerable. Had they been tracking how many resources it took to support the trucking firms, they might have come up with alternative ways of doing business, which is what happened once staff was cut.

TECHNOLOGY, INC.

This company grew from 350 to 35,000 employees in just ten years. It expected to double in size in the next five years. It was hiring at a rate of 1,500 new employees a month and had a 30 percent turnover. The training department had become very efficient at enrolling and delivering technical and HR courses to new hires. The full-time trainers, along with fifteen contract trainers, were so busy delivering classes that taking time for their own development was almost impossible. The logistics of scheduling classes, materials, equipment, and trainers was a full-time job. Attempts at improving coordination by adding Web pages, cell phones, fax machines, and e-mail only made matters worse as the trainers complained that they had too many options for communicating with one another. Information learned from the field about employee relations issues never made it to human resources or those who were delivering the HR courses to new hires.

One of the training managers built a successful case for acquiring a training facility in the North to increase classroom capacity and reduce travel costs. By the time the other trainers found out about it, they could not schedule classes because the rooms had already been rented out to neighboring businesses for meeting space. The training department had inadvertently become a landlord and property management business. At the same time, other training managers were seeing their classrooms disappear because they were being converted to office space. All of the managers began to field questions about travel expenses and were hearing about shrinking company profits. Stock values were falling and the company announced losses. The vice president of training anticipated being asked to cut staff; however, when he asked his people to evaluate the effectiveness of their classes, come up with ways to move away from classroom training, or revisit why they were teaching the classes they were, he was met with an outcry of accusations that he didn't trust his staff. Trainers insisted that customers expected a personal touch and that there was no time to reengineer how work was done.

What happened was that training had created an engine that churned out training hours, without asking at what cost, or why, or to what benefit. The vice president of training wanted his trainers to have time to address issues such as turnover and how to bring people to proficiency faster, not just deliver classes. After failing to meet profit targets three quarters in a row, the company eliminated the HR trainers' jobs. The training department may have been very efficient, but its failure or unwillingness to measure put it in a position of doing the same things the old way. If they had measured, they may not have been able to save all the jobs, but they would have been able to demonstrate where they were inefficient, what they did about it, and the worth of the improvements.

Tool 2.1 is meant to help you focus on those outputs worthy of your attention. There isn't enough time or money to evaluate everything, so you want to measure the things that will more likely generate information you can use to increase the effectiveness of your future efforts.

TOOL 2.1. IDENTIFYING WHAT TO MEASURE

1. List your outputs for the last six to twelve months. What was the problem or opportunity those outputs were expected to satisfy?

2. Who was the customer of those outputs? Who stood to gain the most from what you did?

3. What was the client using as evidence that your output was necessary or would satisfy a need? Was the need immediate or long-term? Was there any kind of analysis done or was the work commissioned because the need was "obvious?"

4. If your output was commissioned to support another larger initiative such as a product launch or the migration to an enterprise-wide computer system, what was the business logic presented to fund the larger initiative? Would the initiative have been successful without your output?

5. If your output was commissioned to support a known deficiency in skills and knowledge such as training new hires, what would have been the cost to the client if your output were not available?

6. What was the assumption on which your output was chosen, for example, was it cost, timeliness, or were you the only game in town?

7. Do you know, as a result of your output, how quickly people achieved proficiency in terms of error rate, the percentage of time spent by supervisors providing direction, or some other metric? Compare this time to how long it would have taken without your output.

8. Those outputs that were the most costly for the client or that, if not provided, exposed the client to the greatest amount of risk are the ones you might want to evaluate in terms of how effectively you fulfilled the promise to the client. However, this presumes you and the client decided on what you would pay attention to as evidence of success or worth. If those measures were not decided on, then meet with the client or other vested parties and ask. It is possible the measurement has already happened or is happening, but you are not privileged to the information. In that case, ask for the information. Those outputs where there is a lack of clarity about the need or how much was at risk are probably not worth any more effort.

Tool 2.2 is meant to help you and your clients discuss expectations, what is being used as evidence of a problem, and what will be used as evidence that things improved as a result of your work. The examples are in no way exhaustive, but are only meant to help you start so you and your client come up with your own examples. Add or change the suggested measures, metrics, and

TOOL 2.2. SAMPLE MEASURES, METRICS, AND DESIRED RESULTS

Sample Measures or Initiatives	Sample Metrics	Sample Results
1. Satisfaction Employee Customers Other departments Investors Suppliers Third party partners	Retention rate # of complaints Rate & % of turnover Cost to service	Higher scores Fewer complaints Less turnover Better ratios
2. Marketing Products Services	% share Speed of penetration # of potential customers Time to market	Greater % Greater penetration Faster times
3. Performance People Product Process	Rating of expectations Means or averages % or # meeting standards Variance Cycle time Quantity Consistency	Reduced variance Higher means Fewer errors Higher quantity
4. Finance Costs Revenues Cash flow Return on investment	Ratio of fixed to variable Ratio of direct to indirect Variance w/budget Cost of service Cost of retention	Better ratios Lower costs Higher returns Better cash flow Fewer defaults Faster collections
5. Growth Agility Resiliency	Time to proficiency # of internal promotions	Faster deployment Greater proficiency Less time # of internal promotions
6. Compliance Policy Laws Regulations Contract terms	# of incidents Frequency of incidents Types of incidents Magnitude of incidents % covered by insurance Loss of revenue Fines in $ amounts Public preception	Fewer incidents Higher compliance Lower fees or fines

expected results to meet your needs. The tool can become a document of understanding and a way to help clarify expectations.

The *measures* in the tool are organized around six categories:

1. Satisfaction of employees, other departments, customers, investors, suppliers, or third party partners

2. Marketing of products and services in terms of size of market or the percentage of market share, rate of market penetration, and so forth

3. Performance of people, products, and processes, in terms of meeting expectations or satisfying standards

4. Finance, in terms of meeting and exceeding goals, variance compared to plan, cash flow, and so on

5. Growth, in terms of increasing the capacity and capability of people and systems

6. Compliance, as applied to internal policies, external regulations, and agreements

The *metrics* are expressed in dollars ($), time (years, months, weeks, days, hours, seconds), percentages (%), means or arithmetic averages, variance or standard deviation (s), frequency (#s), and ratings (numerical or descriptive), and ratios.

How to Use the Tool

- Prior to meeting with the client, build a "straw model" or picture of what you think are the issues and measures the client is focusing on. Complete the table as best you can. You do not want it to be completely filled out; just use enough detail to facilitate the conversation and get the data you need to plan your evaluation efforts.

- During the meeting add to the information you have.
  - Ask about the initiatives for the coming year
  - Ask what the client sees as the opportunities or high priority needs
  - Ask on what basis the client concluded that these are problems or opportunities
  - Ask what the client expects performance to be at a minimum
  - Begin to negotiate over who will be involved and how the data will be collected to determine whether a change occurred (as a result of some intervention)

- The goal of meeting is not to fill out the tool, but to obtain a better understanding of what the client sees as issues and opportunities and why he or she feels that way, and to identify those metrics your work is expected to impact.
- Document and present what was discussed and agreed on to the client.

MISSTEPS

Here are some of the oversights that trainers and training departments frequently make:

1. They fail to take advantage of all the information being tracked already by other departments as indicators of a need, a change, or success. Accounting, sales, marketing, customer service, legal, HR, and quality, for example, track information and identify trends. What they may require from you are performance support tools to track and interpret the results efficiently.

2. They focus too much on results and fail to see the benefits of evaluating and improving the effectiveness of their own processes.

3. They fail to consider the full breadth of possible measures and metrics as useful information to help them improve how they go about work.

TIPS AND TECHNIQUES

Here are some suggestions about how to decide on what to evaluate and how to do it:

1. If you want to show that your training or performance support tool achieves results, then be sure the other elements required to promote the adoption of new behaviors are also in place (clear expectations, management rewards and incentives, well-designed work processes, appropriate tools and equipment, and so on). People change the way they do things because there are consequences if they don't, they have the required minimum resources to do what is expected, and they can monitor and adjust their own performance instead of waiting for feedback from the boss. Having the skills and knowledge is only a part of performing the job well.

2. Court the client, build a relationship that enables you to obtain the inputs you require to judge the importance of the product, plan the environment in which it will be used, and determine management's commitment to dedicating the resources to make it effective.

3. Use the ideas in *The Balanced Scorecard: Transitioning Strategy into Action* (Kaplan & Norton, 1996)[1] to help the client link what is expected of your work to a larger goal.

SUMMARY

It is only by measuring that you will know whether or not you are doing the right things in the right way. Measuring is about purposefully acquiring data and comparing what you find out to some goal or expectation. What data you obtain depends on what questions you want to answer and what information you want to make better decisions. If you don't have any use for the data, then measurement is unnecessary. Yet, avoiding collecting it can put you at risk in the future, as you will be less able to defend the effectiveness of your programs or the efficiency of your operations.

WHERE TO LEARN MORE

Kaplan, R. S., and Norton, D. P. *The Balanced Scorecard: Translating Strategy into Action* (Boston, MA. *Harvard Business Review, 1996*).

Kaufman, R., Thiagarajan, S., and MacGillis, P. (Eds.). *The Guidebook for Performance Improvement: Working with Individuals and Organizations* (San Francisco, CA. Jossey-Bass/Pfeiffer, 1997). See Section VI on Evaluation, Chapters 25 and 26.

Stolovitch, H. *Handbook of Human Performance Technology: A Comprehensive Guide for Analyzing and Solving Performance Problems in Organizations* (San Francisco, CA: Jossey-Bass, 1992). See Chapter 9 on The Function of Evaluation by George Geis, Chapter 10 on Planning an Evaluation Study by Martin Smith, and Chapter 18 on Feedback Systems by William Deterline.

Stolovitch, H. D., and Maurice, J.-G. *Performance Improvement*, 37: 8:9–20.

Van Tiem, D. M., Mosely, J. L., and Dessinger, J. C. *Fundamentals of Performance Technology: A Guide to Improving People, Process, and Performance* (Washington, DC, International Society for Performance Improvement, 2000). See Chapter Seven on evaluation.

Wallace, G. *Lean-ISD* (Naperville, IL, CADDI, 1999). See the chapter on Performance Analysis (2, 21–27).

NOTE

1. Kaplan, R. S., and Norton, D. P. *The Balanced Scorecard: Translating Strategy into Action* (Boston, MA. *Harvard Business Review, 1996*).

Chapter 3

How to Measure Effectiveness

The new buzzword was "accountability" and every department was being asked to produce evidence that it added value and contributed to the organization's goals. Training was no exception, but for the first time it was being asked to show that its programs made a difference.

*T*his chapter is about how to measure your effectiveness (the value you bring to clients). Effectiveness is measured in the number of outputs generated, the degree to which they satisfy a need, and their impact in the short term and long term. What facts you collect will depend on what you want to do with what you find and how much data you collect will depend on how precise you need to be in your findings. How you analyze the facts will depend on how certain you have to be in your recommendations.

EXTERNAL MEASURES

External measures, also known as summative measures, are the facts you collect to confirm how much you produced and the impact on the organization. In the past, people joked about tracking the number of people trained. Trainers and their managers were almost embarrassed to talk about it. Yet, how many people were trained, how many classroom hours were involved, how many modules were accessible on the Web, and how frequently classrooms and training carrels were in use is valuable information, particularly when you add information about what drives you to do the things you do. But they are not sufficient by themselves. You also have to show that something worthwhile came about as a result. You have to ask whether there is a better way to accomplish the same end. External measures are about:

- Evaluating how much you did given the resources you had to work with
- Proving that the behaviors promoted by training were institutionalized or adopted on the job
- Showing that, because of your training and performance support tools, people are more skilled and perform better and that the company is more profitable

Common external measures, both output and outcome related, are explained below.

Output Related

Outputs are measured in terms of *quantity* and *quality*. Quantity is about how much was done. The metrics might include:

- The number of courses developed, scheduled, and delivered
- The number of students registered and who attended versus cancelled or were "no shows"
- The number of courses changed from instructor-led classroom to live Web-hosted classes or that became self-paced CD-ROM or computer-based training
- The number of training or contact hours available to learners
- The number of development or delivery jobs outsourced
- The number of resources dedicated to deployment or delivery versus design and development
- The number of resources qualified to develop (classroom and on-line training), and deliver training
- How many sign-in sheets, tests, and other administrative procedures were processed to help trainers administer courses

You use this information to measure your productivity and you factor it in when measuring the results of your work.

Quality is about how well the output (product, program, or service) met the expectations of the user or the agreed-on design standards. The metrics might be:

- The number of users whose reactions to the utility of product or service were positive
- The degree to which the sponsor reacted positively to the aesthetics of the product's design or elements
- The number of products that met the standard

You use this information to identify when quality fell short of, met, or exceeded expectations and to decide if an intervention is required.

Outcome Related

Donald Kirkpatrick was the pioneer of outcome measures as his four levels are about measuring what happened after the event or solution was implemented. As a professor of management, Dr. Kirkpatrick's thinking closely reflects management's interests. Other writers have expanded on his definition of the four levels of evaluation by adding nuances such as level 5 and even 4a and 4b to distinguish economic and non-economic results. Kirkpatrick's four levels are

Level 1—reaction

Level 2—learning

Level 3—transfer or adoption of the new behaviors to the job site

Level 4—results or solving a problem and adding value

Figure 3.1 shows when Kirkpatrick's four levels usually occur in relation to a learning event.

Figure 3.1. Where Measurement Typically Occurs

Prior to the Event	The Event		After the Learning Event	
Pre-Tests 2	2 1	2 1	3	4

Kirkpatrick requires having agreed-on metrics or success indicators and an ability to track whether they occur. Here are some examples using Kirkpatrick's four levels.

- The test scores of participants one week, four weeks, and six months after training are measures of retention of facts. You compare the scores to identify what information has been forgotten and might be in need of support by job aids, help screens, or another type of cueing system.

- The number of people who are better able to do the job one week, four weeks, or six months after training are measures of learning and transfer. You design the tools to help managers identify the presence of performance indicators from the people who completed the training. You might even want to help managers compare the behaviors of those who completed the training to the people who do the same task but did not complete the training to see if there is a difference between the two.

- The number of people who changed their behavior one week, two months, or six months after the training is a measure of transfer. You would design tools to help managers track the desired behaviors, and together you would use the information to determine what cues, incentives, or other devices are required to reinforce the desired behaviors.

Reaction and *learning*, Levels 1 and 2, are measured with surveys and tests during and at the end of the event. Sometimes tests of learning are given before the event to determine if people have already mastered the content and should be exempt from participating in the event. There is another type of pre-test that does not test learning, but readiness. A test of readiness measures whether people have the prerequisite knowledge and ability before starting a program.

REACTIONS AND LEARNING

A multi-national firm only trains on topics specific to required tasks. A survey is handed out at the end of all instructor-led courses. The instructors are rated on their ability to manage class dynamics, engage learners, respond to questions, explain procedures, and so on. The ratings are tracked, averaged monthly, and used to give instructors ongoing feedback. The annual average ratings are one factor considered in the instructors' performance evaluations. In this situation the role of measurement is to assure that instructors receive feedback. The importance of the feedback is reinforced because it is incorporated into the instructors' annual reviews.

Learners are also tested at the end of each module on the content. The scores are used to give learners feedback, identify deficiencies in the materials or the instructional strategy, and help supervisors plan for further coaching once the learner returns to the job. The role of measurement is to assure the instructional integrity of the materials and provide guidance to supervisors.

LEARNING AND TESTING OF FIELD TECHNICIANS

Job-specific technical training for field technicians is four weeks long. Technicians are tested at the end of each week. The tests are paper and pencil, multiple-choice questions with drawings. The tests are scored, and technicians are given their results at the end of the day. There is no "pass" score, only how many are right or wrong. Technicians are directed to self-study materials based on the topic they answered incorrectly. At the end of the fourth week, technicians are given a comprehensive multiple-choice test on the rules and principles covered over the four weeks. Again technicians are given their scores, but test scores are never shared with their bosses. The combined results of all of the tests are used to identify weaknesses in the training. The role of measurement is to identify learning deficiencies and improve the instructional integrity of the program.

LEARNING AND TESTING OF CUSTOMER SERVICE REPS

Customer service representatives (CSRs) are given tests at the end of each module. The modules are on rules for handling customer accounts and maneuvering through computer screens and different legacy systems. The results are shared with the CSR who is given remediation and coaching where required. There is a comprehensive test at the end of the training that encompasses role plays. The role plays require the CSR to confirm the identity of the caller, efficiently maneuver through screens, accurately locate customer files, follow company protocols using a set of recommended questions, properly execute changes to the customer's file, and accurately answer customer questions. The instructors use a performance checklist to judge the adequacy of the performance. If the CSR makes a mistake or is unable to proceed, the instructor can give cues. CSRs have to achieve a minimum score to pass the test. If CSRs fail the test, they are given a provisional rating and assigned to a workgroup where they are given additional coaching. After one week they are re-tested. If they fail again, they are either terminated or assigned to a completely different job. The role of measurement is to reinforce learning, identify deficiencies in knowledge so appropriate remediation can be prescribed, provide guidance to supervisors who are expected to coach new hires, and identify where the instruction might be strengthened.

Chapters Five, Six, Seven, Ten, Eleven, and Twelve have more examples about how to measure the effectiveness of training and other performance support solutions. Tools 3.1 and 3.2 are about how to measure reactions and learning.

TOOL 3.1. GUIDELINES FOR MEASURING REACTIONS

Here are some suggestions for when you prepare your end of course evaluations or want to find out people's reactions to a performance support tool.

- Only ask questions about those things you are in a position to change or act on. Asking about facilities or the lunch menu when you don't have any control over them sets up unrealistic expectations in the learner or user about what you can do.

- Change some questions periodically to focus on the specific things you want feedback on, rather than asking about all things every time. For example, if you are trying out a new facility, caterer, or testing software and have the option of making changes, then ask more questions of a few learners or groups when you can still act on the information.

- Group the questions by topic, that is, put all of the questions about the environment next to each other. Do the same for questions about the media, the delivery style, the content, the materials, and so forth.

- If the program is instructor-led, allow learners to remain anonymous. You can ask them to sign their names and turn in their responses in a way that the instructor cannot trace specific feedback to the source. This can be as simple as having another learner collect the feedback and turn it in to an administrator or asking learners to e-mail their responses to someone other than the instructor.

- Except for the pilot program, keep the number of questions to the relevant few.

- Allow learners space to write in comments. When you read them, group them by theme and then pull out those you can do something about.

- Make most questions a forced-choice scale, preferably an odd number such as 5. Keep the scale consistent with all the positive meanings to the left or the right of the scale, rather than switching back and forth.

- Allow for a "no opinion" or "not sure" or another neutral response.
- Periodically go back to the same group and ask the same relevant few questions to see whether or not their responses have changed over time. In the case that they do, follow up to find out why.

TOOL 3.2. GUIDELINES FOR MEASURING LEARNING

Here are some suggestions for evaluating to what degree people's knowledge and skills changed as a result of participating in a learning event or using a performance support tool.

- If you want to demonstrate that participants "learned" as a result of the program, you have to give a test at the beginning and at the end and compare the results. The tests should be equivalent and only test what was covered in the training.
- If you want to find out if people have the prerequisite knowledge for a class, then give a test at the beginning that does not cover the content of the training but only what people should know and be able to do to fully accomplish the objectives of the training. Be prepared to direct them to other resources if they lack what is required to participate.
- If you want to find out whether people should be allowed to skip the training because they already have the skills and knowledge covered in the course, then give them a test equivalent to the one given at the end of the training.
- If you want to infer that people can apply what was learned in the event, then make sure your test has a high degree of fidelity or emulates the task and the conditions under which it is done on the job. Give them at least three opportunities during the training event to demonstrate they can apply what was taught. The more times they do it during training, the more certainly you can say, "they can do it" on the job. Because if you find out they are not doing it on the job, then something other than a lack of skills and knowledge is interfering with the application.

Transfer, Level 3, is measured after the event by either observing whether a behavior occurs or by checking a work product. The number of people who adopted a recommended set of behaviors on the job and the number of products that possess the appropriate attributes are measures of transfer.

TRANSFER AND JOB PERFORMANCE

The multinational firm that trains field technicians provides job aids and performance checklists to supervisors to help them measure how effectively learners apply job-specific rules and procedures on the job. The firm believes that it is the job of the supervisor to assure adoption of the learning principles, not of training.

TRANSFER AND QUALITY ASSURANCE

Quality assurance tracks errors made by customer service representatives. Errors that are due to misapplying a procedure or not complying with a rule are communicated to training and to management on a monthly basis. Training and management then meet monthly to identify what other performance support might be required to assure compliance.

Chapter Five on "How to Measure Hard and Soft Skills" and Chapter Seven on "How to Measure Elective Training and Employee Relations Programs" give information on what has to be in place to increase the probability of transfer. Tool 3.3 has suggestions for how to measure the degree to which people's behavior changed when they returned to the work setting as a result of participating in a learning event or using a performance support tool.

Results, Level 4, are whether or not the training satisfied a need or solved a problem. They are measured after sufficient time has passed for the consequences to materialize. Other external outcome measures are

- Acceptance
- Compliance
- Competence or effectiveness, performance, productivity, and proficiency
- Penetration
- Retention and satisfaction

You use this information to determine what needs to be put in place to reinforce the desired behaviors.

Acceptance and *compliance* are about people manifesting recommended behaviors and, perhaps advocating that others do the same. The metrics might be:

- The frequency with which a desired behavior appears or an undesired behavior does not appear compared to the number of opportunities available to manifest the behavior

TOOL 3.3. GUIDELINES FOR MEASURING THE TRANSFER OF LEARNING

If you want to evaluate to what degree people apply the skills and knowledge covered in a training program, and the program has not been implemented, meet with the client to do the following:

1. Find out how soon after training people will have the opportunity to apply what was covered in the program. Use that as a guide for how long to wait before measuring whether or not they do.

2. Identify the barriers to applying what was taught and work with management to address them.

3. If the opportunity to apply is rare or unpredictable, then develop tools such as job aids to support the new behaviors when they are required.

4. Develop tools that help the supervisor and the learner assess if and how well they apply the rules and principles included in the training. An example is an action table that is used as a learning tool in the classroom and later as a check-off sheet by the manager when reviewing employees' performance on specific tasks. Try not to do the observations yourself unless in a quality assurance capacity.

5. Decide what the client will accept as evidence of learning and transfer, as this is the information you collect to determine whether or not people's behavior changed as a result of the training. The evidence might include

   • The adoption or the ceasing of behaviors

   • Behaviors or choices that comply with guidelines

   • Outputs or work products that comply with standards

6. Decide who will collect the data, how, when, and how many times.

7. Determine what help you might give the client to measure whether people are applying the content.

If the program has already been launched, but these questions were not previously answered, meet with the client to do the following:

1. Find out if it is important enough to the client to confirm that people are applying the content of the training. If the answer is no, don't go any further. If the answer is yes, decide how that might be done.

2. Review their expectations of the program. Ask what the measures were that the client planned to use to determine whether or not training was effective.

3. Find out what they are and are not paying attention to that tells them people learned and are using what they learned.

4. Decide what other evidence the client might use to determine whether people are applying the content of the training.

- The number of people who demonstrate the desired behaviors when appropriate
- The number of people whose behavior or work products satisfy some standard
- The number of times a behavior or output did not comply with rules, regulations, or policy
- The frequency with which the target audience advocates or promotes the preferred behavior in communications and by their own actions

You use this information as an indicator that the appropriate behaviors are being reinforced and correlate it with other success indicators, such as customer or employee retention and satisfaction and reduced complaints or rework.

Measures of *competence, effectiveness, performance, productivity,* and *proficiency* can apply to people, products, and investments. You help supervisors by giving them job aids that make it easier for them to (1) identify behaviors, work products, and other results that meet standards and (2) give meaningful feedback. The metrics might include

- The number of people whose work products or outputs were within an acceptable range, at standard, satisfied the requirements of the job, or met expectations
- The amount of work or work products produced within a given time period that satisfied the requirements of the job or met expectations
- The return gained from an investment within a given time period compared to other investment choices
- The percentage of outputs that achieved the desired results compared to the total number of outputs generated

You use this information to identify the need for other support mechanisms, such as job aids, mentors, or help desks, and to show the effectiveness of your programs and solutions.

Penetration is the number of people who participated in your programs compared to the total size of the potential audience. How quickly you penetrated the market is more a measure of your efficiency unless you think of it as a measure of your ability to understand your market and your ability to reach it. Metrics might be

- Percent growth of market share
- Time or speed to market

You use this information to spread your costs across the market, evaluate your marketing efforts, more accurately estimate your ability to promote other programs, and identify the need to engage in other marketing activities.

Retention and *satisfaction* are about how much people's behavior or actions, or a product's performance meet customer and employee expectations. A metric might be

- Customers' and employees' level of satisfaction before and after a program was introduced on the promise it would improve satisfaction

- Customer and employee retention rates before and after a change that was intended to increase retention rates

You use this information to determine whether management requires further guidance on how to better reinforce the behaviors that correlate with retention and satisfaction.

REACTION AND LEARNING AND THE COST OF CUSTOMER SUPPORT

A manufacturer of complex technical equipment trains customers on how to use that equipment. The business goal is to reduce the cost of customer support as measured by the number and length of calls to the help desk. The premise is that less capable customers have more equipment malfunctions and require more support and thus increase costs. The cost of the training includes travel and lodging and meals. Customers are surveyed at the end of the course as to their total learning experience (housing, meals, convenience, and instructor attributes). The survey results are used to identify trends and negative responses that might require a follow-up call from someone in sales and to provide feedback to the hotel where customers stay. Customers are also tested at the end of key modules and at the end of the course. The final test requires customers to operate and perform common maintenance on a piece of equipment. The test results are used in two ways: (1) to identify areas where the instruction might be improved and (2) to track the impact of calls to the help desk. The frequency and length of calls to the help desk are matched to customers' training history. The customers' training history is then correlated with the overall cost of support by the help desk.

LEARNING AND BRAND IMAGE

A manufacturer of industrial equipment contracts with local service centers to repair and service its equipment. The business goal is to preserve brand image and retain customer loyalty. The premise is that customers do not distinguish the brand from the local service center. If the equipment fails or is not properly repaired or made operational within a reasonable time, the customer blames the manufacturer, not the local service center.

The manufacturer trains the technicians who work for the local centers. For the final test, technicians are sent a broken piece of equipment, asked to identify the problem, fix the problem, and then return the equipment. The manufacturer then judges the adequacy of the repair. The manufacturer doesn't care how long it takes to fix the equipment, as it feels it is the job of the local center manager to judge efficiency and productivity. The manufacturer tracks and correlates revenue from the sales of parts, customer satisfaction survey scores, and technicians' training history by center.

REACTION AND CUSTOMER RETENTION

Precision Instruments offers training to customers on the role of weights and balances in statistical process control. The business goal is to retain customer loyalty and to reduce the cost of sales. Customers are surveyed at the end of the course on their reactions to the content, the learning environment, and the instructor's approach. The company correlates customer participation in the program with the purchase of new equipment, the dollar value of the sale, and the length of time after the training before the sale occurs.

There are more examples of how organizations measure the results of their training in the remaining chapters. Tool 3.4 is a set of guidelines for measuring results. It is in two parts. Part A has general guidelines and Part B has guidelines for measuring financial impact.

How to Identify and Collect External Measures

The best way to identify useful external measures is to help the client do it. The client is closest to the situation and in a better position to obtain information. However, if the client is very busy or spread too thinly with

TOOL 3.4A. GUIDELINES FOR MEASURING RESULTS

Here are some suggestions for how to evaluate whether or not a problem was solved or an opportunity seized as a result of people participating in your learning event or using a performance support tool.

- Decide in advance what problem you want to solve or what opportunity you want it to help actualize. Express the problem or opportunity in measurable or performance terms, that is, given [a description of the work environment], people will [the behaviors to be demonstrated or products produced], so that [the criteria that will be used to judge whether business results or consequences were sufficiently changed to conclude training made a difference].

- Make the assumptive base for the training or performance support tool explicit, such as "We believe that if people can do skill X or have knowledge Y, that result Z will happen."

- Decide in advance what the indicators of success will be and how they will be noticed, collected, or monitored. There are many more examples in the following chapters.

- Decide in advance how much time should pass before the impact will materialize sufficiently to be measurable.

- Identify other corroborating evidence that might be available.

TOOL 3.4B. GUIDELINES FOR MEASURING FINANCIAL IMPACT

Here are some suggestions for surfacing financial measures of success.

- Involve the client and someone from the department who knows how the organization accounts for monies and weighs investments.

- Ask what financial measures the client wants to impact and how those measures are determined now.

- Ask how return on investment is currently calculated.

- Ask what information you and the client would have to provide to help determine if a recommended solution should be considered and how it would be measured if implemented.

- Ask how that information would be captured or tracked and who would do it.

Note: Later tools contain sample measures and how to use them.

responsibilities, then you can help by suggesting two or three indicators of success. Try to partner with other functions that collect performance and productivity information. For example, other departments collect information such as the number of callbacks, customer complaints, citations, and budget variances. You can work with them and perhaps suggest ways to format the data so it helps you and the client see trends and draw valid conclusions. If your program is part of a larger initiative, you should partner with the other departments to identify the success indicators they want to monitor and how that data will be tracked.

MISSTEPS

Here are some of the oversights that trainers and training departments frequently make:

1. They avoid evaluating results because they think it is their job and they can't see how they will ever get the information required to prove value. They forget that it is management's job to evaluate performance. The problem is that management will not or cannot dedicate resources to do it. However, it is training's job to create the tools to make it easier.

2. They collect information such as test scores and end of course evaluations but don't use the data.

3. They don't identify interim points of measure but wait until the "end" to see whether the problem was solved. Unfortunately, you and others have changed jobs by the time the "end" arrives and new people are in place who may not know why a solution was chosen and what it was designed to impact.

TIPS AND TECHNIQUES

Here are some suggestions about how to decide on what to evaluate and how to do it.

You don't have to evaluate results after every offering. You don't have to evaluate reaction or anything else all of the time. What is important is that you can and do use the results. So evaluate that which helps you better manage and puts you in a position to show results.

SUMMARY

Measuring acceptance, competence, and so on is as much the job of the manager as it is that of training. Training's role is to assure fidelity and integrity of its programs and to develop friendly tools that make the managers' job of measuring, monitoring, tracking, rewarding, and giving feedback easier. There are many more suggestions and tools on how to measure effectiveness in Chapters Five, Six, Seven, and Eight.

**WHERE TO
LEARN MORE**

Kirkpatrick, D. *Evaluating Training Programs: The Four Levels* (San Francisco, CA: Berrett-Koehler, 1998).

Stolovitch, H. D., and Maurice, J.-G. *Performance Improvement,* 1998, 37: 8:9–20.

Swanson, R. Demonstrating Return on Investment in Performance Improvement Projects, *Handbook of HPT* (2nd ed.) (San Francisco, CA: Jossey-Bass, 1999).

Phillips, J. *Return on Investment: In Training and Performance Improvement Programs* (Houston, TX: Gulf, 1997).

Wade, P. A. *Measuring the Impact of Training* (Irvine, CA: Richard Chang Associates, 1995).

Wallace, G. *lean-IS,* the chapter on Performance Analysis (2, 21–27); and *T&D Systems View,* the chapters on Cost/Benefit Measurement (Naperville, IL, CADDI, 1999).

Chapter 4

How to Measure Efficiency

It was budget time again. The department had some idea about how many new hires there would be, how many new products the company was planning to launch, and what the expected rollout date was for the new computer system. It knew there was never enough time to do a thorough job analysis, much less a needs analysis, and the time and money to evaluate were not there. What they did not know was what it would take in time, resources, or dollars to do the work.

*T*his chapter is about how to measure your efficiency (how you operate). Efficiency is measured in time, speed, and resource consumption. What facts you collect will depend on what you want to do with what you find, and how much data you collect will depend on how precise you need to be in your findings. How you analyze the facts will depend on how certain you have to be in your recommendations.

INTERNAL MEASURES

Internal measures are the facts you collect to determine whether you are efficient in what you do or whether you should improve your processes. For example, by measuring you can learn where to improve. It leads you to questions such as:

- How can we better anticipate customer requests for services?
- How can we better understand what customers are trying to accomplish so we can come up with recommendations that will meet their needs?

- How can we improve our processes in terms of the time they take, the resources they require, and the results they produce?
- What activities consume resources?
- What does it cost to do things a certain way?
- What does it cost to respond to requests?
- What percentage of our time is spent on tasks, doing what, and why?

Then you identify the activities you typically engage in, what causes you to engage in them, how much time each takes, and the number of resources they require. You compare the activities in terms of how many hours, how much equipment, or how many dollars each consumes to identify those which are the more costly to perform and why. If you have access to benchmark data or have access to industry standards, you can compare your activities and hours to those. Some specific examples of internal measures are shown in Table 4.1.

Input-Related Measures

Frequency is about how often you receive certain types of requests. The metrics you might use are

- How many requests are from the same group within a given time frame
- How many requests are from different groups within a given time frame
- How many repeat requests there are
- How often work, plans, or projects were reworked due to changes in the audience profile, modifications made to the content or requirements, or sponsor expectations

This information is useful for identifying the groups you should be in relationships with so you can better anticipate their needs and plan how to service them.

Predictability is about your ability to anticipate the need for your services. It means you have to know what usually causes customers to call, such as

Table 4.1. Internal Measures

Input related:	Process related:
Frequency	Cost
Predictability	Resource consumption
Uniqueness	Cycle time
	Speed
	Variance

bringing on new hires or turnover, meeting regulatory or licensure and certification requirements, supporting new initiatives, product launches, and policy changes. The metrics you might use are

- How many requests you receive that you don't have a process in place to handle
- How many times you did not have a plan in place to respond to requests
- How many requests were not in your budget or work plan

This information is useful for identifying where you need to improve your operational knowledge about your clients or your communications with them.

Uniqueness is about how unusual requests are. For example, orientation for new hires would be a standard request; however, training mechanics in how to reengineer the process for handling electrical outages caused by a major construction contractor might not be typical. Uniqueness is a measure because such requests may require you to engage the help of specialists or go outside of your normal way of doing business. The metrics you might use are

- The number of requests requiring specialists or revised processes
- The number of requests requiring capabilities outside your current abilities or an excessive amount of time, thus jeopardizing other projects

This information is helpful to better identify the resources required to do the work and where you might begin to build relationships with experts inside and outside of the organization.

REWRITES

The human resource development department at a banking firm began to measure how the need for rewrites of its training added costs and delayed launches. Specifically, it tracked cost, time, and the cause of the rewrites. It found that the main cause of rewrites was disagreement within management on what the rules or procedures were. One manager would serve as the "subject-matter expert" but later, when the program was being piloted, other managers and representatives from legal would take issue with the content, necessitating rewrites. The training department used this information to negotiate a new design process that assured the involvement of all the departments with a vested interest in the program's integrity. Costs and political sensitivities were reduced, and overall development cycle time went down.

Tool 4.1 is a discussion guide for you and your team. It is meant to help you better anticipate requests from clients.

TOOL 4.1. HOW TO MEASURE INPUTS

Meet with other trainers or key clients and reflect on where you think the most energy and time was spent over the last three, six, or twelve months for you or for the group. If possible, corroborate your understanding with information from a timekeeping or budget system that gives you the following information.

1. Was the time and emotional energy spent in design, development, production, delivery, client management, vendor management, or other? Which activities were the more costly?

2. What was the driver or cause of what you did, for example, was it new hires, to support the implementation of a new technology or a new product launch, the need to comply with regulatory requirements, a new curriculum roll out, migration to a new delivery system, or what?

3. Will the driver(s) be the same or different? If different, what are they?

4. What do you think will demand the most time and energy in the coming three, six, or twelve months? Design, development, production, delivery, client management, vendor management, or other?

5. If possible, identify which activities have in the past and will in the future cost the most in terms of dollars, time, or emotional energy. The activities that are the most demanding are probably the ones you want to better understand and improve your processes for, particularly if you foresee them continuing in the future.

6. How much of what you did was budgeted for or part of your annual work plan? How much was not?

7. Ask what you could have done to better predict or anticipate client requests for services.

8. Ask what you as a group can do to better anticipate requests and resource requirements in the future.

Use the results of your discussion to identify ways to improve your methods for anticipating work and required resources.

Process-Related Measures

Training's typical processes include:

- Needs assessments
- Job or task analysis

- Design and development of programs
- Production of materials
- Schedules and coordination of sessions
- Registration of students
- Selection and management of vendors
- Maintenance of student records
- Maintenance of program content and materials

Efficient processes consistently and cost-effectively generate outputs that meet requirements. When processes are stable, it is easy to measure their efficiency and effectiveness. When processes are haphazard, untested, not understood, or not followed, it is harder to evaluate whether or not they produce results in a cost-effective way. When evaluation is a strategy, you can question what is known about your processes, identify those that consume an excessive number of resources, and identify those that use very costly resources or take too long. You start by asking questions and then validating:

- What work is before you and what processes will be required to carry out that work
- How efficient those processes are in terms of how many resources they consume, what those resources cost, and how long they take

You take what you learn and direct resources to improving your inefficient and costly processes. Processes are evaluated in terms of their costs, resource consumption, speed, and variance.

Cost is about time and dollars and applies to people, physical assets, materials, and programs. The metrics might include:

- The cost, in hours or dollars, to communicate with clients and stay current in their operations
- The number of hours or dollars required to maintain courses, keep a program current and up and running
- The cost of different delivery systems and media
- The amount of space (a capital asset) in square feet dedicated to training, how frequently it is used, what the capacity is, and how often it is filled to capacity
- The costs to create, produce, pilot, and implement a program

This information is used to build your budget, price your services, and identify areas where you should reduce costs.

Resource consumption is about how many resources (people, equipment, dollars) are used or consumed in the work you do, for example:

- Administrative systems such as registration, billing, tuition reimbursement—how many people it takes to run the systems, how many hours are spent on administration and the cost of the resources, how quickly administrative tasks are done

- Logistics—how many people and how much time is consumed handling the logistics of scheduling and conducting an event, disseminating a performance support tool or pre-course materials, or tracking where learners are in completing a curriculum

- Productivity—how many training hours were delivered by how many trainers within a specific time frame or how many courses were developed by contract developers within a given time frame or dollar amount

- Resource utilization—the percentage of time trainers, course and media developers, and administrative personnel were at task, the percentage of billable time compared to total time, or the percentage of time classrooms and computer carrels are in use

This information is used to identify areas where you should streamline, better leverage your resources, or invest in new systems.

Cycle time is the overall time it takes to produce a product or output. Cycle time includes process time (the time spent doing worthy work) and non-value-adding activities, such as waiting, checking, moving, and reworking. Possible metrics are

- The percentage of time spent on non-value-adding activities compared to the percentage spent on value-adding activities

- The ratio of process time to overall cycle time

This information is used to identify those processes that have a lot of waste and that take an excessive amount of time. You can then decide whether you need to do work differently or do different work.

Speed is about how long it takes or how quickly you can design, develop, produce, and deliver products overall (cycle time). Possible metrics are

- The turnaround time it takes to deliver a plan of action or obtain approvals

- The lapse time waiting for approvals, production, and access to people or equipment

This information is helpful to identify where you need to improve or build new processes.

Variance is about the ability of your processes to produce outputs of consistent quality and usefulness. Possible metrics are

- How much the actual cost of a needs assessment varies from what was budgeted
- How much the actual cost to produce and deploy a program varies from what was budgeted
- How consistently your time estimates for job analyses are accurate

This information is used to identify processes that have cost overruns or that require rework for the results to be useable so that you can dedicate resources to improve them.

The first step to improving the efficiency of your processes is to describe them. There are different ways to describe a process. Whatever way you use, you want the description to capture the following information:

- What activities make up the process
- What and how many resources are consumed by each activity
- How much time is spent on average for each activity
- The relationship of the activities to each other, that is, which are done sequentially and which are done concurrently

You can create a process map or document your procedures with this information. The goal is to create a picture of what you do and in what order, the people involved, and the inputs and outputs of each step. You want enough information to identify the following:

- The information used in each step or activity
- Where that information comes from
- What technology is used in each step or activity
- What and how many resources that technology uses
- The cost of the resources
- The information produced by each step or activity and who uses it

COST DRIVERS

Cost drivers are things that result in the consumption of too many resources or use of overly costly resources. The major cost drivers are

- Inefficient processes
- Inappropriate or misunderstood customer or business requirements
- A lack of standards
- People who perform poorly due to lack of skills or knowledge

Cost drivers are identified by (1) isolating costs, (2) determining what contributes to or makes up those costs, (3) finding out what most influences those costs, and (4) finding out which costs, if changed, would have the greatest impact on a product's or service's cost. The tools you use to identify cost drivers are

- *Budgets* that break out cost components
- *Activity-based accounting* to identify what drives administrative and production costs
- *Process maps* to identify what drives processing costs
- *Needs assessments* to identify the implications of overly satisfying or under-satisfying customers
- *Resource capacity studies* to identify the implications of excess or insufficient capacity

The information gained from these methods can be used

- To do more or less
- To allocate more or less money
- To change the way things are done or what is being done
- To improve people skills and knowledge

The way to manage cost drivers is

- To improve processes, especially a well-designed intake process to clarify and confirm customer expectations and requirements (see Tool 4.2)
- To develop standards for material, such as format, media selection, and review procedures, as they reduce the variance in how work gets done
- To develop support tools to help you and your people execute all of the processes efficiently and consistently
- To support your and your team's professional development

TOOL 4.2. HOW TO EVALUATE PROCESSES

1. With your team, identify what your customers require of you. Consider things such as:
   - Faster turnaround time for program development
   - Reduced lag time between product or technology launches and training launches
   - On-line course registration
   - Qualified educational products, vendors, facilitators, and trainers
   - Current materials and job aids

2. List the processes that most impact your ability to meet client expectations.

3. Select one process in need of improvement that currently negatively impacts your ability to satisfy client requirements.

4. Describe that process:
   - Identify the activities and tasks that make up the process
   - Identify the information available at each activity and task
   - Identify the technology used
   - Identify the resources consumed
   - Identify the cost of those resources
   - Identify where and how activities or tasks shift costs to other processes, departments, suppliers, end customers, or the consumer

5. Look for activities that do not add value and you can eliminate because they
   - are redundant
   - are unnecessary
   - Consume too many resources
   - Force activities on other processes that do not add value

6. Look for opportunities where fewer or less costly resources can be used and still achieve the same or better outcome.

7. Look for instances where false economies exist because the current process shifts costs to other processes.

8. Identify any factors that cause the total time to exceed the actual time required.

9. Identify any policies, standards, or requirements that result in activities or the use of resources that do not add value, add unnecessary costs, or shift costs.

10. Identify any instances where the information used and produced by the process is late, incomplete, or insufficient and results in non-value-added activities or the use of unnecessary or too costly resources.

11. Look for situations where the technologies used by the process result in non-value-added activities or the use of unnecessary or too costly resources.

12. Look for situations where technology might be used to eliminate activities or resources.

13. Consider a time system that allows you to track how much time people spend on specific activities. However, counting all of the task hours, dollars spent, time spent waiting, or resources consumed will mean very little unless you compare the answer to some expectation, goal, or standard. When you compare what you learn to historic data or expectations, you find out how well you are doing and whether there is a need to improve.

14. Identify ways that allow you to compare the time and budget required for the same process when it is done more than once. Use the comparisons to identify any causes for variances in time and budget.

COST ESTIMATES

The learning and performance department at a manufacturer measured what it cost on average to develop every component of its technical training, convert training to the Web, and conduct classroom training at regional centers. At the end of each project, it identified what negatively impacted costs and what activities were the most costly. It used this information to implement better project management controls and to negotiate penalty clauses with vendors. Because of its aggressive tracking of costs, it reduced the variance between its budget and actual expenses. It also used the information to negotiate a different working relationship with operations. Training was able to prove that involving training after a certain point in the development of new products increased costs and delayed product launches.

NEW SOFTWARE

The training department of a major merchandiser tracked the number of times required and the hours and dollars involved to update information for its stores located in all fifty states. The need to update, which came weekly, was driven by the states changing their regulations. Every state had a different set of regulations. Training had to update the information, communicate it to the stores, and maintain documentation for state auditors. It used the results to justify the development of proprietary software that would reduce the cost of updating, deploying, documenting, and generating reports for the individual states.

FORMATIVE EVALUATION

Formative evaluation is a type of internal measure; however, instead of being about how you work, it is about assuring the integrity of the products and programs you develop. Formative evaluation measures work "in process" to determine whether corrections or adjustments should be made before a program is launched. Examples are content reviews and pilot sessions to identify any errors or problems before a program is formally deployed. You can do formative evaluations on all the elements that make up a product, including:

- Media, material, and Web designs
- Instructional and delivery tactics
- Accuracy and sequence of the content

When you do formative evaluation, you measure:

- Accuracy and completeness—whether the rules, procedures, principles, and examples that make up the content are correct.
- Fidelity—how close the examples, practice exercises, or illustrations are to what people actually experience or use on the job. (The closer something is to the real thing, the higher its fidelity. Fidelity is a major strength of virtual reality and some computer simulations.)
- Timing—how long it takes the learner to get through the materials or to do the exercises, or how long it takes the instructor to set up and complete an instructional tactic such as a simulation or role play.
- Utility and ease of use—can the instructor and learner maneuver through the materials, Web page, or job aid easily, and are the directions clear?

Marketing firms and software and product designers do user testing, which is similar to a formative evaluation, for example:

- Marketing looks at receptiveness, aesthetics, and price sensitivity
- Software and product designers look at utility, functionality, and ease of use

In each of these situations, the goal is to assure all elements are accurate and perform as expected. Tool 4.3 has suggestions on how to do formative evaluations.

TOOL 4.3. HOW TO DO FORMATIVE EVALUATIONS

Here are some suggestions for how to evaluate the accuracy and usefulness of a program or product's elements before you commit the resources to produce and deploy it.

1. When checking the accuracy of the content, involve more than the subject-matter experts or high performers you used to obtain the data initially. Use people who were not involved in the development. They will help you identify ambiguities and mixed messages. Confirm that the principles, procedures, and rules on which the training or performance support tool is based are accepted by others. The earlier you discover there is a disagreement on the content, the faster you can resolve it. It is less costly to insist on a resolution early rather than wait until after exercises, job aids, and other learning devices have been developed.

2. When evaluating the clarity of instructions or messages, ask novices, people unfamiliar with the content, to evaluate it. High performers and people who helped you create the materials are less likely to notice logic flaws, deletions, or conflicting messages.

3. When evaluating the user friendliness of a performance support tool, delivery method, or administrative system, ask representatives of the target audience, the people who will use it, not those who helped design it.

HOW TO FIND INTERNAL MEASURES

First, determine what you want to find out. Once you are clear, you can set up systems to capture the information. If you want to better understand the economic ramifications of how you operate, involve someone in your organization who is responsible for capturing and analyzing operating metrics and financial information. The method you use to capture the information might be a training management system that tracks the number of offerings, students, completions, cancellations, and so on. Some organizations set up time records for their exempt staff also, as this allows them to assign time to projects and customers. You can create tools like Tool 1.3 for evaluating your portfolio to identify what you know and still need to confirm about your operation. Other sources of internal measures are industry standards from benchmarking.

MISSTEPS

Here are some of the oversights that trainers and training departments frequently make:

1. They confuse the pilot with the launch. They delay doing a pilot-test of the design, materials, and so forth (formative evaluations) until it is so late in the project that they run out of money and time to make the necessary adjustments.

2. They overly focus on results and fail to see the benefits of evaluating and improving the effectiveness of their own processes.

3. They avoid developing standards (design, media, instructional, and others). Standards and common templates can reduce cycle time, allow for chunking content into reusable units, and make it easier for the learner.

4. They resist formalizing their processes (needs assessment, contracting, design, development, pilot-testing, and so forth), making it harder to measure and improve them.

TIPS AND TECHNIQUES

Here are some suggestions about how to decide on what to evaluate and how to do it:

1. Do your formative evaluations such as pilots early enough in the process that you still have money and time to make adjustments.

2. Look at the work in front of you and identify the processes you expect to use most. Use the work as an opportunity to develop standards and document the processes you follow intuitively.

3. Practice being more stringent on how you capture time (scope out a project, develop a template, covert text to the Web, and so forth). Use what you learn to estimate what it will cost in time and dollars to do similar work in the future. Then compare your estimates with what the actual time was. The goal is not to be perfect or precise, but to become better at estimating. You want your estimates to be close approximations of what it will take to do the work. This ability evolves over time.

SUMMARY

You want to track enough information about what you have to work with and how you work with it to be able to respond to questions about how well you are managing company assets. Management is very interested in keeping resources, such as trainers and training rooms and equipment, busy doing things they think are important. These resources represent cash that is no longer available, so accounting departments in particular want to know that those resources are in use. Companies are looking for ways to reduce the amount of capital they have tied up in physical assets. Buildings, for example, tie up dollars that could be used in other ways. Some methods companies are using include selling buildings and leasing them back and asking people to work at home, while providing only "touch down" spaces at work. Therefore, management wants to know that training rooms and equipment are being used for purposes that benefit the company. They are doing the same thing when it comes to people. Companies are outsourcing non-core functions. They are shifting the responsibility for training and support to suppliers and third-party, after-market partners like distributors. They are willing to pay more for support on a per-hour basis if it means it frees up dollars they can use for other things when the service is not needed. Knowing how many resources you are consuming and how much product you are producing puts you in a better position to do the following:

- Explain what you are doing and why
- Begin to question whether there are better ways to accomplish the same ends
- Be sensitive to what is driving your actions so you can better anticipate the impact when those drivers cease to exist or change in some way

Measuring can help you manage the function better and it can help you anticipate and prepare for change. However, consider measuring all of your processes and protocols for doing work, not once, but periodically. Use the information to improve and publicize your commitment to working smarter. Similarly, measure the effectiveness of your programs and products. Again, you don't have to evaluate every one every time or at every level. Instead, set priorities for the year or for a client, and commit to doing the type of evaluation that will help you and the client appreciate what has been accomplished. Chapters Two and Three continue the subject of how to measure learning, transfer, and results. They contain tools and techniques to help you more effectively evaluate what you do.

WHERE TO LEARN MORE

If you want to learn more about statistical process control (SPC)[1] then check out the following:

Amsden, R. T., Amsden, D. M., and Butler, H. E. *SPC Simplified for Services* (New York: Productivity, Inc., May 1991).

Amsden, R. T., Amsden, D. M., and Butler, H. E. *SPC Simplified: Practical Steps to Quality* (New York: Productivity Inc., 1998).

Amsden, R. T., Amsden, D. M., and Butler, H. E. *SPC Simplified Workbook: Practice Steps to Quality* (2nd ed.)(New York: Productivity Inc., April 1998).

Hupp, T., Polak, C., and Westgaard, O. *Designing Work Groups, Jobs, and Workflow* (San Francisco, CA: Jossey-Bass, 1995). This book contains "how tos" on describing how work is and should get done.

Johann, B. *Designing Cross-Functional Business Processes* (San Francisco, CA: Jossey-Bass, 1995). This book contains "how tos" on describing how work is and should get done.

Wallace, G. *lean-ISD* (Naperville, IL, CADDI, 1999). See the chapter on performance analysis (2, 21–27)

Wallace, G. *T&D Systems View* (Naperville, IL, CADDI, 2002). See the chapter on process improvement.

NOTE

1. Statistical Process Control (SPC) evaluates processes according to the following scale: (1) a *visible* process, where you have enough data to assess the stability of the process and the consistency of the end product or output; (2) a *stable* process, where you experience no unpredictable causes to any variation in the product or output; (3) a *capable* process, where you have enough data to determine that your products and outputs are consistent and within standard; and (4) an *optimum* process, where you have enough data to show that you can produce products or outputs that are within standard and meet customer needs.

Chapter 5

How to Measure Hard and Soft Skills

The organization invested $3M to roll out a leadership program for over two hundred managers. Now questions are being asked such as: Did managers' behavior change on the job? Will the investment help us meet our business goals? Should we have used the money elsewhere? These are all good questions, but other questions should have been asked much earlier, such as: What is the problem we are trying to solve? Why is it we believe leadership behaviors will solve it? What are the leadership behaviors we are looking for? What happens when they are absent? Did the training include sufficient opportunities to apply the leadership behaviors? and Will these new behaviors be supported in the workplace?

*T*his chapter is about the role of measurement to support the adoption of hard and soft skills. You measure:

- To what degree the skill is described in measurable terms
- The presence or absence of the desired behavior, the quality and quantity of the skills' outputs, and the effect of the behavior or output on others and on the organization
- The degree to which the organization's infrastructure and performance management system support the desired behaviors and production of outputs to standard

- To what degree the training has the required elements to build the skills to the level of complexity required
- How effective the training is at bringing learners to the desired level of proficiency
- Whether bringing people to proficiency accomplished the intended goal

If measurement does not occur, it is difficult if not impossible to say that people learned, why they did or did not apply what they learned, and how the organization benefited.

SKILLS AND REQUIREMENTS

Skill is the ability to use one's knowledge effectively and readily in execution or performance. It is the learned power of doing something competently . . . a developed aptitude or ability.[1] The possession or absence of skills shows up in people's behaviors, choices, and work products. We say people are skilled or proficient based on our judgment of the appropriateness of their behaviors and choices and the quality of their work.

Performance requirements are specific to a job but can be independent of skills and knowledge. Performance requirements are things like being twenty-one years of age; being able to lift seventy-five pounds unassisted or reach five and a half feet without the use of a ladder; having 20/20 eyesight with or without corrective lenses; being able to accurately discern colors; holding a commercial driver's license; being drug free; and being available to work certain hours or in specific locations. The role of evaluation is to confirm that the requirements were derived from a valid job analysis or that they satisfy the unique needs of the organization, such as security.

HARD AND SOFT SKILLS

Trainers frequently make a distinction between hard and soft skills. What makes a skill hard or soft is the ability to describe it sufficiently so that its presence or absence can be recognized. *Hard skills* are easier to describe and recognize because they are more likely about how to follow a procedure, for example, wire an electrical outlet, take an x-ray, add a computer to a network, maneuver through a series of computer screens, or operate a piece of equipment. Managers can observe the behaviors and choices and judge the quality of the outputs, for example, the outlet works, the x-ray is readable, the computer can access the network, and employees can locate the correct screen or drive the forklift.

Other skills are harder to observe except in their absence, such as listening, being nice, taking the initiative, and problem solving. These skills are frequently referred to as "soft." However, skills become less "soft" the better you can describe the specific desired behaviors and the work conditions under which they are expected to occur. In reality, however, most tasks are complex and draw on a combination of hard and soft skills such as project management, sales, sales management, and customer service.

Most programs that profess to develop "soft" skills fall into one of three categories:

1. *Reasoning or logic skills*—problem solving, trouble shooting, thinking smart, weighing the odds, making sound financial decisions, qualifying buyers, and anticipating change are some examples. These are actually complex analytical skills that are developed over time through experience. On the surface these skills may seem harder to "see" because the behaviors are not overt, but they manifest themselves in decisions and recommendations.

2. *Interpersonal and communication skills*—listening, relationship management, team building, negotiation, customer service, appreciation of diversity, coaching, and counseling are some examples. These skill sets are more about making appropriate choices about how and with whom to interact and, therefore, depend on personal values.

3. *Leadership, management, and entrepreneurial skills*—supervision, selling, territory management, project management, influencing others, and risk taking are some examples. These, too, are complex skill sets that involve both analytical abilities and personal values.

Organizations have a vested interest in employees learning job-related skills and, therefore, reinforce the application on the job. Many job-related skills are procedural or hard skills. However, when soft skills are required for the job, organizations usually make them part of the hiring criteria. It takes a lot of training, experience, and coaching for people to acquire highly developed analytical or interpersonal skills. It takes a very supportive performance management system to reinforce choices and behaviors that might run counter to people's personal values.

PERFORMANCE SYSTEM

Training's role is to provide opportunities to practice the new behaviors in a safe arena and to give people feedback on how well they do. But training by itself cannot make people perpetuate new behaviors back on the job. If the organization wants people to develop and manifest hard or soft skills, then the behaviors must be rewarded or there must be consequences for not exhibiting them on the job. Once the training is completed, people require feedback and support systems so they can adjust their old behaviors to more closely emulate those that are desired. If you want hard or soft skills to manifest themselves in the workplace, you have to confirm that all elements required for performance are in place, such as clear expectations, feedback, incentives, consequences, performance support tools, and protocols on how to handle exceptions. Figure 5.1 shows the required elements of an effective performance system.

The figure shows that infrastructure, performance management, and performance support are interdependent in terms of contributing to organizational effectiveness. Each has a role to play and each must equally bear the weight to sustain performance over time. The better able human resources is at recruiting people who can satisfy the requirements and who have the enabling technical, professional, self-management, and communication skills, the more training can focus on the skills and knowledge specific to the job. However, when people lack these basic skill sets, training and management have to do more. Training has to either help people develop the enabling skills or develop more on-the-job performance support tools and provide extra coaching. Management may have to redesign the jobs or provide more resources, such as well-documented procedures. The less willing or able management is to provide resources, the greater the burden is on human

Figure 5.1. Elements of a Performance System

Organizational Infrastructure

Vision, mission, values, objectives

Tools and documentation

Information systems

Communication systems

Stable processes and viable procedures

Rules and policies

Job and task design

Facilities and equipment

Performance Management System	**Performance Support System**
Hiring profiles—skills, knowledge	Performance aids and job aids
Job requirements	Help screens
Performance objectives or expectations	Help desks
Performance standards and measures	Developmental assignments
Feedback	Coaches and mentors
Rewards and consequences	Training

resources to attract people who can work with fewer resources—and on training to provide more learning exercises and feedback, make the exercises realistic, and develop job aids and performance support tools. It is through measuring that you can determine the following:

- Whether the desired skills are adequately described
- Whether the organizational infrastructure is in place to support the desired skills
- Whether the performance management system will recognize and reward the new skills
- Whether the performance *support* system is in place to enable and further *support* the application of the new skills

COMMON SENSE

A senior executive lamented that purchasing agents who contracted with suppliers and managed supply chains around the world lacked common sense. The agents' failure to think through commitments damaged relationships, caused unanticipated grief, and drove up costs due to shortages and overstocks. The trainer began by identifying decisions that were examples of poor and good judgment. She used the techniques of defining abstract concepts to identify the attributes that were present in good and absent from bad decisions. Her product was an operational definition (see Exhibit 5.1).

Exhibit 5.1. Operational Definition of Common Sense

The skills, knowledge, and willingness to
    Know what is feasible
    Accept that everything comes with a cost whether it be now or later
    Get to the heart of the issue and quickly get past the tangential (superfluous)
    Set goals whose accomplishment will produce a value greater than the cost (human, financial, and image)
    See and take the simple path
    Identify what is and what is not relevant to the situation at hand
    See what is and what can or cannot be within the larger context
    Select actions and alliances that will most likely achieve the desired outcome at a cost that is acceptable
    Not operate in a vacuum or as an island
    Maintain enough reserves (resources) so another option can be acted on or other possibilities can be created (not put all your fish and bait in the same boat)

The definition provided the basis for discussions about the type of information purchasing agents require for them to make better decisions. Through the discussion, senior management learned that information they thought was available to the new agents was not accessible. This led to a discussion about the roles and responsibilities of training, senior management, and human resources. Training agreed to develop case studies, simulations, and branching exercises that let agents practice making decisions and find out what the probable outcomes were. The exercises required the agents to challenge assumptions, verify information, build future scenarios, and weigh probabilities. Each case and scenario was increasingly challenging to reflect the degree of complexity agents would experience on the job. Senior management agreed to fund the creation of a knowledge management system that provided access to timely, relevant, accurate information about suppliers' historical performance and relationship with the company, economic trends, and consumption forecasts. The business had become too complex to trust the informal communication networks, lore, and insider information that senior management had come to rely on for years. Human resources agreed to create and support a performance management system that reinforced "common sense" behaviors, such as:

- Better hiring criteria so candidates were selected because they had demonstrated in previous work an ability to identify and think through long-term ramifications of decisions

- Improved ways to better communicate expectations in terms of approaching problems, challenging assumptions, weighing probabilities, asking for guidance, and so forth

- Tools to help managers give constructive and timely feedback to less experienced agents

- Ways to reinforce and reward people who demonstrated the desired behaviors

The training manager evaluated the program's effectiveness in the following ways:

- Tracking the number of instances when cross-functional teams met to capture intelligence about suppliers, supply chains, world economic trends, and other information key to making sound decisions and then making that information available

- Periodically interviewing senior management to capture their degree of confidence in the decisions being made and track if and how their level of confidence changed over time

- Asking purchasing to share with her the number of times there were preventable shortages or overstocks

- Tracking the number of times HR asked for training's help to develop feedback tools for managers

She also reported the number of scenarios, simulations, and cases her staff created, the number of people who completed the training within six months of it being available, the initial development cost, and the cost to add new practice exercises annually.

In this situation the process of measuring identified the absent information and support tools that were required for performance. Training could develop the scenarios to build the necessary analysis and judgment skills, but if the company failed to develop the knowledge system or HR did not align its hiring and incentive programs, the training would not be successful.

COMPUTER AND COMMUNICATION SKILLS

I call John whenever my computer system falters and he comes by after work to get it up and running again. Before he does anything, he always asks for my documentation and carefully reads it before making any changes. Before he leaves my house, he talks me through each new procedure, he draws pictures explaining what is part of my wide area network and what is part of my Internet network, and he numbers the steps I go through whenever I shut my system down and later want to bring it up. He even labeled the cables so I know which one belongs to the printer, computer, modem, router, scanner, and so on.

John's regular job is to provide computer technical support to businesses. He answers the phone and talks callers through a series of steps to diagnose system problems. He says the first thing he does when someone calls is to determine the caller's ability and compare that to his ability. Before this job, John was a tax accountant and later a controller for an accounting firm. He wanted to change careers so he signed up for a six-month course to become a certified Microsoft Systems Engineer. He passed all six tests and retains his certification by taking courses and passing an annual test on new product features. Now he works in technical support for a company that sells and supports application software to corporate clients. Once he was hired, he had to complete training on the software, which is divided up into seven modules. At the end of each module is a test that he has to pass. He started taking calls after passing the second test. John brought with him excellent communication skills. He didn't need any training on how to communicate. His certification in systems engineering gave him the skills to visualize the relationship of the computer, its peripherals, and the software. His education in accounting and his experience at the accounting firm helped him develop an appreciation for documentation and the skills to know how to use it. John estimated it took him six months to be fully proficient in his new job.

The tests at the end of each module are how the company evaluates John's level of readiness and the effectiveness of its training. Training had little to do with assuring John had the appropriate skills in communicating and using documentation, as that was done by human resources in its selection process.

CUSTOMER SERVICE

New hires went through a six-week training program to be customer service representatives (CSRs) at a financial institution. The CSRs' job was to respond to customers who called with questions or who wanted to authorize changes to their accounts. The training consisted of the information about the company's business philosophy, lots of rules about how to verify the identity of the caller, what CSRs could and could not say to a customer, and what account changes could and could not be made. Practice was at computer terminals connected to a database created just for training, where new hires learned how to locate and verify information about a customer's account and make changes at the customer's request, such as change the address or phone number or transfer monies from one account to another. After training, the new hires were assigned to a special department for two weeks, where they were given on-the-job experience under close supervision. Everyone was teamed with a "buddy" who was considered proficient. During the two weeks, the new hires took actual calls from customers. The phone routing system assured that most of the calls were from customers with simple inquiries or wanting to make simple changes. At the end of the two weeks, the new hires were assigned to a call center team that handled calls from customers with specific types of accounts.

Training measured the number of people who started and completed the training. During the first six weeks, trainers timed learners' ability to accurately locate account information and make changes. Once new hires were assigned to the interim team, trainers lost contact and were not given any feedback about how well people performed. At no time did the training include "customer service" skills because it was thought it would lengthen the training. Therefore, new hires were not audiotaped so they and the trainer never heard what they sounded like over the phone. There were no role plays or guidelines on how to deal with customers who were nice or not so nice, or whose requests were simple or complex. The goal was to get CSRs on the phones as soon as possible.

There were numerous complaints by managers that new hires lacked customer service skills. The training manager interviewed the team leaders and asked them to evaluate how well training prepared people for the job and how proficient new hires were when first assigned to the team. The managers felt training did a very poor job at preparing people and that the new hires were barely ready to do the job. The managers admitted that the required skills and knowledge varied depending on which team new hires were assigned to because of the type of customers they serviced. The training manager learned that a job analysis had not really been done and that no one in training understood that some teams had more customer contact and required much higher customer service skills. The training manager met with HR and the managers to discuss hiring criteria, training's responsibility, and how to best develop customer service skills on the job.

By measuring, the training manager was able to identify that no one was developing new hires' customer service skills. He was then able to clarify what was expected of training, the supervised on-the-job experience, and from team leaders. Training developed guidelines for how to handle difficult customers and callers requesting exceptions to the rules. The "buddy" was then able to coach the CSR in how to deal with customers. Team leaders had tools to help CSRs deal with more demanding customers.

In this situation, the training manager wanted to find out why managers' expectations were not being met. He found out more about job requirements in terms of customer service skills, what was and was not available to the CSR once on the job, and what was and was not being covered by the training. This enabled him to clarify the roles and responsibilities of training, HR, the buddy, and the managers.

Tool 5.1 has questions to help you convert abstract attributes into measurable behaviors or outputs. You use the results to

- Evaluate the sufficiency of the training design
- Evaluate the adequacy of the performance support tools and the performance management system
- Develop a strategy for how to measure whether people learned and applied what they learned—and the consequences on the organization

TOOL 5.1. QUESTIONS TO IDENTIFY BEHAVIORS, CHOICES, OR OUTPUTS EXPECTED AS A RESULT OF TRAINING

1. What does [the desired behavior or attribute, such as appreciate diversity, make customers happy] mean to you?

2. Why is it important?

3. How does it manifest itself on the job?

4. What are the behaviors or choices you want to see on the job?

5. What are the typical tasks or activities that people engage in that require this behavior or attribute?

6. What opportunities or dilemmas will people face that will require them to manifest these behaviors, make the appropriate choices, or produce outputs to your expectation?

7. How likely are these opportunities to occur?

8. How frequently will they occur?

9. What is it about people's behavior or choices that tell you they have this ability or lack it?

10. What do people have to know to do this?

11. What tools, guidelines, or job aids might be made available to people to help them behave as desired, or make the preferred choices, or produce outputs to your expectations?

12. How is the organization affected when people manifest these behaviors or when they make choices using the variables you think are important?

13. How is the organization affected when people fail to manifest these behaviors or make choices using the variables you think are important?

14. What is the organization willing to do to reinforce these behaviors or choices on the job?

If the client uses abstract words or general phrases to describe the intended outcome of the training, use the questions to better define what is expected. Ask these questions in one-on-one interviews or with groups.

Asking the right questions can improve the effectiveness of training and performance support tools because the answers enable you to better judge whether the objectives and design:

• Accurately describe the desired behaviors, choices, and outputs so that trainers, learners, and bosses can recognize them when they occur

- List the criteria with sufficient detail so that trainers, learners, and bosses can judge the appropriateness of the behaviors, choices, or outputs during and after training

- Specify the conditions under which the behaviors, choices, and outputs are expected to manifest themselves so trainers can emulate them during the training and bosses can identify when conditions change

- Specify the inputs required and assumed to be present for performance to occur so that trainers can supply them during training and bosses can make sure the inputs are in place after training

DOMAIN AND LEVEL

Typically, skills are classified by domain (cognitive, psychomotor, and affective) and level of complexity (recall, application, and developmental). The *cognitive* domain refers to mental functions such as logical thinking or reasoning, the manipulation of data, and the analysis of phenomena. The *psychomotor* domain refers to physical functions like the manipulation of the large and small muscles, or the application of the olfactory, aural, and optical senses. The *affective* domain refers to emotional functions as determined by people's values and priorities and is demonstrated through the choices people make. However, most, if not all, tasks make use of all three domains. For example, people have to know how to (the cognitive), be able to (the cognitive and psychomotor), and choose to do it (the affective). Knowing the domain(s) can help you measure how well:

- The instructional tactics develop the skills required for the expected behaviors

- The on-the-job performance support and performance management systems reinforce the expected behaviors and outcomes

Jobs also require a certain level of skill that may range from simple to complex. For example, some tasks are repetitive. This means procedures can be developed so training only needs to show people how to follow procedures. Other tasks require a higher level of skills because they are non-repetitive or they occur in unpredictable environments. Training can increase people's skill level by (1) providing practice with feedback, (2) increasing the standard, and (3) putting more constraints on the application of the skill. Knowing the required level of complexity will help you measure:

- The adequacy of the practice exercises and the feedback learners get during the training

- Whether or not the standards used to judge proficiency are sufficiently stringent
- Whether the constraints under which people must demonstrate ability are realistic

Frequently, training focuses on the less complex hard skills in terms of the adequacy of the practice and feedback. Unfortunately, this is not always true for soft skills, particularly those that involve the affective domain, such as "be nice." Table 5.1 shows how the skills in each domain increase in complexity; Table 5.2 compares the domains and level of complexity and gives examples of each.

Measuring helps you identify the domains involved in doing a task and at what level of complexity, the context under which people are expected to perform, and what information and tools they have to work with.

Tool 5.2 Tables A, B, and C[2] have verbs to help you describe the desired behaviors for the cognitive, affective, and psychomotor domains. Instructional design texts have similar lists. This list and others help people describe the behavior expected on the job AND the behavior expected at the conclusion of training, which may be different. The verbs can also be used to develop job and task descriptions. Being clear and exact can help you determine how well the training objectives describe the desired behaviors so you can better evaluate the design of instructional tactics and learners' proficiency during and after training. You read the first two tables in the tools from left to right. As you move to the right, the verbs reflect a higher or more complex level of skill. However, be less concerned with where a specific verb shows up on the scale of complexity, and be more concerned with helping clients find appropriate language to describe the expected behaviors. The table for psychomotor skills is simply a listing of verbs in alphabetical order and does not reflect a higher level of complexity.

Table 5.1. Behaviors that Reflect Increased Complexity by Domain

Cognitive	Psychomotor	Affective
Recalls	Repeats	Is aware
Comprehends	Applies to achieve an end	Reinforces
Applies	Applies in a new way	Promotes
Analyzes	or in a new arena	Defends
Synthesizes		
Evaluates		

Table 5.2. Domains and Levels

Domain / Level	Cognitive A person's thinking, ideas, conclusions *People are asked to*	Psychomotor A person's physical actions *People are asked to*	Affective A person's emotions, values, and attitudes *People are asked to*
Least Complex	**Recall** Remember information but not change or process the information: • List the titles of the people in the President's cabinet • State what customer account information can be changed over the phone	**Repeat** Repeat a movement or recognize a sound or sight: • Play a scale on a piano • Play a simple composition on a piano by ear • Disassemble a piece of equipment by removing screws and covers • Discriminate blue wires from green ones	**Be Aware** Recognize the preferred behavior in choices made by other people: • Comment on others giving blood • Comment on the importance of good customer service
	Comprehend • Explain relationships • Explain the balance of power between the Executive, Judicial, and Legislative branches of government • Explain why some customer account information may not be given out over the phone		**Reinforce** • Explain the rationale for why more people should demonstrate the preferred behavior • Distribute flyers on where to donate blood • Follow the prescribed customer service protocols when handling common requests by difficult customers
Moderately Complex	**Apply** • Use information to complete a process or procedure • Explain the process for getting the Supreme Court to hear a case • Explain the process for removing a name from a customer's account	**Apply to Achieve an End** • Play a moderately complex composition on a piano by ear • Create a new composition for the piano and a string instrument	

(Continued on next page)

Table 5.2 (*Continued*)

| | | **Analyze**
• Analyze the decisions of others
• Identify trends in judicial decisions during the terms of office of the past five presidents
• Recognize a pattern in customer requests | • Solder wires with a diameter no greater than *X* millimeters | **Promote**
• Model the behavior
• Give blood
• Volunteer at a blood bank
• Encourage others to follow the customer service protocols |
| | **Most Complex** | **Synthesize**
• Recognize patterns and relationships
• Analyze recent judicial decisions and their implication on the legislative and executive branches of government
• Analyze the implication of a new regulation on call handling times

Problem Solve
• Use information to solve a problem or develop new ideas or applications
• Develop a new government model that still meets the philosophy of the Constitution and Bill of Rights
• Develop new protocols for handling customer requests that satisfy customer expectations while meeting regulatory requirements | **Apply in a New Arena**
• Apply the skill in a new context or under more difficult conditions
• Play piano with a jazz trio
• Compose a composition for an orchestra
• Troubleshoot intermittent equipment malfunctions by visually and tactically inspecting wires and junctions | **Defend**
• Present arguments supporting the preferred behavior
• Regularly speak out on the importance of donating blood
• Give regularly
• Advocate for better guidance on how to handle unusual customer service requests that frequently result in behaviors that conflict with expectations |

TOOL 5.2A. ACTION VERBS FOR THE COGNITIVE DOMAIN

Recall		Application		Developmental	
Knowledge	**Comprehension**	**Application**	**Analysis**	**Synthesis**	**Evaluation**
Define	Categorize	Apply	Analyze	Arrange	Appraise
Label	Classify	Associate	Break down	Assemble	Assess
List	Describe	Calculate	Compare	Combine	Choose
Match	Diagram	Collect	Contrast	Compile	Conclude
Memorize	Differentiate	Compute	Debate	Compose	Criticize
Name	Discriminate	Construct	Determine	Construct	Critique
Recall	Discuss	Convert	Diagram	Create	Decide
Recite	Distinguish	Demonstrate	Discover	Design	Defend
Record	Estimate	Dramatize	Examine	Develop	Develop criteria
Repeat	Explain	Employ	Experiment	Explain	Discriminate
State	Express	Illustrate	Generalize	Forecast	Estimate
Tell	Extend	Implement	Inspect	Formulate	Evaluate
Underline	Identify	Install	Inventory	Generalize	Judge
	Paraphrase	Interpret	Organize	Generate	Justify
	Recognize	Locate	Outline	Hypothesize	Measure
	Reconstruct	Manipulate	Point out	Infer	Rate
	Report	Modify	Question	Manage	Revise
	Review	Operate	Relate	Plan	Value
	Rewrite	Perform	Select	Predict	
	Summarize	Practice	Separate	Prepare	
	Translate	Repair	Solve	Produce	
		Schedule	Test		
		Shop			
		Show			
		Sketch			
		Translate			
		Use			
		Write			

TOOL 5.2B. ACTION VERBS FOR THE AFFECTIVE DOMAIN

Awareness	Reinforcement	Promotion	Defense
Ask	Acclaim	Accept	Abstract
Accumulate	Adhere	Advocate	Act
Attend to	Applaud	Alter	Argue
Be aware of	Approve	Assist	Arrest
Combine	Augment	Choose	Avoid
Control	Commend	Encourage	Balance
Describe	Comply	Help	Debate
Differentiate	Conform	Initiate	Defend
Read	Discuss	Justify	Define
Receive	Follow	Model	Discriminate
Recognize	Obey	Prefer	Display
Reply	Play	Propose	Formulate
Respond	Practice	Subsidize	Influence
Separate	Praise	Select	Intervene
Set apart		Support	Manage
Share		Volunteer	Organize
			Prevent
			Resist
			Resolve

TOOL 5.2C. ACTION VERBS FOR THE PSYCHOMOTOR DOMAIN

Acknowledge	Couple	Maneuver	Secure
Activate	Decrease	Manipulate	Sequence
Actuate	Depress	Mix	Service
Add	Dilute	Measure	Sharpen
Adjust	Disassemble	Monitor	Shut
Align	Disconnect	Move	Shut down
Alternate	Display	Neutralize	Sketch
Analyze	Dissolve	Observe	Splice
Apply	Don	Open	Spray
Assemble	Draft	Operate	Start
Asses	Draw	Perform	Steer
Assist	Energize	Plot	Stop
Backwash	Enter	Position	Store
Balance	Estimate	Prepare	Switch
Begin	Exit	Pressurize	Synchronize
Bleed	Feed	Prime	Tag out
Block	Fix flush	Print	Test
Boil	Formulate	Push	Throttle
Build	Guide	Purge	Trace
Bypass	Heat	Rack	Track
Calculate	Hoist	Raise	Transfer
Calibrate	Hold	Reactivate	Transmit
Call	Immerse	Read	Trip
Center	Increase	Rebuild	Tune
Change	Inform	Re-circulate	Turn
Charge	Inspect	Record	Type
Check	Install	Regulate	Unlatch
Circulate	Insert	Release	Unload
Clean	Isolate	Remove	Unlock
Clear	Job	Repair	Uncouple
Close	Let down	Replace	Vent
Code	Line up	Return	Warm
Collect	Load	Rinse	Warm up
Connect	Lock	Run	Weigh
Cool	Lower	Sample	Weld
Construct	Lubricate	Scan	Withdraw
Cut			

HARD SKILLS—RULES AND MORE RULES

Precision Instruments has an extensive curriculum for its service technicians. The courses include product installation and calibration. The focus of the curriculum is on the rules for when to follow specific procedures, why, and how. During the programs, technicians see demonstrations of the procedures and have many opportunities to practice them. Even the customer service module is about rules—call before you come, show up when you said you would, clean up after yourself, and tell the customer what you did and why. The expected behaviors are well defined in measurable terms.

The program's effectiveness is measured in terms of the technicians' average work order time, customer complaints, and callbacks after the training.

HARD SKILLS—HEURISTICS AND GUIDELINES

A financial consulting firm has an ongoing professional development program for its analysts. The development strategy is one of presenting dilemmas to analysts and encouraging them to engage in a process of self-directed discovery. The objectives are to reinforce specific behaviors about challenging assumptions. The analysts are given guidelines on what constitutes assumptions and how to challenge the thinking behind them. Practice involves giving the analysts increasingly more difficult problems with no one right answer. Analysts are evaluated on their ability to recognize operating assumptions, the economic and political basis for those assumptions, and the socio-political variables that affect the probability of an outcome.

The program's effectiveness is measured in terms of bosses' confidence in the analysts' skills after the training.

Tool 5.3 has guidelines for measuring the probability that cognitive and psychomotor skills will increase through training.

TOOL 5.3. HOW TO MEASURE THE PROBABILITY THAT TRAINING WILL INCREASE COGNITIVE AND PSYCHOMOTOR SKILLS

To measure whether or not the training is designed to increase skill levels to what is required for the job or to the expectation of the client. Find out:

- The number of practice exercises there are and how often learners receive feedback about the adequacy of their performance based on the criteria explained during the training.

- Whether or not the standard used to judge adequacy increased, how often, and to what degree, such as learners have to do something in less time, with greater accuracy or precision, with less help from others, and so on. The greater the ratio of practice with feedback to explanations, the more likely skills will increase.

- Whether or not the constraints on the situation or context under which learners have to demonstrate they can perform a task increase or become more complex, such as the information they have to work with is less accurate or is incomplete, the people they have to interface with are more demanding, the equipment or tools are less compatible or non-traditional, and so forth. The closer the constraints match what people really experience on the job, the more likely they will be able to apply what they learn on the job.

- The degree to which the exercises, standards, and constraints reflect the realities of the job. The higher the fidelity of the exercises, standards, and constraints, the more likely people will be able to apply what they learned.

CONTEXT

Soft skills, like interpersonal and communication skills, are particularly dependent on the work environment or the context under which they are required. It is easy to get along with people who are like us and who share our views of the world. Limitations in these skills become an issue when we have to work with people who are unlike us and have different objectives. The critical factors are (1) the amount of variance or lack of consistency and predictability there is in the workplace, (2) the degree of proficiency required by the work, and (3) the presence of systems to reinforce the desired skill level and enable the organization to recover when the skills are absent.

VARIANCE

Some jobs and work environments require workers to periodically interface with the same people about the same issues. Over time they develop protocols and create language conventions to help them accomplish what they need to do. For example, punch press operators, machinists, landscapers, and assembly line workers use signals to communicate how things are to be done. The way sailors on a flight deck communicate with each other is another example of a job that does not put a lot of demand on language skills. Other jobs require a higher level of interpersonal and communication skills because of the variance that exists in the job. Listening is easy if all you have to hear is the same message. Listening is much more difficult if you are expected to "hear" subtle nuances and the inappropriateness of your response might jeopardize people's lives or international relationships. Customer service representatives and flight attendants, for example, must be able to deal with all types of people, including those who are unskilled at communicating, use a different language set, and are ill or out of sorts. The reason this is an issue is that you want to measure (1) how much variance there is in the workplace and (2) if there are a sufficient number of practice exercises so the training adequately prepares people for the job. Then you are in a better position to measure how effective the training or performance support tool was at helping people deal with the variance.

TOO SENSITIVE

The training director at a major inner city hospital was told that nurses were "too" sensitive and their sensitivity was interfering with their ability to stay focused and at task when assigned to the emergency room. Hospital staff who work in the emergency room witness human carnage first-hand. They see victims of gunshot wounds, domestic and gang violence, torture, automobile accidents, drug overdoses, and fires. Patients are in pain, some are violent, others angry. Some patients are cooperative; others are abusive toward anyone near them. When confronted with the horror, smells, and screams, staff would choke, become paralyzed or unable to respond. Some even left the area. Yet staff was expected to stay focused on cleaning wounds, administering drugs, stopping bleeding, and getting vital information for diagnosis. The required skills were complex and a combination of cognitive (rapid assessment of a patient's need), psychomotor (simultaneous physical manipulation of tools, instruments, and body parts), and affective (choose to stay focused and hold personal reactions in abeyance).

A training program was developed to desensitize nurses and other emergency room medical personnel. The primary instructional tactic was to immerse staff in hours of videotape showing the ugliness and horror they could expect to see while on duty, followed by small group discussions about each person's internal (emotional) reaction.

To measure the effectiveness of the program, the training manager interviewed emergency room personnel one week and one month after the course was given. The interview consisted of questions about their ability to control their reactions to what they saw and heard and stay focused on the task at hand. The training manager also interviewed the doctor in charge of the emergency room. This interview consisted of questions about his observations of staff and reported incidents of appropriate and inappropriate reactions.

In this situation, the role of measurement was to find out the real requirements of the job and the context under which people had to perform. This information was used to develop an instructional strategy (immersion). The training manager only focused on measuring the effectiveness of the training.

BEING NICE

The training department in the same hospital was asked to develop another program to teach nurses to be "nice" after management received a sufficient number of complaints from patients that the nurses weren't nice. The training department began by asking the medical director and the head of nursing to define niceness and the conditions under which "nice" behaviors were expected and to develop protocols for how nurses should respond to unusual situations. They also came up with examples of behaviors that would give evidence of (illustrate) niceness and the lack of it. The training consisted of the rules of behavior followed up with role plays where nurses practiced responding to increasingly difficult encounters and challenges, such as patients who were slow to react or respond, had difficulty understanding directions, were confused or despondent, resisted treatment, were verbally nasty, and were physically violent and abusive. Nurses were told the protocols for dealing with the progressively difficult or unusual situations, such as asking for assistance by another nurse, aide, technician, social worker, or security.

The training manager measured the program's design by counting the number of opportunities learners had to practice, the degree the practice emulated the work environment, and if the sequence of practice exercises became increasingly more difficult. She evaluated the effectiveness of the training by measuring the number, frequency, and type of complaints by patients about niceness after the training. What should have been done, perhaps, was to ask patients what "being a nice nurse" meant. The solution then might have been to give nurses descriptions of the behaviors or variables that are more likely to cause patients to label them as nice and not nice.

Tool 5.4 has guidelines for measuring the probability affective skills will increase through training.

TOOL 5.4. HOW TO MEASURE THE PROBABILITY THAT TRAINING WILL INCREASE AFFECTIVE SKILLS

To measure the probability that training of skills in the affective domain will produce the results required of the job or desired by the client, find out:

1. The number of dilemmas that were presented to learners during training that required them to
   - Recognize the choices made by others and judge the degree those choices satisfied or were in keeping with the expectations of the organization
   - Make choices themselves and explain why they made the choices they did
   - Promote or defend the cause for making certain choices
   - Defend the choices they and others made

2. Whether the practice exercises increased in complexity in ways that seemed probable

3. How choices that reflect the values of the organization will be reinforced on the job, through coaching, decision guidelines, and so forth

4. How choices that reflect the values of the organization will be recognized or rewarded and what consequences there will be for not making choices that reflect the values of the organization

5. How frequently opportunities occurred that required people to make choices and how often the choices made were deemed appropriate by the organization

6. How the organization plans to recover if people's choices are not considered appropriate

Use what you learn to develop a larger implementation strategy that encompasses performance management, performance support, and knowledge management systems.

MISSTEPS

Here are some of the more prevalent missteps when it comes to evaluating hard and soft skills.

1. Trainers promise more change than what the training program is designed to accomplish.

2. Trainers fail to get the client to understand the importance of people having sufficient resources and an effective performance management system

in place to reinforce the behaviors on the job. Training can only do so much. Some managers don't want to hear about this because of cost in time, resources, and expense.

3. Trainers think they should be more rigorous in their evaluation than what the client is interested in, that is, they evaluate and produce measures the client doesn't need or care about.

4. Trainers fail to specify training's role in bringing people to the required level of proficiency compared to the role of the supervisor and HR.

Training cannot replace insufficient resources or counter the lack of incentives or consequences. What training can do is to take the lead in helping the organization to see the importance of having clear expectations, appropriate performance measures, and access to appropriate tools and support systems.

TIPS AND TECHNIQUES

Here are some suggestions on how to evaluate training of hard and soft skills.

1. Find out to what level of proficiency the training is expected to bring learners. For example, is training to bring learners to the level of a novice, journeyman, or master? Then find out if the training provides a sufficient number of exercises with feedback to achieve the level or whether coaching and feedback are available afterward.

2. Check to see if the learning objectives match the level of proficiency expected, not more and not less.

3. Find out if there are a sufficient number of learning events to fulfill the level promised.

4. Find out if it was determined in advance what the client will accept as evidence that the goal of the program was achieved. If it was not done and you want to evaluate whether the program fulfilled the promise, then ask the client what he or she is using to evaluate the effectiveness of the program. Use this meeting as an opportunity to coach or advise the client on what some appropriate evidence might be.

5. If the required skill level of the job is higher than what training can accomplish due to time or budget constraints, then work with the client to assure additional performance support methods are in place to further develop the learners' proficiency.

SUMMARY

To paraphrase the great Joe Harless, there are no "soft" skills, just those that were never defined. What makes skills soft or hard is the degree to which you can describe:

- What a person does
- Under what context he or she does it
- The attributes or outputs that must be present to judge whether the skills were adequate by someone who is qualified to judge

Most tasks involve a combination of hard and soft skills. Most skills have hard (more easily described and measured) and soft (less easily defined and measured) components. Evaluation can play a major role by helping you find out what the expected behaviors are and how the organization expects to benefit from them. It can help guide the design of the instruction and performance management system and clarify the roles and responsibilities of training, management, and HR.

However, management, human resources, and all play a role in helping people become proficient. Management's role is to assure that the infrastructure supports the creation and delivery of goods and services. Human resources' role is to provide a performance management system that attracts the right people and enables them to monitor their own performance. Training's role is to assure people have opportunities to develop the skills and knowledge required to become proficient. The role of evaluation is to confirm all of the elements are in place and in alignment.

WHERE TO LEARN MORE

The following publications will be particularly helpful. They are mostly about instructional design, since training effectiveness depends on the quality of the instruction.

Brethower, D., and Smalley, K. *Performance-Based Instruction: Linking Training to Business Results* (San Francisco, CA: Jossey-Bass/Pfeiffer, 1998).

Wallace, G. *lean-ISD*, the chapters on Performance Analysis (2, 21–27) (Naperville, IL: CADDI, 1999).

NOTES

1. *Webster's Ninth New Collegiate Dictionary, Philippines.* Merriam-Webster, Inc., 1987.
2. The tables are from *Workbook and Job Aids for Designing Good Fair Tests* (Downers Grove: Hale Associates, 1996) and reprinted with permission of the author. The verbs in the tables are a compilation of lists encountered over the years. They are meant to help instructional designers describe the intended outcome of the training.

Chapter 6

How to Measure Required and Mandated Programs

The organization trained 850 new hires a year. It took on average four months after completing the six-week new-hire training course for people to be proficient in their jobs. Management wanted the training department to reduce the cost of the training and the time it took for people to become proficient.

*T*he focus on this chapter is about how to measure the effectiveness of *required* and *mandated* training and performance support tools. What makes a program required or mandated is

- Lack of choice people have in participating or supporting the program
- Presence of consequences for the organization for not enforcing or supporting it

What distinguishes required from mandated is the measure used to judge success. The measures for required training are about *proficiency*, and the measures for mandated training are about *compliance.* How a program is classified is based on assumptions that may or may not be explicit, communicated, or shared about what constitutes a job, what is proficiency, and what is the role of training.

Required Training

Required training assures that people in specific jobs receive the information and skills required to perform their work. Some examples are

- Job training for new hires
- Training on equipment, products, and product updates
- Training on systems and system rollouts

Mandated Training

This type of training includes programs done to comply with regulations or organizational policies. These programs usually specify that the organization must document and report who was trained and when. Some examples are

- Occupational Health and Safety (OSHA) training
- How to handle hazardous materials (HAZMAT)
- Mandated supervisory training, such as sexual harassment, diversity, violence in the workplace, and so forth

This chapter looks at training from the standpoint of why it happens, the *driver*. Some training is done to assure people have the skills and know-how required for the job. Other training is done in response to a legal or regulatory requirement. By understanding the driver, you are in a better position to measure how well the need is being satisfied and whether other solutions might achieve the same end. Being clear on the driver also helps you find out if the organization's infrastructure and performance management system are in place to sustain performance overtime. Tool 6.1 shows guidelines for how to determine the driver.

REQUIRED TRAINING

Required training is job-related and is often called *technical* training, because it is about the rules, procedures, and principles used to execute a task or make appropriate decisions. It is the training given to new hires and employees whenever there is a change in technology or operations. Examples include training on product features and benefits, system operations, and equipment installation and maintenance. Depending on the readiness of the employees and the nature of the new information, the training may just build awareness or it may include extensive skill development through practice exercises. Required training should be derived from a job or task analysis that identifies what people must know and be able to do to be considered proficient. Once you

TOOL 6.1. HOW TO DETERMINE THE DRIVER

1. Meet with the client, a representative of human resources, perhaps someone from quality assurance or risk management, and other appropriate members of the training function. As a group, come to agreement on what the driver is.

2. Ask: "Why are we doing this? What problem are we trying to solve?"

3. Ask if there are consequences to the individual, the supervisor, or the organization if people do not participate in this training program. Ask what the consequences are to the learner, the learner's boss, or to the organization, whether good or bad.

4. If there are no consequences for not participating or supporting the program, then the training is *elective,* even if it is a good idea and there are possible business implications if people lack the skills. If the consequences are about being able to produce documentation on demand about who was trained and when, then the training is *mandated.* If the training covers rules and procedures necessary to perform the job, then the program is *required.*

know that, you can find out the following:

- What people already know before they begin a training program
- What performance support tools are present on the job compared to what should be there
- What information resources are present on the job compared to what should be there
- What behaviors are actually reinforced on the job compared to what should be reinforced
- How much the organization is at risk if people are not proficient
- How much time the organization can afford to give people to become proficient compared to how long it actually takes

What you learn will allow you to then evaluate the training in terms of the following:

- Whether or not there are a sufficient number of practice exercises, given what is expected of learners once they complete the training
- Whether the exercises possess sufficient fidelity (are lifelike enough) so people can easily apply what they learn on the job

- How capable people are by the end of the training and if that is sufficient given the organization's resources and ability to provide performance support on the job

Jobs

Jobs are a composite of duties and tasks that result in accomplishments the organization values. Jobs may also be areas of accountability where the emphasis is on results, not necessarily on how the work gets done. Jobs involve tasks such as:

- Recall and analyze specific information, do mental comparisons or calculations, and draw conclusions, otherwise known as "think"
- Manipulate or operate equipment and tools and use communication and computer systems, using hands, fingers, eyes, ears, lips, and so forth, and also thinking
- Document what they did, the conclusions they drew, and what they recommend as the next steps, otherwise known as "cover their tail"
- Communicate facts and ideas verbally or in writing, otherwise known as "keeping people informed"
- Establish working relationships with individuals or groups, otherwise known as "get along with people"
- Organize information and tasks and set priorities, otherwise known as "manage resources"
- Honor and follow through on commitments, otherwise known as "self-management"

The information people must know and be able to use and the equipment they must be able to operate constitute job-specific training. Other skills, like communication and relationship management, may be expected for the job, but are usually part of the hiring criteria. The organization may provide training in these areas, but usually for professional development reasons.

MEDICAL UNDERWRITERS

A major medical insurer recruits people from the claims department to become underwriters. To underwrite means to accept risk, to assume liability. Underwriters determine if it is in the best interest of the company to assume liability for a person's potential health costs. They examine and verify information about a person's medical history, personal lifestyle, and profile to determine whether the company should grant medical coverage. They also determine what will and will not be covered by the policy. A requirement for becoming an underwriter is consistently high performance ratings, which people receive for being accurate and efficient and for having good job attendance. Recruits attend a four-week training program that meets for four hours a day, five days a week. They return to their jobs in claims in the afternoons. During the morning session, representatives from the underwriting staff come in and talk about what they do. The presentations include common mistakes, pointers on what to watch out for, and tips for assessing risk. There is no training manual, and no one takes notes. At the end of the four weeks, people are transferred to the underwriting department, where they are assigned a mentor.

In this situation, the training is not based on a job analysis, and the information does not follow any organizing principles. Once on the job, the new underwriters are given three large notebooks with decision guidelines about what factors they are to consider when determining what medical conditions will and will not be covered. The decision guidelines function as performance support tools and make the job highly procedural. In the beginning their work is reviewed by the mentor, who is also available to ask questions and direct them in the efficient use of the notebooks. But what is perhaps more important than the on-the-job support tools is how the organization judges proficiency. People are deemed proficient based on how many applications they process within a given time period and their decreasing reliance on the mentor, not the number of claims that result or the profitability of a policy. Those metrics are tracked by other departments and not linked back to individual underwriters. One could argue that to become proficient requires good work habits, the ability to organize information, being detailed oriented, and the willingness to follow rules, all attributes that are considered in the selection process.

Tool 6.2 has guidelines for evaluating the sufficiency of a job analysis.

TOOL 6.2. HOW TO EVALUATE JOB/TASK ANALYSIS

Since the job or task analysis is the basis for most training, it is important that it be done well. The process of evaluation can play an important role in helping clients judge the adequacy of their analysis.

1. *Ask when it was done.* Job or task analyses that are old may not reflect the current complexity of the work environment.

2. *Ask who participated in defining the behaviors, activities, decisions, and so on that make up the job or task.* You are looking for the presence or absence of high performers, customers of the output, vested parties such as regulators, and management. The more voices included the greater the chance the results reflect the full range of required activities.

3. *Ask if the results were validated, such as by observing a high performer and comparing what was observed with what was expected.* The closer the match, the better the analysis.

REQUIRED TRAINING MEASURES

The two most important measures of effectiveness of required training are

1. Time to proficiency

   • How long it takes (in hours, days, weeks, or months) for people to reach the level where they can do a task with little or no supervision or support from others

   • How long it takes for people to produce a product that meets the standard

   • How long before the boss expresses confidence in a person's decisions or actions

2. Cost of proficiency, that is, what it costs in direct and indirect dollars to bring people to the level where they can perform a task adequately, which is measured by:

   • The cost to recruit and place a person in a position

   • The cost to orient the person to the organization and the job

   • The combined costs to develop, administer, and deliver the training (instructional designer, trainer, facilities, materials, equipment, and so forth)

   • The time the learner is away from the job being trained

   • The time the person is in the position but not fully proficient

   • The percentage of time the supervisor or team leader has to spend directing, checking, or coaching after the training

Time and cost of proficiency depend on the effectiveness and efficiency of the selection process and on the development and implementation of the program. Other measures that are subsets of time to and cost of proficiency are

- *Learning.* Do people know the content after having completed the training, that is, the terms, procedures, rules, and principles which can be measured by (1) how many people answered how many questions correctly on a test and (2) how many people demonstrated an ability to appropriately apply what was taught in the training event.
- *Application.* Do people apply the rules, procedures, and principles back on the job, which can be measured by direct observation or by checking the output (product) of their work.
- *Lapse or Lag Time.* How long in days or weeks people have to wait before they can attend or participate, which can be measured by the number of people on the wait list or the time lapse between when people register and actually attend or participate in a program.
- *Efficiency.* How efficient you are in developing or acquiring the program, which is measured in terms of the work hours and dollars consumed in creating or customizing the training product or the cost to purchase it.
- *Ongoing Costs.* The ongoing costs to deliver, administer, and maintain, which is measured in terms of the number of hours, dollars, and other resources consumed to enroll people, prepare and distribute materials, set up the facility, conduct the training, evaluate test scores, update materials, and report results.

You track the time to and cost of proficiency because these are two measures you want to improve. Through the process of measuring, you can identify what contributes to time and cost. Bringing people to proficiency faster and at less cost is how you prove training's effectiveness. It is also how you show that the time to and cost of proficiency are affected by the adequacy of the infrastructure and the alignment of the performance management system.

Table 6.1 lists the common measures for required and mandated training.

Table 6.1. Measures for Required and Mandated Training

Internal Measures	External Measures
Cost to	Learning
• Develop	Time to proficiency
• Disseminate	Cost of proficiency
• Maintain	Correlation with performance, incidents, and
• Administer	other business metrics
• Document	Degree of market penetration
Speed of market penetration	

PROFICIENCY AND THE ROLE OF TRAINING

Proficiency is about being able to do the routine tasks under normal circumstances, not the exceptional tasks under unique circumstances, which is *mastery.* Proficiency can be synonymous to competence. People are proficient when they actually do a job in ways the organization deems appropriate, not that they are just capable of it, but they actually demonstrate their capability by doing something of value. People are proficient when they do the job consistently to standard. However, proficiency presumes there are requirements and standards; otherwise how would you know whether or not a person is competent.

Performance standards, too, are specific to the job; however, they are about the skills and knowledge required to obtain the minimum expected results, measured by quality, quantity, accuracy, timeliness, speed, safety, and satisfaction.

The *role of training* is to bring people to some predetermined level of proficiency. How long people have to become proficient is a factor that affects how training is designed and how its effectiveness is measured. For example, new hires go through training, but may not be expected to be fully proficient at the end. Instead, their proficiency is expected to increase as they apply the procedures and rules they learned on the job. They may receive coaching on the job or be assigned a "buddy" or partner who checks their work and provides ongoing feedback. Over time they require less supervision and coaching. Eventually, they are fully functional in the job. However, some jobs require people to start out fully proficient. There is no tolerance for on-the-job development because it puts people or assets at risk. Airline pilots and operators in nuclear power plants are two examples.

The more proficient people have to be at the end of the training event, the more opportunities they require to practice and to receive feedback, and the more the practice has to emulate the real job environment. To evaluate the integrity of the instruction, identify to what level of proficiency the training is expected to bring people. Next, determine whether there are sufficient opportunities for practice and feedback. How much practice depends on the degree of mastery required and the sufficiency of other performance support systems available on the job.

For example, if you wanted to evaluate how effectively your program teaches swimming, you would design it based on what you think is the minimum amount of practice required to bring learners to a certain level of proficiency. If the learners are just recreational swimmers who want to better enjoy the community pool, your training would teach the basics. You might "pass" those who demonstrated they could swim to the opposite side of the pool. If your training prepared people to be lifeguards, you would increase the constraints and conditions under which they must demonstrate their ability to swim because a higher level of capability is required of lifeguards. If your program prepared people to be Navy Seals, the training would be even more rigorous, as the conditions and constraints under which they must swim are very severe.

NEW HIRE TRAINING—FINANCIAL SERVICES

An international financial management firm hires new college graduates with degrees in mathematics, economics, and finance to be financial analysts. Its new-hire training program is in three phases that combine classes and team assignments. Phase one is orientation. It starts with two days in a classroom, where the new hires process their benefit forms, complete other required paperwork, and are told how to operate the e-mail system. It ends with them spending three days with the team they will be assigned to. Phase two is a week of formal classroom training on computer basics and a week with the team, where they are given simple assignments that reinforce what was covered in the training. Phase three consists of two weeks of practice—specific training that involves solving problems, doing calculations, and working through case studies. A different field consultant comes in each day and guides the class though the problems and practice exercises. Students are given large notebooks full of job aids and other documentation they are to use when on the job. When they return to their team, they are assigned a coach and they are to meet with the boss for one-on-one sessions every month to discuss career goals. Currently it takes from nine to twelve months before analysts are thought to be fully proficient, yet 30 percent leave the firm within the first six to nine months of employment.

In this situation the organization would benefit if it did a more thorough job task analysis, focused its training on what was learned from that analysis, found out why people leave, and, based on that information, put programs in place to increase retention. However, without measuring, the training department can only operate on conjecture about what new hires require, what they expect, and how that matches what the organization has to offer.

NEW HIRE TRAINING—PICK AND PACK

A large distribution center hires people to sort, pick, pack, unpack, check for damage and spoilage, and repack clothing and other merchandise. Industrial engineering studied those people who had consistently higher production rates at these tasks to identify what they did and how they did it. They used these people to set the production standard. Training then teaches new hires how to do the task using behaviors that will result in a person meeting standards. The training for these jobs lasts from 59 minutes to 180 minutes. The training consists of

- Demonstrating specific movements and procedures
- Explaining the rationale or benefit to the movement or procedure
- Coaching the employees as they demonstrate the movement or procedure

Employees who meet standard become members of the 100 percent club. Productivity above 100 percent results in extra bonuses. It can take a person a couple of months to reach 100 percent, and some never make it. To encourage people to apply the recommended behaviors, new hires are given a bonus if they reach production milestones within a certain period of time. For example, they receive a bonus if they reach 80 percent within thirty days of employment and the bonus goes higher as performance goes up. The goal is for everyone to reach 100 percent as quickly as possible.

Large bulletin boards are posted at each job site showing the average daily production rate and the amount of merchandise in the queue to be worked on. Employees can even find their specific rate for the previous day. Measurement played and continues to play a significant role in the setting of standards and in the design of tasks, feedback systems, and training.

NEW HIRE TRAINING—SERVICE TECHNICIANS

The laboratory division of a manufacturer of precision weighing and dimensioning instruments is responsible for training its service technicians and sales personnel. The basic course for service technicians includes how to install, service, calibrate, repair, and integrate the instruments with other process controls used in a client's operation. It is offered twice a year. The course consists of three weeks on the basics of servicing the instruments, with a fourth week on how to repair them. Students travel from all over the world to attend the class in Europe. Class is limited to ten participants. At least 80 percent of the time in class is spent on practice servicing the instruments they will encounter when back on the job.

Learning is evaluated through tests that are administered at the end of the first three weeks and at the end of the fourth week. Test scores are used to evaluate the effectiveness of the training, not the performance of the technicians, because evaluating job performance is considered the responsibility of the supervisor, not the training department. The trainers examine individual and class scores to identify trends, which they use to improve the materials, practice exercises, and visuals. Supervisors have performance standards they can use to measure productivity. Supervisors also have surveys they can use to measure customer satisfaction. Technicians are expected to be 100 percent proficient on servicing those instruments used in the majority of traditional laboratory settings by the end of the training. The cost of bringing technicians to proficiency is significant. Travel costs and compensation are the responsibility of the servicing unit the technician works for. The manufacturing division that provides the training is responsible for

- Housing, local transportation, and meals
- All other direct and indirect costs related to delivery of the training, such as facilities, equipment, materials, and trainers compensation

A major cost, however, is the lapsed time or the cost of lost productivity due to the limited number of offerings.

Tool 6.3 has guidelines for how to measure the effectiveness of required training.

TOOL 6.3. HOW TO EVALUATE REQUIRED TRAINING

If you want to evaluate required training, and if the intent of the program is to build skills and knowledge, then:

1. Meet with the client and other knowledgeable parties to define proficiency in terms of attributes, outputs, or other indicators the client will accept.
2. Determine whether the performance management system has the elements to reinforce the skills.
3. Determine whether the infrastructure will provide the resources required to apply the skills on the job.
4. Next, identify the overall average cycle time to achieve proficiency.

   a. Ask the client how long after training learners manifest or demonstrate the attributes of proficiency.

   b. Decide on a unit of measure or metric of time, such as hour, day, week, or month, and use it consistently.

c. Start with the day hired or reported for assignment.

d. Add the lapse time waiting to be trained from the day of hiring or assignment.

e. Add to (d) the time spent in formal and on-the-job training.

f. Add to (e) the time spent being coached or receiving guided practice in between formal training events.

g. Add to (f) any time spent gaining experience if not already included above.

h. The time from (a) to (g) is the average cycle time to proficiency.

5. To identify the cost to achieve proficiency.

a. Ask the client what the average cost of recruitment is.

b. Ask if there are any sign-on bonuses to be factored into the overall cost and add it to (a).

c. Add the cost of compensation for the average cycle time to proficiency to (b).

d. Ask what percentage of a coach's or supervisor's time is dedicated to reviewing work and giving feedback up until the time proficiency is achieved and add the cost of that time to (c).

e. Add the cost of materials to (d).

f. Ask how delivery costs such as trainer's time and use of the system might be prorated or allocated to a specific learner. Add that cost to (e).

g. Ask how overhead costs such as facilities, training equipment, and so forth, can be prorated or allocated to specific learners. Add that cost to (f). This gives you the average cost to bring a person to proficiency.

h. This figure does not include any other related costs, such as overtime incurred by proficient workers or lost revenue while waiting for a person to become proficient.

6. To measure learning as a result of the training:

a. Meet with the client and other vested parties and decide how you want to use the results, that is, judge the ability of the learners or the effectiveness of the training.

b. Develop a test. Map or chart each question to the course objectives and course content to assure the test measures what is covered by the training and not something else.

c. Make sure the test items (questions or problems) are at the level of the course objectives, that is, if the content stresses learning definitions or rules, then the items should be at the recall level; if the content has practice applying the rules, then the items should be at the application level.

d. If you are going to use the test results to make judgments about the learner's capability, then administer the test to a group of people who are known to know or are able to apply the content. Their cumulative average score gives you the top range of what learners should achieve on the same test. Next, administer the same test to a group who are known to not know the content. Their cumulative average score gives you the bottom range of what learners should achieve on the same test. Target the passing score somewhere between the two average cumulative scores.

e. Administer a test at the beginning of the training to establish a baseline.

f. Administer the same or an equivalent test at the end of the training and compare the results to (e). This is a measure of growth, or how much more learners know or can apply as a result of the training.

g. Now compare the learners' test results to the average cumulative score of those who were known to be competent and the target passing score. The learner's test score is a measure of mastery. The traditional standard is 90 percent of the learners score at least 90 percent on the test; however, the Department of Energy uses 80 percent as its standard.

h. Administer a survey at the end of the training event to measure learners' reaction to the training. The cumulative score is a measure of acceptance of the course content.

MANDATED TRAINING

Mandated training is done to satisfy either a regulatory requirement, like those imposed by the Occupational Safety and Health Agency (OSHA), Environmental Protection Agency (EPA), Department of Labor (DOL), and the Department of Transportation (DOT), or internal policy, such as corporate values and ethics. Policies are usually developed in response to some external pressure, such as public or customer image, insurance requirements, accidents, or quality failures. Some examples of mandated training are safety procedures, lock-out tag-out procedures, HAZMAT (how to handle hazardous materials) procedures, rules related to sexual harassment, and guidelines on how to handle violence in the workplace. A significant amount of mandated training could be classified as information programs rather than skill building, as they are designed to create awareness or serve as a reminder. Exceptions are those safety training programs that require people to demonstrate they know the rules, such as the annual classes in cardiopulmonary resuscitation (CPR) procedures, where people must demonstrate they can apply the principles on life-size models of adults and children. OSHA mandates that a powered industrial trucking course combine one hour of classroom with one hour of hands-on training.

Some job-specific training can be classified as both required and mandated because there are laws or regulations that specify that people must complete a curriculum and pass a test to demonstrate proficiency before being allowed to do the job. Such programs are more about complying with the law than about developing skills, so they would be classified as mandated programs. This is usually the case when poor performance puts people or assets at risk. In this situation, regulatory agencies usually require people to be licensed or certified. Some examples are pilots, beauticians, architects, and physical therapists. Measurement plays a role by (1) confirming that the tasks that make up a job actually require a credential and (2) helping management compare the cost of hiring people with the licenses and certifications to the cost of developing employees to the point where they can achieve the credential.

The primary measure of mandated training is how well the program satisfied the mandate. The internal measures are

- Speed to deploy, or how quickly the training department was able to have a program available
- Lapse or lag time, or how long people have to wait to enroll and participate in the training
- Initial cost to purchase or develop the program
- Ongoing costs to deliver, administer, and maintain
- Cost to document compliance, or the hours spent in checking rosters, updating files, and producing summary reports of who did and did not receive training

The external measures include how many were trained, how frequently, and the number of documents that must be submitted compared to how many are required and by when. There is an increasing trend to require organizations to measure that learning occurred, that is, people know the rules and can apply them appropriately. When learning is expected, then the metrics might be test scores or the frequency of demonstrated compliance on the job.

SAFETY

A manufacturer mandates that every Wednesday supervisors meet with staff for fifteen minutes to review safety rules. One technique supervisors of office personnel use is to divide staff into teams and have them engage in a contest to see which side can accurately recall basic first aid principles, such as the symptoms of heat exhaustion, what to do in case of a fire, how to treat an open wound, and so on. In the plant, however, supervisors pull people off task and meet with them as a group. The supervisor then reads a set of safety rules to the group. Which set of rules depends on what the group does; however, within a year, the supervisor has to show that all of the rules were reviewed.

The manufacturer is complying with the law. The intent of the mandate is to remind, refresh, and reinforce safe behavior. However, actual reinforcement is best accomplished through a performance management system, not by training, by rewarding or punishing supervisors who do and do not reinforce the appropriate behaviors of staff and work crews.

POTTY MOUTH

Steve supervises union people in the building trades, including electricians, plumbers, carpenters, painters, and mechanics. His company announced a new policy about not tolerating the use of obscenities on the job. Steve was required to train his crew in the policy. His training consisted of meeting with them as a group, reading the policy aloud, and concluding with the statement, "You now know the policy. What you also need to know is that I will enforce it, so you have a decision to make." The training was just formally informing people. However, changes in behavior will be the product of his enforcing the policy and modeling the behavior, not just telling people what it is.

Tool 6.4 has guidelines to measure the effectiveness of mandated programs.

TOOL 6.4. HOW TO EVALUATE MANDATED TRAINING

If you want to evaluate mandated training, and the intent is to build skills, then use the same tool as you use for evaluating required training, with the following additions:

1. Meet with the client to develop a mechanism to determine whether and how often exceptions are made to
   - Requiring attendance or participation in the training event
   - Requiring people to complete the training, its exercises, and tests
   - Accurately tracking and documenting attendance, learning, and skill attainment

2. Meet with the client to determine how many resources are involved in capturing and documenting the information required for reporting.

3. Develop a mechanism to determine the cost of complying and not complying with the regulation or policy.

4. Meet with the client to develop a mechanism to measure whether and how often the organization is at risk due to non-compliance of the regulation or policy.

MISSTEPS

Here are some of the more common mistakes that trainers make when they evaluate the effectiveness of required and mandated training:

1. They fail to determine what the driver is behind the training, which leads them to select inappropriate measures.

2. They fail to measure the adequacy of the performance management system and the infrastructure when evaluating the effectiveness of the training.

3. They believe new measures are needed. However, what the organization currently uses to measure should be used to the maximum extent possible. It costs money to develop and implement new measures. It is also harder to convince management of the need for new measures.

4. They fail to confirm the job or task analysis was based on input of high performers, not just the opinions of subject-matter experts or other trainers. Opinions are nice to know, but they are not as useful as facts.

5. They fail to consider the cost to administer tests or the importance of deciding in advance how test results will be used.

TIPS AND TECHNIQUES

Here are some suggestions about how to evaluate required and mandated training:

1. Select measures that are appropriate based on the driver (required or mandate) and the intent (build skills or inform).

2. If you use costs as a measure, identify whose costs. Ask that group to help determine what the costs actually are.

3. If the training uses tests, make sure the tests only measure what was covered in the training. The more tests look like real job assignments, the more defensible they are.

4. Be a little cynical. Believe what people tell you, but remember they are sharing what they know. They only have a partial view of the situation, so validate the information they give you by asking for or seeking corroborating evidence.

5. Find out what is used as evidence of proficiency, and compare that to what is covered in the training. If there is disconnect, work with the client to modify either the standards or the training.

6. Use the current measures of effectiveness to the maximum. Only introduce new measures if you can show managers new ones will help them make better decisions than the ones currently used.

7. Determine how proficient people should be when they exit training.

   • Meet with or interview supervisors and managers and ask how long it takes for people to become proficient.

   • Compare this to how proficient they are when they complete training.

   • Ask what they think it costs to bring people to proficiency.

   • Ask what they can afford to bring people to proficiency faster or how they would benefit if people were proficient sooner.

   You don't know how proficient you want people to be when they exit the training until you know what the cost or consequence is of their not being proficient.

8. Determine the standard or measure of proficiency.

   • Meet with the client and other vested parties and ask them to identify what distinguishes competent performers from those who are not competent. Have them consider factors like the quantity and quality of outputs (work products), the amount of required supervision or checking, the ability to handle unusual or unexpected demands, and the performer's impact on others' productivity.

   • Ask what they use to judge the proficiency of those expected to do the job or task under consideration. Compare this answer to the ones given for the previous question.

   • Ask how and when performers are informed of what is used to judge their performance.

   • Ask how performers might be better informed so they can use that information to monitor and self-regulate their own performance.

   • Ask if it is worth evaluating the effectiveness of the feedback system.

9. Here are some of the things you can do through the process of measurement to *reduce the time to proficiency*:

- Ask how long it takes on average for people from the time they are hired (or assigned) to become fully proficient. This is the number to reduce.

- Ask how close they are to being proficient at the conclusion of the formal training. You won't know if they should be more or less proficient at this point until you know what it costs to bring them to proficiency.

- Identify what people already know and can do and then check that they are only trained on what they don't know or can't do.

- Check to see how much fidelity there is in the practice exercises. The more they look like the real job, the easier it is for the learner to transfer the rules, procedures, and so forth, to the job.

- Find out which procedures or content elements can be and were made into job aids the learner can use as a tool after training. Aids used during training that can also be used on the job reinforce the content and shorten the time to proficiency.

- Find out what the hiring profile is and compare the entry-level skills and knowledge with the training design.

- Find out what support people receive once they complete training. The more support, the greater the likelihood they will be proficient sooner.

SUMMARY

It is important to understand the reason why an organization chooses training as a preferred solution. Some training is done because it is the only viable way to assure that people have the skills and knowledge required to do a job. Other training is done in response to external regulations or management policy dictates that it be done. Whatever the reason, if the goal is to assure people are proficient, then other things must be in place as well. The organization has to provide direction, tools, and resources. The performance management system must be designed to attract candidates who satisfy the job's requirements, establish and communicate what is expected, and outline how proficiency is judged. By evaluating you can measure (find out and compare the current situation to what it should be):

- What people actually know and can do when hired
- What they must know and be able to do to accomplish the expected outputs of the job
- What resources they have to work with

- How well the job is designed, or how stable the work process is
- What other performance support tools are available on the job
- How proficiency is judged
- Whether people have been informed of what is expected and about how their performance will be judged
- How the organization intends to provide people with feedback

You can then discuss training's role and how to best measure its effectiveness. Provide adequate and timely feedback so performers can measure their own performance.

WHERE TO LEARN MORE

Hale, J. A. *Performance-Based Certification: How to Design a Valid, Defensible, Cost-Effective Program* (San Francisco, CA: Jossey-Bass, 2000). There is a chapter on how to do a job task analysis and guidelines on how to measure knowledge and proficiency.

Tufte, E. R. *The Visual Display of Quantitative Information* (1983), *Envisioning Information* (1995), *Visual Explanations* (1997) (Cheshire, CT: Graphics Press).

Wallace, G. *lean-ISD,* the chapters on Performance Analysis (2, 21–27); and *T&D Systems View,* the chapters on Governance & Advisory Systems, Strategic Planning, Cost/Benefit Measurement, and Process Improvement (Naperville, IL, CADDI, 1999).

Chapter 7

How to Measure Elective Training and Employee Relations Programs

Time management, presentation skills, coaching, team building, and more—the company had made a significant investment in its "performance excellence" curriculum. Trainers genuinely believed these programs made people more effective in their jobs, but they didn't know how to prove it. Human resources believed the firm's commitment to training helped the company attract and retain better employees, but they couldn't show a correlation between participation and the cost of recruitment, retention, or business performance. Management was proud of the firm's commitment to professional development, but they had never thought to link the programs to business performance.

*T*he focus of this chapter is on how to measure the effectiveness of *elective* training and *employee relations* programs. What makes such programs elective are

- The amount of choice employees and their bosses have about whether or not to participate or support the program
- The lack of consequences for participating or not in the program
- The measures used to judge success

Elective training and employee relations programs are usually done to satisfy a belief that they are an appropriate solution. However, the driver, the assumed need, is not always based on good data nor clearly understood by those who must develop and implement the programs. By understanding the driver, you are in a better position to measure how well the need is being satisfied and whether other solutions might achieve the same end. Being clear on the driver also helps you find out if the organizational infrastructure and performance management system are in place to sustain performance over time. Some examples are

- Professional development programs that may or may not be stipulated in individual development plans, such as communications, finance, writing reports, and so on
- Supervisory and management development programs that may or may not be a prerequisite for promotion, for example, the basics of supervision, leadership, coaching and counseling
- Employee relations programs, such as smoking cessation, financial planning, pre-retirement planning, or others

ELECTIVE TRAINING

There are a number of reasons why organizations support programs other than what is required for the job or to comply with a regulation. Most of those reasons fall into one of three categories:

1. Human resource sponsored programs that are intended to improve employee relations
2. Management championed or sponsored programs that are intended to fulfill the goals of visionaries
3. Professional, management, and employee development programs that are done in response to a perceived current or future performance deficiency

What makes these programs elective is that knowing or applying the content is rarely linked to performance expectations or reinforced back on the job. If people wanted to apply the information or new skills, there are few support mechanisms to give them feedback or guide the application. The organization's communication and information systems and work processes may not support the new behaviors. There are rarely formal consequences to employees or their bosses if people choose not to participate. Participation in the programs, even if they are heavily promoted, is discretionary. All of this means that it is very important that you decide in advance:

- What you want to find out from measuring
- What questions you want to answer
- What you will do with the information you gain

Then you will be in a position to select the appropriate measures and capture the information that leads to better decisions. Table 7.1 lists the common internal and external measures of elective training and employee relations programs.

HUMAN RESOURCE SPONSORED PROGRAMS

Human resource departments support programs because of the belief such programs:

- Are good to do
- Help attract better job candidates
- Help retain employees
- Are legitimate and therefore the right solution

Table 7.1. Measures of Elective Training and Employee Relations Programs

Internal Measures	External Measures
Cost and ease to	Presence or absence of current measures
• Develop	Evidence of a need or opportunity
• Promote and market	Presence or absence of elements within the infrastructure that will enable the new behaviors
• Deliver	
• Administer	Presence or absence of a performance management system that will reinforce new behaviors
• Maintain	
Speed to penetrate the market	Target audience's reaction
	Learning and adoption of new behaviors
	Degree of market penetration
	Correlation of participation with performance or some other business metric, such as the cost of performance or retention

Some examples are programs like pre-retirement planning, smoking cessation clinics, anger and stress management courses, and health and fitness. It is by measuring that you collect information about the following:

- What the need or goal is

- Whether or not the need or opportunity warrants a solution

- How much change is required to justify the investment in a solution

The goal is to collect enough information to state what the assumptions are about doing a program. For example, the belief might be that a program will positively affect turnover, recruitment, or employee satisfaction. Once you decide that a solution is warranted, you can continue to gather information to help you decide the following:

- Whether or not to purchase a vendor's program or develop one yourself

- If you use a vendor, which vendor's program is best suited for your needs

- If you do it yourself, whether or not to outsource its design, development, delivery, and maintenance

- If the program is best done off site or on site

- When it is time to reduce the amount of resources used to promote a program because the market has been saturated

- Whether or not to continue, add similar programs, or cease to offer such programs

If you know or can estimate what it costs to deliver, market, administer, and maintain a program, you can compare your costs (dollars, time, space, and equipment) to that of a third-party provider, such as a training vendor or community college. Unfortunately, it is rare that these programs are based on a needs assessment or evaluated on whether or not they actually contribute to employee satisfaction, recruitment, or retention. Yet they consume and compete for resources, time, and money.

GETTING ALONG

The director complained that managers didn't get along with one another and would leave the room whenever they began to "argue" over program goals or resources. The director repeatedly announced she wanted everyone to get along with one another and be team players. The director hired a consultant to come in and lead a day-long retreat on communication styles. Had the director done some measurement before the retreat, she would have discovered that none of the managers had cooperation, collaboration, or team effort as part of their performance goals. None of the people who work in the different departments have assignments that require working as a team and there are no systems in place to support working as a team. Therefore, the only suitable measures for evaluating the retreat are

- The number of people who participated compared to the total number possible
- Participants' reaction to the event
- The direct and indirect costs to do it

MANAGEMENT SPONSORED OR CHAMPIONED PROGRAMS

The second major type of elective programs are those that are done because someone in the organization thought it was a good idea. The program makes sense to that person. Perhaps the individual or group wants to leave a legacy. This is how some corporate universities begin. It is also how programs are adopted and stay around long after the champion has moved on in his or her career. Examples of such programs are creative thinking, how to be an entrepreneur in the workplace, business economics, and the like. By evaluating at the time of the request, you can find out:

- What the sponsor sees as the need or hopes to change
- What the sponsor plans to do to facilitate the change
- What the sponsor is using as evidence that a solution is warranted (the current state)
- What the sponsor expects to happen as a result of the proposed solution (the future state)
- What to measure in the beginning, during, and at specific milestones to determine whether the need was satisfied or the change occurred (cost/benefit)

If you are evaluating after a solution was implemented, you can find out:

- What the sponsor saw as the need or hoped to change
- What the sponsor did to facilitate the change
- What the sponsor used as evidence that a solution was warranted (the original measures)

- What the sponsor expected to happen as a result after a solution was implemented (the intended future state)
- What the sponsor expected the cost/benefit to be
- What to measure so you can compare the original to the current state

You can then measure to see whether or to what degree a change occurred and whether the benefit outweighs the cost.

EPIPHANY

A senior executive of a large manufacturing company attended a two-day program titled "Diverse Thought: Insights for the Next Century." He found the program personally inspirational. He asked the training department to make the program available to all managers and major suppliers of the firm. The training department contacted the provider and arranged to offer the program on site. Managers and major suppliers were informed via e-mail. A few months later, training was asked to evaluate the program. Since training had failed to identify what the expectations were of the program, all it could do was report on these dimensions:

- The number of sessions held
- The number of attendees compared to the number invited
- The cost to deliver each session and all of the sessions in total
- The participants' reactions to the program
- Participants' conjectures about how the content might affect the way they conducted themselves in the future

---

Tool 7.1 has guidelines for how to measure the effectiveness of elective and employee relations programs.

PROGRAMS BASED ON A PERCEIVED NEED

Some elective programs are done in response to a perceived current or future need, such as changing customer expectations or a foreseeable loss of key talent due to retirement. Some examples are time management, communications, project management, customer service, basic supervision, business economics, and culture change.

By measuring *before* a program or solution is implemented you can find out:

- What the assumptive base is behind the proposed solution
- What the evidence is that a problem exists

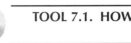

TOOL 7.1. HOW TO EVALUATE ELECTIVE TRAINING AND EMPLOYEE RELATIONS PROGRAMS

1. If a program is already in place:
   - First recollect or find out why the program was instituted.
   - Ask what the beliefs or assumptions were on which the decision was made to purchase or implement the program.
   - Based on the assumptions, ask what the situation was at the time the program was introduced. (This information will allow you to compare what was to what changed.)
   - Ask what was used as evidence that this solution was the appropriate thing to do. (This will given you the measures to determine success.)
   - Find out the intent of the program, that is, was it to build awareness or to develop skills.
   - If the program was intended to build skills, use the tools in Chapter Two to evaluate the integrity of the design.
   - If the program was intended to increase awareness, use the other tools in this chapter to measure reading level and format.
   - Use what you know about the program, why it was done, and what it is expected to accomplish to measure the effectiveness and cost/benefit derived from the program.

2. If the program has not been implemented, ask what the program is expected to change or to do.
   - Ask how certain people are that a need or opportunity exists.
   - Ask what indicators they are using now as a basis for their decision.
   - In collaboration with the client or sponsor, identify the factors you want to track or monitor to determine whether the program is a success.
   - Decide how you will obtain the information and who will do it.

- Whether or not an analysis was done to determine the cause of the problem
- How pervasive or widespread the need or problem is
- What the known or perceived current cost (economically and non-economically) of the problem is
- What the cost is of not solving the problem

- What has to change to prove the program was worth the investment (key success indicators)
- To what degree the infrastructure and performance management systems will support (enable or reinforce) the expected change
- What vendors or community colleges have a similar program and what elements must it possess to meet your need

After the program or solution is implemented you can measure:

- Who and how many participated in the program or were affected by the solution
- How many of the participants changed their behavior as a consequence of participating in the program
- If and to what degree the key success indicators changed

CLEAR TALK

A company developed a program to reduce accidents due to miscommunications between technicians and radio dispatchers. The program was very successful—so successful that after the original audience had taken the program it was extended to anyone in the firm who was a supervisor or higher. Even suppliers were invited to attend. The reason the company decided to make the program available to others was to recover the investment cost to create the simulation. The company had made a significant investment in the development of the program and the simulator that allowed people to experience the consequences of miscommunication. It cost $1,000 an hour just to run the simulator. The role measurement played was to

- Point out that the needs of the target market had been met
- Track the number of hours the simulator was in use to spread the dollars across a larger population
- Ask what the company intended to accomplish by making the course and the use of the simulator available to people outside the target group

As a result, the company is redesigning the course so it is better suited to supervisors and contract administrators.

MEASURING PROBABILITY OF ADOPTION AND LONG-TERM CHANGE

Training organizations support the launch of programs only to see those programs disappear, perhaps fade away. Some programs are only intended to serve short-term needs. However, others are meant to institutionalize new behaviors or processes, that is, change the way people do their jobs. When this is the case, a number of assumptions come into play about what will remain the same and what might change. Change can erode a program's integrity; when this happens the investment made to create it may be lost. When evaluation is a strategy, you are in a better position to discuss assumptions about the future that might support or undermine a program's effectiveness. For example, you can ask:

- The likelihood a sponsor of a program might leave, change positions, or become distracted by other priorities. You can then discuss how to link the program to a business initiative instead of to the person or how to best replace the person so continued support is assured.

- How the goal of the program is documented so others in the future can be reminded of what it was and what the expected results were. You can then discuss how the expected results will be monitored over time and who will retain ownership of the program.

- The probability that the business will reorganize and how that might jeopardize either the ownership or the ongoing implementation of the program. You can then start a conversation about who and how the organization's infrastructure and performance management and performance support systems might stay aligned to sustain the integrity of the program.

- The dependence on a technology being in place that the program is designed to support or use and what happens when the technology is upgraded or replaced.

- How skills will be maintained because they will degrade over time if they are not reinforced. You can ask about the plan to reinforce skills, who will do it, how anyone will know if they are not in use or are degrading.

Tool 7.2, Measuring Probability,[1] along with its discussion guides and worksheets, is designed to help the team identify what might happen in the future that could put at risk or undermine your work. The guides and worksheets are to be used together. Collectively they will help you and your clients begin to understand what the future might hold and how different futures will affect the success of your plans, programs, and working relationships. The tool is designed to facilitate discussions about what the future might look like. There will be a future, but what it will be is shaped by the social, political, and economic environment as well as by decisions made internally about how to operate.

TOOL 7.2A. MEASURING PROBABILITY

Purpose

To drive meaningful discussions about the following:

- How probable is it that the future will be relatively the same?

- What decisions, actions, or events might make the future be different from today?

- How probable are those decisions, actions, or events?

- What might be the impact on the function responsible for training, HRD, and performance improvement?

- How might measurement play a role?

This tool helps you guide clients' discussions about their beliefs related to the predictability of external and internal factors. It allows you to introduce different scenarios and talk about the probability of them happening and the effect on your programs.

Steps

1. Identify people who have a stake in how you operate and the services you offer.

2. Develop a plan to
   - Poll their assumptions about the future
   - Get them to participate in identifying factors that could produce alternative futures
   - Have them determine the probable impact of those futures on your plans and programs

   You may want to use a combination of data-gathering techniques, such as the Delphi, nominal group, focus group, and open interviews.

3. Generate a list of questions to start the discussion, such as:
   - What do we assume to be true about the future?
   - What might change, that would significantly affect the success of our plans, programs, and client relationships?

4. Create a discussion guide like the one in Tool 7.2C that lists some of the assumptions they may have about the future. Ask how probable those assumptions are and what the effect might be.

TOOL 7.2B. DISCUSSION GUIDE 1

Today	The Future
Key stakeholders and people of influence. Someone had to obtain the stakeholders' support to launch the program. They were identified and enrolled.	They will leave or move to different positions. Where will they be in three years? Five years? How will we orient and enroll their replacements so the new leaders can continue to support the behaviors and practices your programs depend on?
Sponsorship. You probably had a sponsor, someone in senior management who championed the program or plan. More than likely that sponsor was rewarded for the successful launch and deployment of a program.	Eventually no one's bonus will depend on continuing to sponsor a program. Call the question. Ask: "Who has the program's continued success as part of his or her performance contract? Whose bonus will be affected by the program's future success or demise?"
Ownership. The goal of most programs is to shift ownership and accountability for the new behaviors and results.	Over time the responsibility will shift back to HR or the staff organization. Develop scorecards and other reporting devices that track and publicly communicate people's progress using the new behaviors or new program. Continue to celebrate adoption.
Competition for attention. Keep your initiative or program on management's agenda.	New initiatives will compete with your program for attention and space on the agenda. How many initiatives were there over the last three years? There will be that many or more in the next three. How will you identify them early so the program can be linked or seen as an enabler, and not pushed off the agenda?
The promise. Your program was funded on the promise it will produce positive business results. The promise may or may not be in economical terms, but it should be measurable.	As time passes, an understanding of the promise will get distorted. What will we do to assure a continued understanding of the promise and what was agreed to as evidence of success? How will we continue to report progress, impact, or results?
Organizational structure and reporting relationships. Your ability to influence is enhanced or limited by your position power.	We will reorganize. We will see mergers and takeovers in our industry. Reporting relationships will change. On average, 90 percent of employees have their workspace relocated at least once a year. How will this affect our ability to sustain attention and accountability for the performance we want to institutionalize? How will this affect our ability to sustain support? How can we prepare management for the impact of such changes on this program?

Technology. Your program or initiative was launched on the premise of some technological capability.

New technologies will emerge. Some will support greater autonomy; others will enable greater centralized control. How might future developments in technology affect this program's long-term effectiveness? How will we identify and anticipate those new developments so management is prepared for the impact?

Tools and Training. You probably launched your program or initiative with a series of training programs. You may even have developed brochures, set up a help desk, and produced job aids.

Behaviors will cease without reinforcement. People will need tools to help them become confident in the new behaviors. Pay particular attention to tools that guide decisions like how to assign merit pay and select people for jobs. Also consider tools that help the managers give feedback and coach.

TOOL 7.2C. DISCUSSION GUIDE 2

Purpose

To identify different probable futures and discuss the implications on what your function does, the programs it provides, and how it operates.

Possible Factors Affecting the Future

If *growth* stays or does not stay the same, what are the implications?

If *turnover* stays or does not stay the same, what are the implications?

If no *new technology* emerges or if one does emerge, what are the implications?

If *customers' economic behavior* stays or does not stay the same, what are the implications?

If *internal champions* stay or do not stay engaged, what are the implications?

Other

Ask for Each Factor

What would be the consequences?

- Economic and non-economic?
- On how we operate as a unit?
- On our programs?

What should we pay attention to and track to see if any of these changes are happening?

Where might we find the data that might signal a change?

Alternative Future 1: There Is Little Change

Growth stays the same

Turnover stays the same

No new technology emerges to replace the current technology

Ask

How probable is this future state? Very, maybe, unlikely?

What would be the impact on how we operate as a unit?

Customers' economic behavior stays the same

Internal champions stay engaged

Other

What would be the impact on our programs?

Alternative Future 2: One or Two Factors Change

Ask

Growth does not stay the same (accelerates or slows down)

Turnover stays the same

A new technology emerges to replace the current technology

Customers' economic behavior does not stay the same (increased or decreased spending, or spending on different solutions)

Internal champions move on

How probable is this future state? Very, maybe, unlikely?

What would be the impact on how we operate as a unit?

What would be the impact on our programs?

Alternative Future 3: Assume a Different Set of Factors Changes

Ask

List your assumptions here.

How probable is this future state? Very, maybe, unlikely?

What would be the impact on how we operate as a unit?

What would be the impact on our programs?

TOOL 7.2D. ALTERNATIVE FUTURES WORKSHEET

Purpose

To drive meaningful discussions about the impact of possible future states. This tool is very similar to the tool on cost/benefit analysis; however, it focuses attention on assumptions about behaviors and outcomes, instead of just on costs. You use the results of your discussions from the previous discussion guides to hone in on how different futures might affect behaviors, outcomes, and costs.

Steps

1. Create a worksheet similar to the one shown below, except put in real behaviors, outcomes, and costs wherever you can.

2. With your team, identify the behaviors and consequences of the current state.

3. Identify your assumptions if you do nothing (Action Set 1).

4. Identify a set of actions that you might do (Action Set 2) and your assumptions about how they might affect behaviors, outcomes, and costs. Actions might be things like "outsource more," "make increased use of technology (the Web)," "catalogue training in reusable chunks," and so forth.

5. Identify another set of actions that you might do (Action Set 3) and your assumptions about how they might affect behaviors, outcomes, and costs.

6. Put your assumptions on a worksheet so everyone can comment, edit, disagree, and discuss.

TOOL 7.2E. SAMPLE COMPARISONS WORKSHEET

Now	Action Set 1 (Do nothing) Assumptions	Action Set 2 (Do A) Assumptions	Action Set 3 (Do B) Assumptions
Behavior X	Behavior X	Avoid Behavior X	Avoid Behavior X
Behavior Y	Behavior Y	Reduce Behavior Y	Keep Behavior Y
Behavior Z	Behavior Z	Keep Behavior Z	Reduce Behavior Z
Outcome M	Outcome M	Lessen Outcome M	Avoid Outcome M
Cost A	New Outcome N Reduce Cost A Add Cost B	Avoid Outcome N Add Outcome O Eliminate Cost A Avoid Cost B Add Cost C	Lesson Outcome N Avoid Outcome O Add Outcome P Reduce Cost A Avoid Costs B & C Add Cost D

TOOL 7.2F. PAYOFF TABLE WORKSHEET

Purpose

To continue the discussion about the probable economic and non-economic consequences of different action sets given different futures. It is not the goal to be precise or come up with definitive answers but to identify the phenomena or changes you will want to monitor over time so you are better prepared and can adjust appropriately.

Steps

1. Create a worksheet like Tool 7.2E.

2. Across the top, list two to three probable futures, such as a change in sponsorship, a loss of institutional memory, a reorganization, a new technology, or the atrophy of skills.

3. In the first column, list two to three possible actions you might follow through on, such as outsource more, make increased use of technology (the Web), catalogue training in reusable chunks, and so on.

4. In each cell, note what the payoff (good and bad) will be for each combination.

5. In the last column, total or summarize the payoffs for each row. The action with more positive outcomes, independent of futures, is the one with the highest expected value.

6. Use the exercise to develop a plan for the coming year.

7. Possible discussion questions:

   • How probable is Future #1?

   • Given the occurrence of Future #1 and the implementation of Action Set #1, what is the expected outcome economically and non-economically (payoff 1,1)?

   • Given the occurrence of Future #1 and the implementation of Action Set #2, what is the expected outcome economically and non economically (payoff 1,2)?

   • Given the occurrence of Future #1 and the implementation of Action Set #3, what is the expected outcome economically and non-economically (payoff 1,3)?

8. Repeat the questions for the other futures across each action set. Which action set has the highest expected value given all three futures?

TOOL 7.2G. SAMPLE PAYOFF TABLE

Alternative futures	Future #1	Future #2	Future #3	Expected Value
Action set #1	Payoff 1,1	Payoff 2,1	Payoff 3,1	Expected value A
Action set #2	Payoff 1,2	Payoff 2,2	Payoff 3,2	Expected value B
Action set #3	Payoff 1,3	Payoff 2,3	Payoff 3,3	Expected value C

PROGRAMS THAT INFORM

Two other measures are often overlooked, yet are very important to the effectiveness of elective and mandated programs in particular. These measures are about *readability* and *format.* A lot of elective training is designed only to "encourage" or persuade people to adopt certain behaviors or attitudes. The assumption is that people have skills, but choose not to behave or make desired choices because of some personal value set. A lot of mandated training is about communicating rules; therefore, it is very important that the information be expressed clearly and the format of the message support understanding by highlighting the key points.

Readability is about the ease of understanding. There are two standard methods of measuring readability. One is called a "fog index" and the other the "Flesch-Kincaid Index." The term "fog index" is from a definition of fog, "that which confuses or obscures because the meaning is hidden behind a fog of rhetoric."[2] Both methods calculate the reading level of a passage and compare it to a grade level. For example, Hemmingway's short stories are written at the fourth-grade level. The *Reader's Digest* is at the sixth-grade level. *The New York Times* is higher. The Gettysburg Address is at twelfth-grade level.

Some word processing software will automatically calculate the reading level of a passage. However, the benefit of doing it yourself once in a while is that you are reminded of the factors that result in good writing. Information that is easy to understand is chunked into small pieces. The paragraphs are short, and the sentences are simple, not complex. The words used are also simple and the passage is written in the active not passive voice. The variables that reduce or make a passage harder to understand are

- *The ratio of active to passive voice.* Active voice is easier to understand. Ninety-seven percent of the sentences in Hemmingway's short stories are in the active voice.

- *The length of the paragraphs.* Short paragraphs, and the use of bullets to mark off lists are easier to understand.

- *The length of the sentences.* Short sentences are easier to understand because long sentences tend to be complex. It was the length and complexity of the sentences in Lincoln's Gettysburg Address that increased the reading level.

- *The number of words with three or more syllables.* Short words are easier to understand.

Format affects readability.[3] Most simply format is about the size of the type and margins, the organization of the content, and the use of icons and maps to help people understand the relationship of the content. Readability is helped by large clean typeface and wider margins. Printing conventions such as type size and the use of boldface, italics, underlining, and initial capitalization can be used to signal a change in topic, stress importance, and show the relationship of the topics to each other. Examples are using a different typeface for titles and main subject areas. To improve the readability of this book, each chapter is structured in the same way. Each chapter has section on missteps, tips, and suggestions on where to learn more.

Readability applies to training independent of the delivery format. Web-based training, help screens, and information on CD-ROM can benefit by consistently using a standard format. Authoring systems and word processing templates are tools to help you standardize training materials. A benefit of consistently following a standard format is that learners become familiar with how the content is presented and have to spend less energy learning how to maneuver through the materials. They can spend their energy on understanding the content.

GOOD LABORATORY AND MANUFACTURING PRACTICES

The Food and Drug Administration requires manufacturers of drugs to train laboratory personnel in good laboratory practices (GLPs) and manufacturing personnel in good manufacturing practices (GMPs). One firm satisfies this mandate by requiring all new hires to read the GLPs and the GMPs and then sign a statement that they read and understand the material. The documentation new hires read ranges from two hundred to five hundred pages in length. The information is not well-written. The information does not describe the specific procedures in a step-by-step manner. The sentences do not follow the rules of grammar, and the people who prepared the documentation did not follow any standard template or format. English is a second language for many of the new hires. Whether English is a first language or not, the literacy level of most new hires was very low.

The manufacturer actually relies on the first-line supervisor to demonstrate the proper procedures and then enforce compliance. Call it what you will, training—whether to inform or build skills—did not happen. What happened was a charade done only to comply with the letter not the spirit of the law.

Tool 7.3 has guidelines for measuring the effectiveness of programs that just inform. The tool is in two parts.

TOOL 7.3A. HOW TO EVALUATE PROGRAMS THAT JUST INFORM

Here are some suggestions for how to evaluate a program that is intended to inform, whether called training or not. The important thing is that the program does not build skills, as it lacks practice exercises with feedback.

1. Measure (gather information about) dissemination:
   - How long it took to roll out the program and be available to the target audience and compare what you find out to the client's expectations
   - How many people participated compared to the number in the target audience and compare what you find out to the client's expectation

2. Measure people's initial reactions, specifically to the utility of the information and the likelihood they will apply it and compare what you find out to the client's expectation.

3. Measure the direct and indirect cost to develop, deliver, and deploy it and compare this to the budget for the program.

If the expectation is that people will use the information in some aspect of their job, meet with the client to do the following:

4. Identify how the information is to be used, what will be accepted as evidence of use, and what the consequences will be of applying or not applying it (to the organization and to the people).

5. Decide how the client will reinforce the information and the importance of its appropriate use over time.

6. If the information is required for the job, meet with the client or other knowledgeable people to determine the cost to create and disseminate the message.

   a. Ask what it costs to create or acquire the message.

   b. Add to (a) the cost of the learner's time to receive, listen to, or read the message.

   c. Add to (b) the cost of the person's time to deliver the message.

   d. Add to (c) any costs incurred to deliver the message not already accounted for.

   e. Add to (d) the cost of any time spent clarifying or interpreting the information. This gives you the average cost to inform a person.

7. Meet with the client and agree on a desired reading level and message format.

   - Determine what percentage of the materials are at the desired reading level
   - Determine what percentage of the materials or message follow the desired format

8. Determine whether or not the client's expectations, evidence, and

consequence of use or non-use were communicated during and after the program and give the client the results.

9. Periodically meet with the client to offer support to reinforce the appropriate use of the information.

10. If the client does not want to do the items listed in Steps 4 through 8, don't spend any more energy on evaluation.

TOOL 7.3B. HOW TO DETERMINE THE READING LEVEL OF A MESSAGE

Many word processing systems will do this for you. However, doing it yourself once in a while will help you understand and remember the factors that make written passages harder or easier to understand.

The Variables

- *The number of sentences in a passage.* Long paragraphs are harder to comprehend than short ones. Count compound sentences (sentences joined together with and, but, or, so, or other connecting words) as more than one sentence.

- *The number of words in a sentence.* Long sentences are harder to understand than short ones. Long sentences also tend to be complex, that is, contain multiple phrases.

- *The number of words with three or more syllables.* Long words are harder to understand than short words.

Here are the steps to calculate a reading level.

1. Select a passage of at least one hundred words. It can be in one or more paragraphs.

2. Count the number of sentences in the sample.

3. Divide the number of words in the sample by the number of sentences to find an average number of words per sentence.

4. Count the number of words with three or more syllables. Overlook three-syllable words ending in *es* or *ed*.

5. Divide the number of words into the number of three or more syllable words to find the percentage of polysyllable words. Multiply the answer by 100.

6. Add the average number of words in a sentence to the percent of polysyllables to establish a base value.

7. Finally, multiply the base value by .4 to get an estimate of the reading level.

MISSTEPS

Here are some of the common difficulties trainers and training managers get into when they evaluate elective training and other employee relations programs:

1. They fail to document the rationale for the program and establish baseline measures they can use later to determine whether the program was effective.

2. They fail to consider the shelf life and market size of a program and extend it beyond what is useful.

3. They fail to do a cost/benefit analysis comparison of (a) the worth of a solution compared to the cost of the problem or (b) one solution compared to another.

4. They assume there is a market for the program and that people will automatically sign up. Promoting a program has a cost. The cost may be in time or money.

5. They assume they have to be more precise in their measurement than what is required to answer the question.

6. They assume evaluation is optional.

7. They fail to develop job aids to help managers support the transfer of the new skills to the job.

8. They fail to evaluate how well materials follow good message design principles or a standard template, or they fail to check the reading level of the materials. This is especially important when the "training" is actually about informing and there is little opportunity to practice, obtain feedback, or ask questions.

TIPS AND TECHNIQUES

Here are some suggestions on how to evaluate elective training and employee relations programs:

1. State aloud the reason for or assumption behind a program. You may even want to suggest language that describes what is believed to be the problem the program will solve: "So the reason we want to do X is we believe it will impact Y. Is that right?"

2. State aloud what the suggested solution is intended to accomplish: "So the assumption is that if we do X, Y will happen. Is that how you understand it?"

3. If you are asked to evaluate a program after it is launched, whether or not the rationale for doing it was based on a careful analysis or well-documented, find out how the results will be used. Don't be more rigorous or more precise in your evaluation efforts than what is useful.

4. Figure the cost of packaging and selling a program into the overall cost. Considering the hidden costs will help you make a better decision about whether to buy an off-the-shelf program or to develop one yourself.

SUMMARY

It is important to understand the reason why an organization chooses to support elective programs. You want to determine if programs are implemented based on assumptions or on data. Either way, you will be in a better position to decide how much measurement is warranted and what variables to use as evidence of effectiveness. The assumptions might be a belief that a program will satisfy a perceived need or about the organization's willingness and ability to support the adoption of new behaviors. Measuring can open the door to meaningful dialogue and inquiry about what is assumed to be true, what the organization can and is willing to do, and what the consequences might be of implementing and maintaining specific programs. By measuring, you can contribute data to the conversation. No matter what the driver is, identifying in advance what is and is not in place will help you predict whether a program is likely to fulfill its promise and be a wise investment of time and money.

WHERE TO LEARN MORE

Wallace, G. *lean-ISD*, the chapters on Performance Analysis (2, 21–27); and *T&D Systems View*, the chapters on Governance & Advisory Systems, Strategic Planning, and Cost/Benefit Measurement. (Naperville, IL, CADDI, 1999).

NOTES

1. Qualitative probability theory is an extension of Aristotle's deductive logic, where you reduce the argument to specific hypotheses.

2. Both the Gunning Fog Index and the Flesch-Kincaid Index are used by the more popular software programs to measure readability. Measuring readability is the cumulative work of many people. Robert Gunning in his book *The Technique of Clear Writing* (New York: McGraw-Hill, 1952) developed the Gunning Fog Index. Gunning's other publications are *How to Take the Fog Out of Business Writing* (Chicago, IL: Dartnell, 1994) and *New Guide to More Effective Writing in Business and Industry* (Boston, MA: Industrial Education Institute, 1962). Peter Kincaid, former chief of Naval Education and Training, re-normed and adapted the Flesch Reading Ease Formula for use with Navy enlisted personnel. It is referred to as the Flesch-Kincaid. To find out more, check out P. J. Kincaid, *Derivation of New Readability Formulas: Automated Readability Index, Fog Count and Flesch Reading Ease Formula* (Millington, TN: Naval Air Station Memphis, 1975).

3. Check www.timetabler.com/reading.html to find more information on readability.

Chapter 8

How to Evaluate Delivery Alternatives

Organizations are changing the way they deliver their training and HR programs, for example:

- A company with hundreds of field locations moved all training to the Web.

- An international firm with offices all over the world requires learners to complete pre-work that is sent to them by e-mail before they can participate in any classroom, satellite broadcast, live intranet, or videoconference session.

- A manufacturer put its safety training on CDs and mailed it to field personnel.

- Another manufacturer put 90 percent of its training for production line personnel on laminated job aids.

- One company's legal department demands that the course on sexual harassment for first-line supervisors be classroom, instructor-led, and two days long.

- A company requires its product managers to train sales personnel at regional sales meetings; the training is to consist only of demonstrating the new products' features. However, production line personnel are to be trained on the production room floor and in increments no longer than fifty-nine minutes.

These organizations are adopting new delivery methods. Whether or not the new methods are more "effective" than what was previously done depends on what they hope to accomplish with the change, such as lower costs, increase accessibility, make content reusable, or shorten the time to proficiency.

*T*his chapter is about how to measure the effectiveness of delivery systems. Delivery systems are how information and instruction are packaged, formatted, and deployed or made available to the target audience. Organizations are looking for ways to deploy information and instruction to wider audiences, more quickly, and at less cost. At the same time they want delivery systems that allow for "just-in-time" access, provide practice and feedback, track participation, automatically grade tests and update professional development records, and signal payroll to issue tuition reimbursement checks. Organizations are asking for a lot and they may not always understand the implications or tradeoffs of trying to have one system meet all of their needs. The range of possible delivery systems is extensive, and they are difficult to compare because of the number of variables you might consider. For example, you might choose to compare systems by whether or not they are

- Self-paced or group-paced
- Instructor-led or self-administered
- Paper or electronic, including CD-ROM, e-mail, Internet, intranet, video, audio
- Designed for limited or unlimited access
- Just-in-time and on-demand or fixed and scheduled
- Organized by modules or by course or curriculum
- Synchronous (live, real time) or asynchronous (not live or real time)
- With or without animation or graphics
- Real (as in on-the-job using actual equipment and data) or simulated
- Text alone or with audio and video
- Full narrative or just job aids
- Combine multimedia, instructional strategies, and performance support tools or have discrete functions

The reason for considering all of the variables is to help you identify any assumptions you might have about what you hope to accomplish and on what basis you might select a system. Therefore, the questions are

- What do you hope to accomplish by adopting new or different delivery systems?
- What do you want to accomplish through the process of evaluation?
- What criteria will you use to compare alternatives?

THE DRIVER

Organizations are embracing new delivery systems for a number of reasons. Most of the reasons come down to cost and speed. For example, as organizations become international or their workforce is more dispersed, it becomes increasingly costly to convene employees to update them on policies, regulations, and product changes, much less train them on how to do their jobs. This is also the case when there is an increase in the people who have to be informed and trained, because the people keep changing due to reassignments or turnover or the information and procedures keep changing. Therefore, one of the main drivers is to reduce or avoid cost. Organizations are focusing on costs associated with

- Time away from work, whether for participation or travel
- Travel, including airfare, lodging, meals, and other expenses
- The use of facilities, whether rented or owned, shared or dedicated
- Headcount, such as full-time instructors, course and meeting administrators, instructional designers, media developers, webmasters, and so on
- Content updates, whether because of new regulations, products, or policies, that require changes to the information, examples, practice exercises, or tests
- Program administration, scheduling, enrolling, checking eligibility, shipping materials
- Test administration including scoring
- Report generation about participation, cancellations, and test scores
- Translation of print, visuals, and audio recordings into other languages
- Printing, duplicating, and shipping of materials
- Delivery infrastructure for e-learning

Therefore, one of the things you might want to measure is if, or to what degree, the type of costs listed above or others are reduced or avoided by the adoption of a different delivery system. Start by asking if the cost of the previous or current delivery system is known so you will have a point of comparison. If the costs are only roughly captured and recorded, you can use best guesses. However, you must also factor in any other associated costs of the new delivery system, such as acquiring the equipment and materials, paying for leases, training people how to use it, and maintaining it.

Similarly, organizations want people to get the information and skills they require faster without sacrificing accuracy or utility. Speed, like cost, is relative and is sometimes confused with accessibility and usefulness. Sending out information through e-mail is fast, but not everyone may be at a desk to retrieve it, be able to apply it at that moment, or have rapid access to it when they need it at a later date. The same is true of voice messaging, Web pages, and CDs. A job aid that fits in a pocket may be preferable, as it is fast and people have it when they require it. Therefore, in evaluating alternative delivery systems, consider cost, speed, usability, and accessibility as separate criteria.

If the goal is to reduce the cost and time to proficiency and to provide support for all components of instruction (not just information), then you must consider the degree the new system allows the following:

- Practice and feedback
- Fidelity or reality base of the practice and the conditions of performance
- Remediation or development of enabling skills
- Reinforcement of rarely used procedures or rules once the person returns to the job

If the goal is to maintain a contingency workforce or maintain proficiency in rarely used skills, then you should consider how well a system allows for periodic, distributed practice and feedback sessions. Rarely used procedures are best supported through performance support tools and by standards or well-documented procedures. Both rarely used procedures or skills and complex skills and procedures (such as flying an airplane) degrade rather rapidly over time. Therefore delivery systems that allow for periodic practice and feedback can help workers retain their proficiency.[1]

If the goal is to get people to more thoroughly learn the underlying principles behind a task so they can apply that knowledge to new situations, the more important it is for a system to provide practice and feedback sessions. If workers are known to take "shortcuts," then the practice and feedback should reinforce the preferred procedures and performance standards.

Another driver is risk management when you want to reduce the probability of errors by assuring that people have been informed and are capable. Risk management is why organizations want delivery systems that test learners' knowledge and skills at the end of the training event. In performance assessment, the goal is to measure the degree to which actual and desired performance match. Certification is a type of performance assessment where the goal is a formal review of an individual's or group's ability to perform. Certification can become an important factor in risk management, because certification implies that the "certified" individual or group has proven ability to perform a given task.

THE CRITERIA

Understanding the driver behind the search for a solution is only one part of the equation. The other part is the *criteria* that will be used to compare new alternatives with the current way of doing business and different options. Criteria can include:

- *Accessibility*—If it is available when needed, compared to only at fixed time intervals; if it can be retrieved remotely, compared to only at a specific locale; and if the users have the equipment or materials required to access and use it.

- *Administrative support*—What costs might the organization have to absorb to fully utilize the alternatives that are not immediately obvious, such as training people to use it or making people available to maintain records or support users.

- *Content stability*—How often some or all of the content has to be updated due to changing regulations, new technology, product rollouts or enhancements, and so forth.

- *Cost*—To purchase, customize, implement, maintain, use, and convert from a previous system to a new system. The cost may be fixed (independent of volume or use), variable (dependent on volume and use), direct (attributable to specific users, products, or functions), or indirect or hidden (not attributable to specific users, products, or functions).

- *Cultural tolerance*—To what degree an alternative supports or is counter to the organization's culture or traditional way of doing business.

- *Fidelity*—How true to life the message is; how much translation, explanation, interpretation, or extrapolation is required for learners to comprehend the information and its application and to gain skill and confidence in their ability to apply the content.

- *Functionality*—What functions it can provide or support beyond conveying information, such as practice exercises, feedback, testing, maintaining learner records, cueing or reminding people of specific rules or steps in a procedure, and so on.

- *Motivation*—How the system impacts the motivation of the target group. When analyzing competing delivery systems, each component of motivation (attention, confidence, relevancy, and satisfaction)[2] must be considered. If a delivery system cannot positively impact each element of motivation in the target group, that delivery system will almost certainly fail, as people will "vote with their feet."

- *Performance management*—To what degree an alternative requires the adoption of behaviors that are not supported by the current performance management system, such as clear expectations and incentives, and the consequences for not using the system.

- *Risk*—To what degree it puts people, data, or other assets at risk or exposes them to hazards that jeopardize the safety of the process, image, or investment.

- *Speed*—How quickly the system and the information and instruction it is expected to deploy can be made available to the target audience.

REDUNDANT SYSTEMS

A firm of 45,000 employees with hundreds of field offices put its performance management system on-line. This system allows employees to access and update information in their personnel records, such as change of address. Supervisors can record employee performance goals, reviews, and development plans. Even salary adjustments are done on-line. However, approximately two thousand employees cannot access the system because they do not have access to a computer on the network and do not need it for their work. The company decided to maintain the old paper-based and inter-office mail system; therefore, it has not reduced or avoided costs because it must now support redundant systems.

DISTRIBUTOR SALES STAFF

A manufacturer of electronic equipment provides training to its retail partners on selling skills and its products' features and benefits. The manufacturer trains up to 10,000 salespeople a year due to the high turnover in the retail business. The manufacturer's field training staff goes to the stores and to the retailers' regional meetings. Since the bulk of the training was to convey information about products, the manufacturer decided to migrate the more proven and elementary content to CD-ROM.

Why the change? Management set a goal of doubling revenue and tripling margin, a $40M impact. Achieving this goal required a combination of increasing sales and reducing the cost of sales. The cost of training, specifically its delivery, was a major component of the cost of sales. Using CD-ROM to deploy the more stable content allowed the trainers to focus on modeling and coaching the desired sales behaviors. However, there was an unanticipated cost of putting the training in an electronic format. The training relies on the use of computer-generated graphics and photographs to convey key product features. The manufacturer discovered it did not know what rights had been secured with regard to ownership of these images. In some cases contract course developers who created the images had retained the copyright. Therefore, the firm had to either be licensed to use them or create new images under terms that would provide clear title. In this situation the only measure being used to compare the new solution with the old is overall cost of sales training, particularly the migration of the content to the new format and its impact on delivery costs.

VIRTUAL REALITY[3]

In the past, surgeons learned by watching more experienced surgeons operate. The operations were done in small amphitheaters with students sitting above and on all sides of the operating arena. The surgeon would explain aloud what was being done and why. Later, cameras were used to capture the surgeon's actions and broadcast them on televisions mounted around the amphitheater. Students developed the required fine motor skills and eye-hand coordination by practicing on animals and later patients under the guidance of an experienced surgeon.

Today the medical profession is using technology, specifically "virtual reality" simulations, sophisticated real-time computer programs, to give students practice executing complex medical procedures. The programs replicate the senses of sight and sound and touch and motion. The performance goals are

- To decrease the time to proficiency
- To reduce the cost of training while reducing risks to the patients
- To lessen the dependency on animals and human subjects
- To make more effective use of instructors' time
- To build learner confidence in their abilities

As medical liability becomes an increasingly important aspect of the business of medicine, another important goal is to create objective, performance-based, standardized certification programs. In addition, the simulations provide both formative and corrective feedback as well as a database record of learner performance.

The manufacturers of medical equipment (known as original equipment manufacturers or OEMs) have created another goal for medical simulations—the ability to demonstrate and train new or potential users on new medical devices. In the past, these activities required an OEM's sales force to demonstrate or train health care professionals on new equipment, using the actual equipment. This required an enormous expense in time and materials. In addition, the FDA has been increasing its requirements on OEMs to demonstrate the quality of their new equipment training programs. High fidelity, virtual, medical simulations meet these needs at a fraction of the cost required for traditional methods. The measures used to compare the technology solution to the traditional methods are

- Sensory fidelity of the program
- Medical accuracy of visuals and touch sensations
- Number and type of practice scenarios available
- Relative time to proficiency as demonstrated through tests that are simulations
- Impact on instructor availability
- Effect on building learner confidence in their own abilities and acceptance of the delivery methodology
- Lessening dependence on animal and human subjects
- Ability to practice sufficiently to gain skill without risk to others
- Cost to purchase the simulation
- Scientific viability of certification tests

PLUMBERS AND PIPE FITTERS[4]

The plumbers and pipe fitters union has invested millions of dollars in training. As a result, union members and apprentices can go to any local union hall and log on and participate in a variety of distance learning modules. Some students are even assigned a password that allows them to log on from a remote location such as their home or the local library. Some of the courses that make up the curriculum are listed in Table 8.1.

Table 8.1. Plumbers' and Pipe Fitters' Curriculum

Residential and Commercial Plumbing	Back-Fill Procedures	Math and Calculus
CFC Refrigeration	Welding	Blueprint Reading
Medical Gas Installation	Red Cross Safety	Science
Boiler and Steam Heating Systems	OSHA Safety	Customer Relations
Fiberoptics	Test Balances	Plumbing Estimating
Hydraulics	Pipe Cutting and Soldering	Supervising

The modules use computer-assisted design (CAD) to show each step in a task and how the object looks before, during, and after each step. Every module has practice tests and a final test. At specific points in the curriculum, students go to a local union hall with a practice lab where they practice the procedures under the guidance of the instructor. One instructor, who works out of the Bloomington, Illinois, local hall, is available to answer questions from local students and those on-line. He sees from 90 to 120 students a year. Many of the courses prepare students to be certified by third parties, for example, a representative from Hartford Insurance certifies students in up to twenty-nine different welds. Some courses are recognized by colleges and can lead to an associate's degree. The process of evaluation helped the union identify what it required of a delivery system for this curriculum. The drivers were

- Provide access to learners across the country, thus reducing travel and housing costs
- Spread the cost of developing a Web-based series of modules across local union halls
- Make sure students know the basic rules and concepts before taking up valuable time and space in a lab
- Assure consistent dissemination and explanation of the rules and concepts
- Reduce the need for instructors
- Provide transcripts and maintain a database of student training history
- Correlate students' performance at the centers with their success at completing the state licensure exams

Once the union was clear on what it wanted to accomplish, it was able to put together a workable combination of delivery methods. The measures were the cost of training per person, the percentage of graduates who successfully passed the state license exams, and increased access by people in other states.

LACK OF INFRASTRUCTURE

An international firm has manufacturing operations in both developing and developed countries. It wanted to reduce the cost of training its human resource (HR) generalists. The courses in the HR curriculum included staffing and recruiting; employee and labor relations; compensation and benefits; health, wellness, and accommodation; expatriate issues; project planning; change management; and succession planning. Delivering the training to plants in developed countries was not difficult. Materials were sent by way of e-mail to the generalists, who would download them, print them out, work the exercises, and then send their assignments back to corporate training by e-mail. The same system did not work for the developing countries where the generalists did not even have access to a fax machine, much less a computer. They did not read English and may not have been proficient in their own language, as the opportunity to learn English or go to school was rare. The decision was to train the plant managers in the HR curriculum and make them responsible for the development of their HR generalist. Plant managers were better educated and proficient in English. The materials were mailed to them. They would then complete the assignments and return them for review and feedback. In this situation, access to the training materials by all of the countries was an important consideration when deciding on a delivery system. The correlation of incidence of complaints, turnover, production, and profitability to the number of courses the plant manager completed was how the company evaluated the results of training plant managers in HR.

TECHNOLOGY SOLUTION

A company with a geographically dispersed workforce compared a number of vendors' products. Before doing the comparison, training managers from the different sites were asked to review a survey listing the criteria. They added some criteria. Next, the survey was sent to all locations that would be affected by the proposed new system. Training managers were asked to rate the functions (1 being necessary and 5 being not necessary). The surveys were collected and data was compiled and weighted to determine the optimal system. Six vendors were contacted and given a list of the capabilities so they could submit how well their solutions fit the required functionality requirements. The top three vendors (based on the weighted criteria) were asked to prepare and deliver functional demonstrations of their products. Managers from Technology Solution individually and privately rated the vendors' products and assigned percentages for how well each vendor met the criteria. Table 8.2 shows the criteria the managers applied and the cumulative percentages of their comparisons.

The firm decided to purchase Vendor B's product because the difference in the functionality when compared to what Vendor A offered was not sufficient to offset the difference in cost and the loss of the investment already made. Vendor C's product was the least costly, but had much less functionality compared to Vendor A's. In this situation the most important criterion was the overall want satisfaction value of three products.

Table 8.2. Product Comparisons

Category Description	Vendor A	Vendor B	Vendor C
Classroom Instruction	90.6%	98.4%	87.5%
On-Line Self-Paced Instruction	100%	81.5%	79.5%
Skills and Performance Mgmt	100%	89.5%	83%
Employee Access	100%	96.3%	90%
Reporting Capabilities	85.1%	95.3%	87.5%
Facilities and Equipment	100%	100%	97.5%
Miscellaneous Characteristics	100%	79.1%	80%
Lending Library	32.6%	91.6%	60.5%
Totals	94%	92.9%	83.19%
Cost of acquisition	Very costly	Costly	Least costly
Leverage current investment	Not owned	Already in use at one site	Not owned

Tool 8.1 contains guidelines for comparing different delivery alternatives. This tool is to be used by you, your team, your clients, and any other groups with a vested interest in a delivery system. You want to be sure you identify people's assumptions about what they want a delivery system to accomplish. The tool is meant to drive meaningful discussions about what is known and assumed to be required. It has three worksheets that you can add to or modify to meet your needs. It walks you through the steps of weighing and ranking the measures you decided on and the alternatives you are considering.

TOOL 8.1A. DECIDING ON THE CRITERIA

Give everyone a copy of this worksheet (print, e-mail, or Web) and ask that they complete it as well as possible or hand it out and discuss each item.	Place your answers in this column.

1. Of the products or programs you want the delivery system to support, what percentage:

   • Are job specific or required?

   • Are mandated?

   • Are done for professional or management development reasons?

   • Of the content is stable?

   • Are done to support HR employee relations initiatives?

   • Are to build awareness or keep people informed?

   • Require documentation, records of participation, completion, and so forth?

   • Require test administration, including delivery, scoring, and reporting results?

   • Require administrative support, such as enrollment, scheduling, and sending out of materials, certifications, or notices to bosses?

2. The audience your products and programs are intended to support. Include in this the audience's access to technology and the type of constraints under which they work.

   • How widely dispersed are they?

   • How many are there?

   • How much turnover is there?

   • What electronic and technological capability do they have or not have?

   • What constraints do they have about usage or access?

   • What incentives are there for them to use new or different systems?

TOOL 8.1A. (Continued)	

3. The problem you are trying to solve.
 	
   • Cost, what costs, whose costs? (See Tool 6.2.)
 	
       Dissemination
       Updating or maintenance
       Administration
       Development
       Other
 	
4. Which of the following is required?
 	
   • Faster dissemination
   • Increased access
   • Increased fidelity of the content
   • Provide more practice with feedback
   • Do better assessments of readiness
   • Do better assessments of accomplishment
   • Be better able to reuse discrete pieces of the content
   • Be better able to link solutions to development needs
   • Other
 	
5. The size of the problem. Are you looking for a solution for
 	
   • One course or program, some, or all?
   • One audience, some or all?
   • A limited time frame or an ongoing solution?	

Compile everyone's answers to the above questions, share them with the team and clients, and discuss them. Based on the information you gained from looking at your current situation, ask the team and clients to generate a list of system requirements that one or a combination of systems must have to (1) solve your problem, (2) work within the constraints of the audience, and (3) fulfill the goals of the curriculum or programs. *Note:* It is very unlikely one system will meet all of your requirements; therefore you might want to focus your efforts on an optimum combination of systems. To complete your list of requirements, you might want to do a nominal group technique (see Chapter Ten). Use the results for comparing systems (see Tool 8.1, Worksheet C). If you decide you want to do something other than a nominal group technique, follow the guidelines in Tool 8.1, Worksheet B, Rating and Ranking Criteria.

TOOL 8.1B. RATING AND RANKING CRITERIA

System Requirements

Directions

1. From Tool 8.1, Worksheet A, list the requirements you want a delivery system to satisfy. Add as many rows as you require to the form below.

2. Give a copy of the list to everyone (print, e-mail, Web). You may want to convert this worksheet to a spreadsheet to make tallying the results easier.

3. Let people add requirements (rows) if they think of them later.

4. Assign each person a column (letter) and ask him or her to privately assign a value to each item on the list under his or her column.

Values

5 = must have; 4 = desirable; 3 = nice to have;
2 = could be useful; 1 = not necessary

List factors here	Respondents					
	A	B	C	D	E	Total
Total						

5. Once you have everyone's values (5 through 1) for every requirement, share them with everyone who participated.

6. Discuss each person's assumptions behind the values he or she gave.

7. Decide on a process to come up with a final list and set of values. You might want to let people change their values once they hear other people's ideas or calculate the averages.

8. Ask the group if there are variables they would like added, such as cost, availability, compatibility, and so on.

9. Use the results to evaluate systems under consideration (see Tool 8.1, Worksheet C).

TOOL 8.1C. COMPARISON OF SYSTEMS TO REQUIREMENTS

Requirements	System A	System B	System C
List the requirements agreed on here, adding as many rows as necessary.	Put rating here	Put rating here	Put rating here
#1			
#2			
#			
#			

List any other factors that might influence your decision.

- Cost
- Availability
- Compatibility
- Other

Ask everyone to evaluate each system under consideration separately using the following scale. Apply the scale to each requirement.

5 = fully meets; 4 = mostly meets;
3 = meets some; 2 = meets a little; 1 = does not meet

Summarize everyone's ratings (average them, list them separately) and discuss. Use Tool 8.2 to do cost comparisons of different solutions.

Tool 8.2 explains how to compare the costs of different delivery alternatives. Sometimes you know what delivery method you want. Now it is a question of cost. Tool 8.2 is designed to help you compare the cost of one or more alternative delivery systems. Costs that you might consider are listed in the first column. Add any other costs that are unique to your situation. Add a sufficient number of columns to handle the number of options you are considering. You may want to put the table in an accounting or spreadsheet format to help calculate values. *Fixed* costs are those you incur but are not dependent on volume of usage. *Variable* costs are dependent on how many users you have. Some fixed and variable costs may be *direct* in that they can be assigned or

Costs	Alternative A	Alternative B	Alternative C
TOOL 8.2. COST/COST COMPARISONS			
Initial or Start-Up Costs			
Fixed/Direct			
• Facilities			
• Equipment			
• Software			
• Licenses			
• Materials			
• Personnel			
Learners			
Trainers			
Instructional designers			
Administrators			
Experts			
Logistics personnel			
Variable/Direct			
• Facilities/usage			
• Licenses/usage rate			
• Air or broadcast time			
• Print volume			
• Postage volume			
• Materials consumption			
• Assessment			
• Personnel time			
Learners			
Trainers			
Administrators			
Vendors or contractors			
• Travel			
• Lodging			

TOOL 8.2. (continued)			
Costs	**Alternative A**	**Alternative B**	**Alternative C**
Ongoing Costs			
Fixed/Direct			
• Facilities rent, maintenance			
• Equipment maintenance			
• Personnel			
• Software licenses			
Variable/Direct			
• Facilities rent			
• Equipment repair, upgrades, and so on			
• Software, new installations			
• Licenses usage rate			
• Materials reprints			
• Assessment			
• Personnel			
• Travel			
• Lodging			

allocated to a specific function, group, project, product, or user. Other fixed and variable costs are *indirect* and difficult to assign so they are spread across functions, groups, projects, product, or users.

Tool 8.3 can be used to help you compare the cost/benefit of different alternatives. This tool is to help you identify and compare the cost and worth of different alternatives. Even if you do not have all of the facts, the tool will help you to identify what is known and what is assumed and to see the positive and negative aspects of different alternatives. The intent is to help you make a more informed decision. Complete the chart with other members of your team. Fill in the costs you know and what you think they might be given your understanding of the situation.

TOOL 8.3. COST/BENEFIT VALUING ALTERNATIVES

Now Do nothing Assumptions	Action Set 1 Do A Assumptions	Action Set 2 Do B Assumptions
List the costs of your current system • Which are fixed? • Which are variable? List any expected added costs if you continue to do what you are doing now	List current costs that remain the same List those current costs that will be reduced List any future costs that will be avoided List the costs that this solution will require	List current costs that remain the same List those current costs that will be reduced List any future costs that will be avoided List the costs that this solution will require

MISSTEPS

Some of the common oversights people make when choosing a delivery system are

1. Not having measures on the current method, making comparisons difficult.

2. Not using existing performance measures.

3. Not fully understanding current costs so they don't know what drives costs, which costs to focus on, or how to compare the value of reducing one cost over another.

4. Not defining what a new system is expected to accomplish.

5. Thinking all training is equal in purpose and in design and, therefore, one delivery system will satisfy all needs.

6. Failing to recognize that the culture and performance management system do not support the behaviors required for an alternative to be effective, such as doing pre-work, using an on-line learning system, or exercising self-initiative to participate in a program.

TIPS AND TECHNIQUES

Here are some suggestions on how to better evaluate different delivery systems:

1. *Determine what you want to accomplish* as an outcome of evaluating a delivery system. For example, is the goal:

   • To measure the effectiveness of the current delivery system?

   • To compare different systems so you can decide what delivery system to use?

- To prove that a specific delivery system is more or less effective?
- To assess the feasibility or probability of a system being effective?
- To determine if and how well a delivery system will satisfy your requirements?

2. *Decide on the criteria you will use.* Invite stakeholders to help develop and rank the criteria. Include those who will fund the acquisition of a system and those who are or will be most impacted by it. At a minimum consider criteria such as:

Accessibility	Fidelity
Content stability	Functionality
Cultural tolerance	Required administrative support
Congruence with the current	Risk
performance management system	Speed

3. *Identify and prioritize* the attributes a system must have to satisfy your needs versus what would be nice to have.

4. Once you have identified one or more delivery alternatives with the attributes to satisfy your needs, *compare them to each other and to your current system* in terms of the initial and ongoing costs.

5. Once you implement your choice *measure* how well it actually satisfied the need.

6. If the driver is cost, *find out whose costs and what costs are fixed, variable, direct, and indirect.* Accounting departments have developed conventions to help them classify and allocate costs. You should find out how your client does it and find out how costs for a particular delivery system are classified. Ask about fixed, variable, direct, and indirect costs. The more specific you are, the easier it is to measure if and how well the new delivery system affected costs.

   - *Fixed* costs are those that are *not* dependent on volume, such as classrooms and computer labs.

   - *Variable* costs are dependent on volume, such as license agreements that bill you based on the number of learners who use a product or the number of hours a product is in use.

   - Some fixed and variable costs may be *direct* in that they can be assigned or allocated to a specific function, group, project, product, or user. For example, all costs associated with training field technicians might be assigned to the service department.

- Other fixed and variable costs are *indirect,* because they are difficult to assign to specific functions or programs so they are spread across functions, groups, projects, product, or users. For example, the employment costs of instructional designers, media developers, and trainers who support more than one user group (sales, service, headquarters, field operations) might be spread either equally or in some proportion across all user groups.

7. Identify what makes up the *current costs* to deploy training or other human resource programs. Then separate those costs that are dependent on the delivery system from those that are independent. For example, if the delivery method is classroom, the *dependent* costs include instructor, facility, travel, and material costs. *Independent* costs are those that would be incurred no matter what the delivery system was. Examples include developing the content, practice exercises, and tests. Identify the dependent costs the delivery system increases, reduces, or avoids.

8. Be sure to identify the costs of *not implementing* the intervention, since doing nothing or continuing to do the same thing is not necessarily inexpensive.

9. When comparing different delivery systems, be sure to do the following:
   - Confirm that users, sponsors, and other vested parties are in agreement on what they expect a system to do, what needs it is to satisfy, and what costs it should avoid or reduce.
   - Confirm the capability or functionality of the system, particularly the assumed conditions under which it works. It may not be possible for you to replicate those conditions.
   - Confirm who owns what, whether you are leasing or buying. Annual licenses can be a last-minute and unpleasant surprise.
   - Confirm if there are any costs to upgrade, discontinue, or modify the system. Sometimes the cost to disengage is so high it prevents innovation and future migration to a better solution.

10. Review the current learning objectives and identify those that are about conveying information versus demonstrating a procedure or providing practice. Consider a different delivery solution for the information, demonstration, and practice with feedback component.

11. Identify what percentage of the current curriculum content is relatively unchanging. Consider different delivery systems for that which is stable compared to that which is volatile (ever-changing). For example, CD-ROM and multimedia are expensive to update compared to the Web.

SUMMARY

This chapter is meant to help you identify appropriate measures for evaluating different delivery alternatives. The ideas will help you identify what you require of a delivery system and compare alternatives. The delivery system can make up the largest cost component of a training curriculum or program, as it drives, reduces, or eliminates the need for other costs, such as travel, instructors, meeting space, and so on. The tips, guidelines, and tools are meant to help you identify both what you know or assume to be true and what you should verify to make better decisions about an appropriate combination of systems.

WHERE TO LEARN MORE

Here are some resources to learn more about different delivery alternatives.

Rossett, A., and Gautier-Downes, J. *A Handbook of Job Aids* (San Francisco, CA: Jossey-Bass/Pfeiffer, 1991).

Heinich, R., Molenda, M., Russell, J., and Smaldino, S. *Instructional Media and Technologies for Learning* (5th ed.) (Englewood Cliffs, NJ: Merrill Prentice-Hall, 1996).

Newby, T., Stepich, D., Lehman, J., and Russell, J. *Instructional Technology for Teaching and Learning: Designing Instruction, Integrating Computers, and Using Media* (Englewood Cliffs, NJ: Merrill Prentice-Hall, 1996).

Rosenberg, M. *E-Learning: Strategies for Delivering Knowledge in the Digital Age* (New York: McGraw-Hill, 2001).

Stolovitch, H. *Handbook of Human Performance Technology: A Comprehensive Guide for Analyzing and Solving Performance Problems in Organizations* (San Francisco, CA: Jossey-Bass, 1992). See Chapter 23 on Classroom Instruction by Stephen Yelon, Chapter 25 on Video-Based Instruction by Diane Gayeski, Chapter 26 on Computer-Mediated Instruction by Ruth Clark, Chapter 27 on Printed Self-Instruction by Murray Tillman, and Chapter 29 on Structured On-the-Job Training by Ron Jacobs.

Schank, R. C. *Designing World-Class e-Learning* (New York: McGraw-Hill, 2002).

Sugrue, B., and Clark, R. E. "Media selection for training." In S. Tobias and D. Fletcher (Eds.), *Training and Retraining: A Handbook for Business, Industry, Government, and the Military* (pp. 208–234) (New York: Macmillan, 2000).

NOTES

1. Ormrod, J. E. *Human Learning* (3rd ed.) (Upper Saddle River, NJ: Merrill, 1999, p. 355).
2. Keeps, E. J., and Stolovitch, H. D. (Eds.) *Handbook of Human Performance Technology* (2nd ed.) (San Francisco: Jossey-Bass, 1999, p. 378).
3. To learn more about medical simulations, check out Immersion Medical, a company located in Gaithersburg, Maryland. It has been producing medical

simulations that not only replicate the senses of sight and sound, but also the senses of touch and motion. Its simulations include: Colonoscopy (using a scope to navigate a colon to view and biopsy suspected cancerous tissues); Bronchoscopy (using a scope to navigate the tracheobronchial tree and adjoining anatomic structures to view and biopsy suspected cancerous tissues); Vascular Access (starting an IV or drawing blood in pediatric, adult, and geriatric patients).

4. To learn more about what the plumbers and pipe fitters union is doing, check their Web page at www.UACOTE.com.

Chapter 9

How to Sample People and Documents

The training department wanted to do a needs assessment to find out what training would be required in the coming year. Some trainers suggested interviewing all of senior management; others wanted only to survey the exempt staff. Managers of staff functions complained that sales got all of the attention and wanted a process that included their opinions. Field offices complained that corporate got all of the attention and wanted a process that gave them an equal voice.

*T*his chapter is about how to sample an appropriate number of people and documents. Measurement happens in the beginning when you want to find out whether or not there is a problem or opportunity that should be addressed. It happens as you implement actions to find out if they are working as expected and at major points in time to find out if what you did produced the changes you expected. However, the decision to measure at every point brings with it other decisions, such as how precise to be, how much data to gather, and from whom or where.

MEASUREMENT PLAN

To begin, develop a plan that includes what you want to discover or measure, how you will go about it, and how you expect to use the results. The plan will help guide your decisions about how precise you should be and whose opinions to include. As a rule, include more than one source or audience in your data-gathering efforts, particularly when the goal is to discover needs or uncover opportunities. One audience can only give you one perspective. Other audiences can validate the results from the first audience and may add information that will lead you to a better understanding of the scope of the problem and possible contributing factors. More than one audience can also help when the goal is to measure change, as you can find out about unexpected consequences, both good and bad, that happened as a result of a change. Your plan should include more than one audience so you can gather corroborating data. For example, you might interview sales representatives to find out what they believe is needed to improve sales, whether to close more sales, shorten the sales cycle, develop more leads, qualify potential customers, or other ideas. However, sales representatives are only one voice. Therefore, you might also want to ask for information from sales management, customer service, billing, and customers themselves. Similarly, if a program were implemented to improve sales and you wanted to measure its effectiveness, you might include the voices of customer service and accounts receivable to determine if there were any unforeseen consequences.

PRECISION AND COST

One of the dilemmas you will face is how precise you have to be in your measurement to be confident in your findings and recommendations. There is a tradeoff. The more precise you want to be, the more costly the evaluation effort. Your need to be precise depends on the following:

- The type of decisions that will be made based on the data, for example: Will decisions be made about who will be hired, what the performance standard and basis for bonuses will be, or what projects are funded?

- What will be promised based on the data, for example: Will guarantees be made to customers, investors, employees, or the public about safety, product performance, or financial returns?

- The risk associated with the decisions, that is, the consequences of your being right or wrong. Usually high-risk decisions are not based on one set of information but incorporate other factors such as expert opinion, historic data, and the findings from other independent sources.

- The availability of data that might corroborate or add support to your findings. The availability of corroborating data may lessen the burden on you to be precise.

Your degree of precision and the cost of the evaluation effort are affected by

- The size of the sample you use to obtain the data
- How rigorous you are in the data-gathering process
- Your access to and your ability to use corroborating data
- Your budget and how quickly you want to produce findings that may help you or others make informed decisions
- Your ability to leverage other departments' data-gathering efforts

POPULATION AND SAMPLING

One of the earlier decisions you will have to make is about where or from whom to obtain information. Sometimes you want to collect opinions; other times you will want to check actual work records or production reports. Still other times you will want to watch people at a task to find out what they really do and how they do it. Whether you want information from people or from documents, you have to decide from whom, where, and how many. Therefore, start by defining the population. A population is a group of people or of work outputs, for example, the people who develop business cases for the organization or the actual business cases. Find out if and how

- The people's behavior changed, for example, they follow the recommended procedure for developing business cases to get funding
- The attributes of the business cases changed, for example, they adhered to the recommended format and include the same type of information
- The consequences or results changed, for example, the organization was able to obtain funding sooner

Define the Population

Defining the population appears simple, but it is not. Continuing with the example on business cases, here are four ways you might define the population:

1. Everyone who participated in the training program on how to develop business cases from the time it was introduced.
    - However, if the program was introduced five years ago, some of those people may have moved on to jobs where they no longer develop business cases, meaning the intent of the program is no longer relevant to them (they may even have left the company).

- Some of the people who attended may not actually develop business cases but supervise those who do, that is, they are not really members of the target audience.

2. Everyone who participated in the course and is currently in a job where he or she is expected to develop business cases and apply the content.

- However, some of these people may have just finished the program and may not have had time to develop a business case, that is, apply the procedures with enough frequency to show a difference.

3. Everyone who participated in the course within the last six months to two years and is currently in a job where he or she develops business cases and has applied what was covered in the program.

- However, some of these people may work in parts of the world where the procedure has been modified to accommodate local conditions.

4. Every business case developed since the program was introduced.

Tool 9.1 has guidelines for defining a population.

TOOL 9.1. HOW TO DEFINE A POPULATION

Define the population. This guideline applies to people, documents, and work samples.

A. Describe the attributes the population must or must not have. Include attributes such as

  a. Recency—How far back will you go in time?

  b. Currency—Must they still be in use or active?

  c. Preparation—Must they satisfy some pre-qualification such as certification, training, experience, or use?

  d. Time—What percentage of their time must be dedicated to the task or behavior?

  e. Environment—Must they work or be in use in a specific environment that may differ from other environments, such as countries, languages, in an office or at remote sites, and so forth.

B. Once you have defined the population, the next questions are

  a. How big is it or how many are there in it?

  b. Do you know who or where they are?

  c. Can you get to them, that is, do you have access to them?

d. Are there differences among them that might affect how they apply the procedures covered in the program?

e. Do you need to include all of them, or can you include just some of them?

f. What is the incentive for them to participate?

Define the Sample

A sample is a sub-set of the population. Because the sub-set came from the population, it should possess the same attributes as the larger group. If you only train ten field technicians a year, and you know where they work and how to reach them, you would want to include all of them. However, if 45,000 employees were trained, you will probably want to include just some of them, that is, take a sample. The primary reason for sampling is because including the whole population is too costly and labor-intensive. For example, if you have 30,000 managers, 3,500 work tickets, or 120 products, sampling will be faster and less costly, yet still produce useful results. There are three common methods for selecting samples: (1) representative samples; (2) random samples; and (3) stratified samples.

A *representative sample* is one where you nominate people or things because you believe they represent some aspect of a larger group. For example, you might ask seven teams to each nominate one person or one product (document) to represent them or the quality of their work. You depend on the people or products that were nominated to accurately portray some attribute of the larger group.

A *random sample* is a technique where everyone in the population has an equal chance to be included or omitted. Statisticians have shown that if you use a sufficiently large enough random sample its attributes will reflect the population.

A *random stratified sample* is a combination of a representative and a random sample. You would still pull a random sample, but add a requirement that specific segments in a population are equally represented. For example, you may want to interview managers, but you also want to make sure you include those from different branches, business units, geographies, age groups, ethnic groups, and so forth. In this situation you would identify the subgroups (strata) and pull a random sample from each strata based on the size of the strata. Frequently, stratified samples are done to assure clients that everyone who might represent a specific viewpoint is or will be included. It is not unusual that regional offices and different functions believe that their requirements are unique. Sometimes it is wiser to do a stratified sample just to see if it is true. This can avoid battles in the future about findings not being relevant to a specific group. A stratified sample may point out legitimate differences in subgroups.

Confidence Levels and Intervals

Statisticians have also come up with two conventions, confidence level and confidence interval, that are helpful when deciding how large of a random sample is required, given what you want to find out and how precise you want to be.

Confidence level is a percentage that reflects how certain or sure you want to be. For example, in the human resource arena people reporting results say they are 90 percent or 95 percent certain. In other arenas such as manufacturing operations that apply statistical process controls people may report they are 99 percent certain. Your level of certainty depends on the confidence interval.

Confidence interval is a plus or minus figure, for example ±5, and is about how precise or exact you want to be. The ± can apply to any value, such as time (milliseconds, seconds, minutes, days, weeks), size (millimeters, centimeters, inches, yards, miles), weight (grams, ounces, pounds, tons), counts (tens, hundreds, thousands), and so on. It means that you are 90 percent or 95 percent sure about a result plus or minus some value. The wider the interval or the higher the value, the more certain you can be that a value (time, quantity, production rate, and so on) demonstrated by a sample is the same as that of the larger population.

For example, if you want to measure how the time required to do a task changed as the result of some intervention (training, job aid, or change in how work is scheduled), you would decide how certain you want to be (90 percent certain) and how precise you want to be (±15 minutes). Knowing how certain and how precise you need to be helps you decide on how large a sample you will require. In this situation, you might pull a random sample of work tickets to measure the amount of time technicians spend doing the specific type of repair. Work tickets tell you how much time they reported, not how much they spent. The only way to actually know the time spent is to observe people doing the task, but that is very labor-intensive. If the times reported average forty-five minutes, you could say that this type of repair takes on average of forty-five minutes, plus or minus five minutes. If you were less confident, you could give a larger value such as ±10 or ±15 minutes. Confidence intervals are affected by the following:

- *The size of the sample.* The larger the sample, the more confident you can be that its attributes (behaviors, choices, results, times, and so forth) represent those of the population as a whole.

- *The percentages of people or things in the sample whose behavior, results, or attributes are the same.* For example, the more work tickets showing 45 ±5 minutes, the more confident you can be of that time.

PAINTING WALLS

The airport was experiencing a significant increase in the number of requests for work by people in the trades. The number of requests was now over 3,500 a year and was expected to double every six months. The work requests fell into five categories:

1. *Repair*—Fix the electrical, plumbing, carpentry, mechanical, upholstery, and paint.
2. *Service*—Add, relocate, or change something like an electrical outlet, wall, window, door, light, or other item.
3. *Support*—Chaperon contractors while they are in secured sites, answer questions about specific facilities, interpret drawings, and so on.
4. *Projects*—Be on a team to do work that involves more than one trade, requiring a licensed architect and approval by a code official.
5. *Preventive maintenance*—Do periodic checks as required by warranty or law, replacement of parts, and routine maintenance (change filters).

Four out of the five categories involved painting. What troubled management was the amount of time spent on painting walls and other surfaces. The time spent ranged from minutes to hours for what seemed like comparable work. The airport had facilities spread over twenty-five miles. All of the trades reported their time in five-minute increments but did not break out time according to preparation, travel, and task. The result was wide variance in reported times, mostly because of the time spent traveling from one site to another.

The recommendation was to ask painters to break out their time by travel, preparation, and painting. They still reported time in increments of five minutes. It was learned that the need to travel from one side of the airport to the other was increasing because of new construction and remodeling of buildings. A decision was made to schedule work by zones and better equip the trucks with the required supplies to reduce the need to travel. Management then compared the amount of time spent in traveling and at task to what it was before. Rather than check all work tickets, they pulled a random sample of ninety tickets or about 3 percent of the three thousand tickets that involved painting. This sample size would give them a confidence level of 95 percent and confidence interval of ±10 minutes. The intervention was the improved reporting, scheduling, and coordination of jobs. A by-product was better data about how time was spent and why.

ON-LINE PERFORMANCE MANAGEMENT SYSTEM

Human resources (HR) decided to move many of its data management functions on-line, such as salary inquiries, benefit changes or enrollment, reporting of time, training registration, and so forth. Employees can go on-line and check the status of or arrange for direct deposit and make changes to the personal contact information, such as address or phone number. They can register for courses and even take on-line assessments to help them judge their readiness for a new position or a training program. The last function to go on-line is performance management. This function will require supervisors to post employees' goals and performance measures, when they met to review the goals, what performance standards are being used, what developmental decisions (if any) were made, and what the year-end rating was—all on-line.

There are about 45,000 employees in the company and about 30,000 have one or more direct reports. Human resources could do a representative sample of some percentage by function, a random sample of ninety-five managers (see Tool 9.2B), or a stratified random sample of 982 managers. Human resources decided to use a stratified random sample to see whether usage differed by function and to assure the fourteen senior managers that each of their areas was equally represented. The computer could poll those managers' files that were designated to be part of the sample, so the cost was minimal. Four of the senior managers were responsible for small corporate functions such as legal, public relations, accounting, and HR. The remaining ten managers were responsible for regions and each had approximately three thousand managers under them. Table 9.1 shows size of the sample for each of the fourteen senior managers.

	Corporate					Regions								
Senior Managers	1	2	3	4	5	6	7	8	9	10	11	12	13	14
Managers with Direct Reports	2	10	25	90	3k	3k	3k	3k	3k	3k	3k	3k	3k	3k
Sample Size	2	10	25	45	90	90	90	90	90	90	90	90	90	90

Table 9.1. Stratified Sample

Note that senior managers 5 through 14 have approximately three thousand managers in their functions. The variance in size was thought to have little affect on the size of the sample. This sampling will allow HR to be 95 percent confident that some percentage (the result of the analysis) of the managers are or are not using the on-line systems ±10 percent.

Tools 9.2A and 9.2B have charts to help you select the appropriate sample size. Table A is for very small populations and assumes you will corroborate your findings through other efforts.

Table B is for small to medium size populations and it shows how the sample sizes, confidence levels, and confidence intervals are interdependent. It compares the sample sizes with a confidence level of 95 percent with intervals of ±5 and ±10 of some value. The percentages have been rounded to the nearest whole number.

TOOL 9.2A. SAMPLE SIZES FOR SMALL POPULATIONS

Size of the Population	Percent in the Sample
6 to 50	100%
51 to 100	50%
101 to 250	25%
251 to 500	10%

TOOL 9.2B. SAMPLE SIZES FOR SMALL TO MEDIUM SIZE POPULATIONS

Size of the Population	Size of the Sample @±5	Percent in the Sample	Size of the Sample @±10	Percent in the Sample
100	80	80%	49	50%
250	152	61%	70	28%
500	217	44%	81	16%
1,000	278	28%	88	9%
5,000	357	7%	94	2%
7,500	365	5%	95	1.5%
10,000	370	4%	95	1%
15,000	375	3%	95	.6%
20,000	377	2%	95	.5%

MISSTEPS

Here are some of the common mistakes people make:

1. They don't decide how to select documents or work samples to review, but arbitrarily pull examples. It is difficult to generalize without selecting a sufficient sample.

2. They fail to balance the number required for a valid sample with the need to include a sufficient number of people for the results to be believable. Sampling theory usually requires you to engage fewer audiences and documents than what people tend to believe.

TIPS AND TECHNIQUES

Here are some suggestions for how to sample people or things:

1. *Sampling documents or files.* If you want to pull a sample of documents or reports, you don't have to number them ahead of time, but they do need to be in a form so you can count them. Decide on how many you want in the sample (see Tool 9.2, Tables A and B). Collect a sufficient list of random numbers based on the size sample. Assume the first report is #1, the second is #2, and so on, and pull those whose numbers match the random numbers. For example, if your random numbers are 12, 18, 3, 1, 77, and 111, you would pull files numbered 1, 3, 12, 18, 77, and 111.

2. *Stratified sample of documents or files.* If you want to pull a stratified random sample of documents or reports, they must be in some order (alphabetical, by date, by location, by person) to match the desired strata or subgroup. Decide on how many you want in each subgroup (see Tool 9.2, Tables A and B) and make a sufficient list of random numbers for each one. Do not use the same numbers for every subgroup, but pull new ones. Be sure to include those numbers pulled for previous subgroups so every report has an equal chance of being selected or omitted. For example, if you pull #33 for the first subgroup and do not return #33 to the list of possible numbers, then files #33 in other subgroups can never be selected. Assume the first report in each subgroup is #1, the second is #2, and so on, and pull those whose numbers match the random number. For example, if your random numbers for the first subgroup are 17, 9, 23, 6, 2, and 103, you would pull files numbered 2, 6, 9, 17, 23, and 103. You would pull another six numbers for the second subgroup. It is okay if the same random number comes up for more than one subgroup.

3. *Create an audit trail.* Document what you did, who or what were the sources of your data, why and how they were selected, and why you chose the methods you did. Documenting what you did and why will help you be more effective and efficient in future efforts.

4. *If you want a representative sample* decide what attributes the representatives must have to be included. Determine if there are any factors that might exclude a person or document, such as being retired, having been

disciplined, being on a temporary assignment, being under investigation, having been subpoenaed, or whatever. Consider attributes such as:

- Location
- Years of experience
- Group membership or affiliation
- Products or reports produced by a specific group of people
- Rank or position

5. *If you want a random sample,* first define the population, then:
    - List members of the population, or put them in a form where you can number them
    - Decide how confident you want to be (your confidence level)—90 percent, 95 percent, or 99 percent
    - Decide how far off you can be (your confidence interval)—±5 or ±10
    - Decide on the size of the sample (see Tool 9.1, Tables A and B)
    - Decide on how or from where you will get your random numbers (Software packages do this for you and there are tables in books on statistics you can copy and keep handy)
    - Select a sufficient quantity of random numbers for the sample size you want
    - Pull a random number and match it to one of the numbers used to identify members of the population

6. *If you want a stratified random sample,* decide on how many strata you want, identify the size of population in each stratum, and pull a sample from each stratum that is of the same proportion.

SUMMARY

This chapter was about how to sample a group of people so you can find out:

- Their opinions and preferences
- What they know and do not know
- What they do and how often
- What they use
- How skilled they are

It also covered how to sample documents and work products so you can find out what attributes they possess and whether or not they reflect what is expected. In summary, sample size depends on the following:

- The size of the actual population
- The level of precision you require, that is, the confidence interval
- How certain you want to be, the confidence level
- The statistical treatment that you will use, as some methods are better suited for small or large samples (This is discussed in greater detail in the next chapter)
- How many other audiences or other sources of data you will draw on to corroborate your findings

WHERE TO LEARN MORE

If you want help deciding on a sample size, check out www.askjeeves.com. Type in the words "sample size" and then select the sample size calculator.

Chapter 10

How to Collect Data

Survey, interview, and observe—the list of possible ways to find out what the current situation is or what has changed can be endless. The challenge is figuring out what the more appropriate methods might be, given time and money constraints.

*T*he focus of this chapter is about when and how to use the more common data-gathering methods. One of the decisions you will have to make is how to obtain the data you require. What methods you use depends on what you want to measure or discover. Sometimes you want to find out what people care about or what is going on today. In these situations you should use a data-gathering method that is especially designed to uncover what the issues are. If you want to find out whether your training made a difference, then you should use methods that are better suited for measuring change.

The more common methods are interviews, surveys, observations, and document reviews. Generally, most evaluation efforts begin with a series of interviews. Depending on your purpose, you follow them up with other techniques such as the following:

- A critical-incident question to identify the key attributes or behaviors

- A sociogram to discover group dynamics and communication patterns

- The Nominal Group Technique to make a more comprehensive list of requirements or desired and undesired behaviors

- Direct observation to confirm what and how something is done, in what sequence, and under what conditions
- A review of documents or actual work samples to validate what you learned earlier

Then, based on what you learn, you might want to expand your inquiry with the following:

- A survey to find out how pervasive an issue is or how widely held an opinion is
- A structured interview to compare other people's opinions with what you learned from those you interviewed or observed earlier

Always use two methods. One can be somewhat intrusive, like an interview, and the other less intrusive, like a records review. How many people you involve and how many methods you use in total will depend on what you want to measure and on how confident you have to be in the conclusions.

Tool 10.1 is in two parts. The first part, Table A, briefly explains the uses and limitations of the more common methods for collecting data. The second part, Table B, shows when to use each method.[1,2]

TOOL 10.1A. DESCRIPTION OF COMMONLY USED DATA-GATHERING METHODS

Individual Interview Methods

Open Interviews:

Are effective at gathering first impressions, experiences, conclusions drawn from those experiences, and the feeling (positive and negative) behind them or the degree of confidence a person has in his or her experience

Can be used to uncover rationale or logic behind a conclusion, feeling state, or rule

Can generate a set of scenarios to be used to develop practice and test scenarios

Are less effective at generating a list of variables

Are best done with individuals and in person or on the phone

Sociograms:

Are very effective at identifying who in a group has the most or least influence, who is the leader, and if cliques exist

Are effective at measuring group cohesiveness

Are best used in conjunction with other methods

Are less effective at identifying the rationale behind a behavior or outcome

---

TOOL 10.1A. (Continued)

Can be done (the interview) in person, on the phone, or via e-mail

Are interventions themselves, as their power is in the presentation of the results

Structured Interviews:

Are best done after a comprehensive list of variables has already been made

Can be used to determine how many share perceptions and to compare responses to previously held ones or to another group's responses

Require very skilled interviewer to classify the responses

Can be done in person, on the phone, and on-line

Critical-Incident Interviews:

Can identify key variables or discriminators

Can be done with individuals and groups

Are best done after another method was used to generate a comprehensive set of variables

Require a great number of interviews to generate a comprehensive list of variables

Can be done live, in person, on-line or via the Web

Can be done with individuals and groups

Questionnaires/Surveys:

Require that a set of variables or issues be generated by another method

Can determine the degree to which a larger group agrees or disagrees on an issue

Can measure if and how much a group's opinions changed over time

Are very effective at reaching a wide or widely dispersed audience

If open-ended, are costly to analyze

Can be done with members of a group

Can be done live, in person, on the phone, on-line, or through a Web page

---

Group Interview Methods

Focus Group:

Is done with a group who share a common concern and may or may not be from the same work unit

Is best used to gain a better understanding of data derived from other sources or to gain an initial understanding about an issue

Is less effective at generating a comprehensive list of variables

Is less effective at controlling group bias

Is best done live and in person

TOOL 10.1A. DESCRIPTION OF COMMONLY USED DATA-GATHERING METHODS (Continued)

Nominal Group:

Can be done with an intact work group or with people who share a common concern

Can effectively and efficiently generate a comprehensive set of variables

Allows people to rate the importance of a variable

Is effective at controlling group bias

Is less effective at gaining an in-depth understanding of a variable

Can be done in person or on-line, but should be live, real time

Process Mapping:

Is usually done with an intact work group

Is used to capture and record how work gets done—activities and their sequence; interfaces with equipment, technology, information, people, and so on

Identifies activities that add value and those that do not

Requires multiple meetings

Produces a picture "map" of the activities involved in executing a task

---

Observation Methods

Direct Observation:

Done to identify what is done, how, and how often

Labor-intensive to administer

Does not identify the reason for behaviors

Can be real time or videotaped for later evaluation

Requires developing a tool to capture what is observed for later analysis

Flanders Interaction Analysis:

Identifies who communicates with whom, the type of communication that occurs, and the length and frequency of the exchange

Validates how groups communicate

Is labor intensive to administer

Can be done real time or videotaped for later evaluation

Requires forms to capture the data

May require the ability to track specific time intervals.

TOOL 10.1A. (Continued)

Time and Motion Study:

Is designed to track the time consumed in doing work and how that time is used (waiting, moving, examining, getting directions, setting up, using equipment)

Requires multiple observations

Requires developing a tool to classify activities and capture time spent

Is done real time and on site

Performance Checklist:

Is not a method, but a tool designed to support observations

Requires a qualified observer

Can identify deficiencies and strengths

Can be used to qualify people based on their performance or work product

---

Document Searches

Work Samples:

Can be used to compare work to a set of standards

Require a performance checklist to control rater bias

Can measure change in quality

Do not determine the cause of the change

Statistical Process Control:

Is designed to measure processes that are stable and to identify controllable and uncontrollable causes of variance in either production quantity or quality

Can identify trends and measure the effectiveness of changes

Requires standardized data collection and a person trained to interpret the charts

Before and After Production Reports:

Can measure change

Can identify trends

Unless other variables are controlled, do not determine the cause of a change

Activity Logs:

Can measure how people use time and the activities they engage in

Can identify trends

Do not determine the reason for the activity

Require a standardized tool with activity classifications and time intervals if you want to compare the results

TOOL 10.1B. BEST USE OF DIFFERENT DATA-COLLECTION METHODS

Data Gathering Method	Best Suited for Discovery	Best Suited for Measuring Change or Improvement
Individual Interview Methods		
1. Open	X	–
2. Critical Incident	X	–
3. Structured	X	X
4. Sociograms	X	X
5. Questionnaires	X	X
Group Interview Methods		
1. Focus groups	X	–
2. Nominal groups	X	–
3. Delphi studies	X	–
4. Process mapping	X	–
Observation Methods		
1. Direct observation	X	X
2. Flanders interaction analysis	X	X
3. Time and motion	X	X
4. Performance checklist	X	X
Document Searches		
1. Work samples	X	X
2. Statistical process control reports	X	X
3. Pre- and post-production reports	X	X
4. Performance checklists	X	X

Some methods are better suited for discovery or assessment, others are better for measuring change, and some can be used for both purposes.

INTERVIEWS

There are four commonly used interview techniques: (1) open or unstructured; (2) structured; (3) critical-incident; and (4) surveys. What distinguishes them is (1) the amount of control each places on the interviewer and on the person being interviewed and (2) what they measure. All of them can be done on the phone or in person, through regular mail, e-mail, or a Web page.

Open Interviews

The method is referred to as an "open" interview because the people being interviewed are free to answer any way they wish. Unlike some surveys, people are not forced to choose an answer. However, the interviewer does not have the same amount of freedom. The interviewer follows a procedure. The questions and the order in which they are asked have been decided on in advance. Because the interviewer follows a procedure, he or she can ask other people from the same or different audiences the identical questions and later summarize and compare the answers. The interviewer starts with a plan, documents the questions, tests the questions to confirm they are clear and address the topic at hand, and decides how to capture the full essence of the answers (audiotape them or write them down).

Open interviews are ideally suited for initial discovery and for identifying what to study next. Therefore, they measure the degree management or a representative group is in consensus on what the issues and priorities are. They also provide the information required to construct other data-gathering instruments such as structured interviews and surveys.

NEW COMPETENCIES

An international retailer purchased a major catalogue outlet chain. It decided it wanted its buyers and inventory managers to service both the retail and the mail order parts of the business. Management had already promoted one hundred buyers and inventory managers to the new position. Human resources was asked to develop a program to equip the buyers and inventory managers to handle the mail order business. Human resources decided to conduct a series of open interviews with senior management. To plan for the interview it created a matrix that listed what they wanted to find out and who would be the best person to interview. Exhibit 10.1 shows the matrix and the topics.

Exhibit 10.1. Open Interview Plan

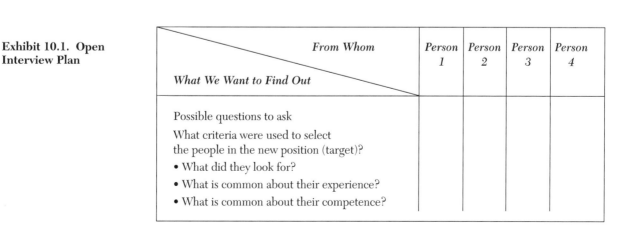

What We Want to Find Out / *From Whom*	*Person 1*	*Person 2*	*Person 3*	*Person 4*
Possible questions to ask What criteria were used to select the people in the new position (target)? • What did they look for? • What is common about their experience? • What is common about their competence?				

Exhibit 10.1. *(Continued)*

What We Want to Find Out	*From Whom*	*Person 1*	*Person 2*	*Person 3*	*Person 4*
Who will the target have to work with or through in this new role (shippers, suppliers, and so forth) that is different from in the past? • How is this relationship different/same from what has been done in the past? • What's the incentive for those new relationships to work with the target? • How are their objectives interdependent? • How are the other people evaluated? • What are they expected to accomplish? • What have the others been told or what do they know? • How have they been prepared for this new relationship?					
What must they know? • What will the target have to know beyond what he or she knows now to be effective? • Who has the information or where would we find it? • How much information is volatile or ever-changing? Or is it steady?					
How will they be evaluated? • How will the target be evaluated? • What are they expected to accomplish?					

The plan helped HR identify what it felt it needed to know and possible ways to find out information beyond the interviews. The plan also helped them identify resources they would not have otherwise considered.

Tool 10.2 is in two parts. The first part explains how to design and conduct an open interview. The second part is a tool for documenting who you want to interview and what you want to find out. It can be modified for your specific use.

TOOL 10.2A. RULES FOR DESIGNING AND CONDUCTING AN OPEN INTERVIEW

Purpose

The primary reason for doing open interviews is to get a feel for a potential or known situation. They are done to discover what people want and need, what they are or are not getting, and what they anticipate changing. Depending on what you discover, you may want to delve deeper into the subject.

Rules

1. Plan the process.
   - Be clear on your purpose. What makes you think that an open interview will gain you the information you require to proceed?
   - Identify the people who might be in the know, who have the history or the vision that you think will add meaning to your purpose. Focus on a few people. If you want to reach more people later, you can do so with a less labor-intensive method.
   - Do your homework. Find out if anyone has information about the topic that would be helpful and get it. Don't waste people's time giving you information that you could have easily gotten elsewhere.
2. Design the interview.
   - Scope out your questions and match them to the people who are more likely to give you the information you want. Focus on a few questions. You can always probe for details during the interview if the person has the time or ask for more time later.
   - Put the number 1 (most important) question in the second position and use the first question to orient the person to the topic.
   - If time is limited, open with your most important question.
   - Practice the questions aloud. Sound serious yet conversational.
   - Prepare your opening statement about the purpose, why the person was chosen, and what will be done with the results.
   - Decide how you will capture the information. Will you take notes, use a tape recorder, ask someone else to take notes for you, or some combination.
3. Arrange for and schedule the interviews. They can be on the phone, but preferably would be in person. Be prepared to explain the purpose, why the person was selected, and what you plan to do with the results.
4. Conduct the interview.
   - Explain the purpose, go over the topics in general, ask permission to tape record or explain that you may pause to take notes.

- Pose the first question.
- If the person is vague, ask him or her to give an example, tell you more, explain how it came about. Seek specifics, not generalizations.
- At the end, thank the person for his or her time. Restate how the data will be used and, if asked, tell the person what you can or cannot share at the conclusion of all of the interviews.

5. Record or transcribe your notes.

TOOL 10.2B. PLANNING THE OPEN INTERVIEW

What Do You Want to Find Out? / From Whom	Name	Name	Name
What will you ask about the topic or issue in general?			
Add questions to go deeper (history, thinking, driver, and so forth) if time permits.			
What will you ask to get to the assumptions or the underlying premises behind the issue (steady state, new pressures, and so on)?			
What will you ask to find out about the conditions surrounding the issue?			
What will you ask to find out about incentives, whose they are, and whether they are in conflict?			
What will you ask to find out how relationships will/might be affected? Which relationships?			
What questions will you ask to find out if people will require a different set of skills?			

Structured Interviews

Structured interviews are experienced by the people being interviewed in the same way as an open interview, that is, they can answer any way they want. However, the interviewer has anticipated the answers and has only to classify the response according to what was expected. The interviewer derives the anticipated answers from open interviews or other methods, such as a focus group. The structured interview measures (1) the degree to which the people being polled agree on what the preferred answer is among those that were anticipated and (2) the degree to which the preferred answer agrees with what management or another standard says it should be. The process requires the interviewer to do the following:

- Document the questions and the anticipated responses
- Create a checklist to record people's responses
- Conduct the interview
- Classify people's answers
- Count how many people chose which answer

If someone gives an unexpected answer, the interviewer need only add it to the list and include it as a choice in future interviews. Exhibit 10.2 has two

Exhibit 10.2. Sample Structured Interview Questions

1. What is the most important role facility managers play in their corporation?
   (Possible answers, but not given to the person being asked the question)

	Respondents					
	A	B	C	D	E	Total
Plan for new space, facility, and equipment						
Coordinate changes with vendors and tenants						
Protect and make wise use of assets						
Communicate current rules, policies, and changes						
Blank						
Blank						
Notes:						

Exhibit 10.2. (*Continued*)

2. When it comes to budgets and finance, what do you have to do to be an effective facility manager?

	Expected	Respondents					Total
		A	B	C	D	E	
Prepare budgets							
Use available assets wisely							
Maintain security							
Know inventory space and costs	X						
Blank							
Blank							
Notes:							

examples of structured interview questions in a format to capture and tally responses. The second example has a place to put the preferred answer, whether it came from management, an outside authority, or an industry standard.

Tool 10.3 is in two parts. Part A has the rules for designing and conducting a structured interview. Part B is a template you can modify for your own use.

TOOL 10.3A. RULES FOR DESIGNING AND CONDUCTING STRUCTURED INTERVIEWS

Purpose

The structured interview technique was developed to take advantage of the positive features of both open-ended questions and forced-choice interview formats while minimizing their weaknesses. To accomplish this, the questions, their sequence, and even the answers are determined in advance. The interview is conducted so that the person being interviewed (the respondent) does not see or hear the choices. Only the interviewer knows what the choices are. Respondents experience the interview as if they were being asked open-ended questions, that is, they may answer any way they wish. However, because the answers have been anticipated, the interviewer has to classify the responses.

Rules

1. Plan. Define your purpose or be clear on why you are doing the interview, that is, what information you want to either verify or expand on.

2. Develop a comprehensive set of questions that support the purpose of the interview. Ask representatives from management, exemplar performers, or another stakeholder group to review the questions and help generate an anticipated set of answers.

   • If the purpose is to determine what people know (or if what they know is correct), the list of responses might include what experts say, what opposing experts say, commonly held misconceptions, and frequently made oversights. (Recall)

   • If the purpose is to determine whether people know a procedure, the list of responses might consist of the preferred steps (or sequence), acceptable alternative steps, incomplete procedures (with the more frequently left out steps missing), and inaccurate procedures. (Procedural)

   • If the purpose is to determine whether people can appropriately apply a concept, principle, or rule, the list of responses might include correct and incorrect applications. (Application)

   • If the purpose is to determine whether people can solve problems, the list of responses might include the attributes of effective, less effective, minimally acceptable, and unacceptable solutions. (Problem Solving)

3. Develop the lead-in statement you will read to each respondent explaining the purpose of the interview and how it is done.

   • Practice reading the lead-in statement and the questions so you do them the same way each time.

   • Pilot test your questions, answers, and forms.

4. Create a form to capture the responses that allows you to tally how many you receive for each anticipated answer. (See Tool 10.3, Part B Sample Structured Interview Form.)

5. Conduct the interview; classify and record each respondent's answer after every question.

6. Analyze the data, paying particular attention to how frequently each alternative was chosen. If appropriate, compare the group's responses to an expected set of responses.

TOOL 10.3B. SAMPLE STRUCTURED INTERVIEW FORM

Question goes here

	Mgmt	Respondents					
		A	B	C	D	E	Total
List of expected answers							
Answer #1							
Answer #2							
Answer #3							
Blank							
Blank							

Notes:

Critical-Incident Questions

Critical-incident questions are especially designed to identify key attributes.[3] They rarely constitute an entire interview themselves, but are embedded in other data-gathering methods. For example, they might be part of an open or structured interview or a survey. They are used to discover critical attributes and measure the degree to which a group agrees on them. The technique asks people to recall an incident they personally witnessed, identify the behaviors that occurred, and describe the consequences. It can be administered to individuals and to groups.

INDEPENDENT MANUFACTURER SALES REPRESENTATIVE

Manufacturers wanted to find out what customers expected of independent sales representatives. The manufacturers sold their products through their own dealerships and through independent sales representatives.

Independent sales representatives represent products from more than one manufacturer and sell both directly to facility managers and through interior designers. The manufacturers interviewed a representative sample of eleven facility managers and six designers by telephone, using a series of open interview questions and two critical-incident questions. The questions were written down to assure that each interview was conducted in the same way. Exhibit 10.3 lists the questions that were used.

Exhibit 10.3. Open and Critical-Incident Interview Questions

The open interview questions were

1. Do you use the services of an independent manufacturer's representative now? If so, why? If not, why not?

If yes:	*If no:*
• What do you expect of him or her?	• If you were to use his or her services, what would you expect of him or her?
• What does he or she do for you?	• Of those services, which are the most important?
• Of those services, which are the most important?	• If you were looking for a unique or special piece of furniture, fixture, or equipment, what would you do to find it?
• How did you come to use the rep you use now?	
• Did he or she find you, or did you find the person?	
• If you were looking for a unique or special piece of furniture, fixture, or equipment, what would you do to find it?	

The two critical-incident questions were

1. Think of a rep you have used who is very good at what he or she does. What does that person do that makes you consider him or her outstanding?
2. Think of a rep who fell short of your expectations. What did that person do or not do that did not meet your needs?

Tool 10.4 describes how to design a critical-incident question.

TOOL 10.4. RULES FOR DESIGNING AND USING THE CRITICAL-INCIDENT INTERVIEW TECHNIQUE

Purpose

The Critical-Incident Technique is best used to identify the discrete behaviors or actions that distinguish one group (usually competent people) from another group (usually less competent people). The technique is especially effective when used as part of an open interview or as a follow up after conducting the Nominal Group Technique. The Critical-Incident Technique results are used to develop assessment instruments, particularly performance checklists. They are also used to refine data derived from other methods about what competent people do that distinguishes their performance from that of others.

The process is to interview people individually or in a group and ask them

- To recall an incident where someone did a job or task very well
- To identify the behaviors that led them to that conclusion
- To describe the consequences of the person's performance

Next, you ask them

- To recall an incident where someone did a job or task poorly
- To identify the behaviors that led them to that conclusion
- To describe the consequences of the person's poor performance

A disadvantage of critical-incident interviews is that they require people to recall what they observed or remember what they did. Depending on the amount of time that has passed, their recollections could be faulty. Therefore, these interviews are best when people are asked to recall a recent incident. Another disadvantage is that it is very difficult to generalize what behaviors other people should or should not exhibit based on what just a few people did. There-fore, you should either validate the desirable and undesirable behaviors through another process or conduct a sufficient number of interviews to be able to gener-alize with confidence.

Rules

1. Before you conduct the interview, develop a set of forms to record people's responses. If you are using the technique with a group, give them forms that restate the question and have space to write what was observed and the consequences.

2. Define the situation to be observed or that should have been observed. If you want to ask people about an incident they may have witnessed many times, ask them to focus on a more recent happening. As much as possible, explain what it is you want them to focus on as they recall

the incident, for example, do you want them to describe:

- The situation that led up to the incident
- What the person did or said
- What events triggered or led up to the person taking action or responding
- How others reacted to the person's behavior
- What the outcome or consequences were

3. Come up with sufficient criteria so that the participants can determine if the behavior they observed is relevant to the purpose of the study.

4. Develop a form for recording both positive and negative effects of behavior.

5. If this is the only type of interview you are doing, start with a more general or open-ended question rather than the first critical-incident question. The goal is to cause reflection and get them oriented to the subject.

6. Prepare participants so they are
   - Familiar with the function (situation or incident) they are expected to have observed
   - Oriented to the purpose of the activity
   - Familiar with the criteria for judging what to include and how to value it
   - As specific as they can be in their description of the behavior, events, or consequences

7. Present the first question.
   - Record and classify results immediately
   - Use specially prepared forms to record data

8. Go to the next question.

9. If working with a group, share everyone's answers and note where they are in agreement and how many variables they identified.

10. Compare the results to data derived from other sources, or select techniques to validate the data, or conduct a sufficient number of interviews to permit making generalizations.

Surveys and Questionnaires

Surveys and questionnaires are also a type of interview. They can be done in person or on the telephone. They can also be in a printed or electronic format and distributed through mail or e-mail. They measure demographic data,

Exhibit 10.4. Sample Survey Questions

1. The most important skill a supervisor should have is coaching.

   Totally agree   Agree somewhat   Not sure   Disagree somewhat   Totally disagree

2. How many times has your supervisor met with you to discuss your goals in the last twelve months?

   More than 3   3   2   1   Never

3. How effective is your supervisor at explaining what is expected of you in your job?

   Very   Pretty good   Average   Somewhat   Very Poor

opinions, familiarity with a topic, and degree of satisfaction. They may consist of a series of questions or statements. Some surveys ask people to rate or rank their opinions or positions on a scale. Exhibit 10.4 shows examples of survey questions.

PROVING WORTH

The Full System Company trained third-party distributors to install and service its equipment. The training was very extensive and costly to deliver. The Full System Company's advantage was its ability to set up complex simulations that included equipment from different manufacturers and of different technologies, a situation distributors faced on a daily basis. Competitors could only train on single systems.

A question was raised about how to prove that distributors were more effective on the job after completing Full System's training. The evaluation plan was to conduct a phone survey with a random sample of seventy technicians (plus five alternates) who had completed the program within the last six to nine months. The survey consisted of twenty-four questions. People who were selected were sent a letter that asked them to participate, explained the purpose of the interview and how the results will be used, and described the process for scheduling the phone call. Some of the questions focused on the technician estimating the economic benefit of the training to the distributor. All of the technicians were able to estimate some economic benefit. Full Systems used the results to promote its programs' effectiveness.

Tool 10.5 has guidelines for designing surveys and questionnaires.

TOOL 10.5. RULES FOR DESIGNING AND USING SURVEYS AND QUESTIONNAIRES

Purpose

A forced-choice survey or questionnaire is one on which the respondent sees or hears the question and the answers. The person then has only to pick the one answer that best reflects his or her position. The purpose is to poll a large number of people about a topic. A well-designed forced-choice survey instrument has three characteristics.

1. As indicated in the name, it forces the respondent to choose a supplied response.
2. All items (questions) contain the same number of choices arranged in the same way along a continuum.
3. It contains enough items to be evaluated statistically.

Rules for Developing Surveys

1. There should be more than twenty items. This is to make sure the data can be treated statistically.
2. There should be fewer than fifty items. This is to keep the time needed to fill out the survey to ten minutes or less.
3. The introductory paragraph for the survey should tell respondents why the survey is being conducted and how the results will be used.
4. There should be instructions for responding to every type of item used. These should be located directly before the item in the survey so respondents don't have to look them up.
5. Every item of a type should be constructed the same way as the others of its type. The scale should go from good to bad the same way for each. There should be the same number of possible responses for each. The construction and format should be as similar as you can make them.
6. If possible, the question should be a single simple sentence.
7. Stick to the subject. Avoid questions about areas of interest that aren't related to the objectives being measured.
8. Use a Likert scale (odd number of alternatives with a neutral position in the middle). Providing an odd number of alternatives gives the respondent the choice of not taking a definitive stand on an issue. When you use an even number scale, you force people to take a position that they may not agree with. A non-committal is valuable information.
9. Provide a continuum of possible answers. Many times a survey contains items that have only two alternatives, for example true/false. Include a third choice like "I don't know" or "Maybe."

10. Watch the wording. It's best to keep references general and in the third person. Make sure the words are understood by every one of your intended respondents. The recommended reading (fog) level for this type of writing is six, that is, it should be easily read by an average sixth grader.

Process for Constructing a Survey

This is similar to developing structured interviews. The steps are

1. Define the purpose and the topic you want to measure.

2. Write the questions with the audience in mind. Make every question as easy to interpret as possible. The reading level should be about sixth grade no matter who the audience is.

3. Design the survey. Have at least one question for every point you want to cover.

4. Write the questions. Use simple statements or questions. Keep the number of possible responses the same for each question and make them plausible. If you use absolutes such as "all" or "none," put them at the extremes of a continuum. If possible, use the same continuum for all questions.

5. If you use continua:

   • Label the ends of the continua with the extreme opposite positions expected from this audience. (Remember to keep the continua similar to each other from item to item.)

   • Use a Likert scale (odd number of positions) and label the central choice so it is neutral, that is, doesn't represent either side of the continuum.

   • Intermediate positions may be left unlabeled if the audience can easily understand their intermediate nature.

6. Provide a line for comments. If the survey is done on the phone or in person, ask if the person has any final comments. Many respondents will want to say something more than appears in the answers you have supplied.

GROUP DATA-GATHERING PROCESSES

Sometimes you may want to poll the opinions of a group of people at the same time. The two more commonly used methods are focus groups and the Nominal Group Technique. What distinguishes these two methods is the degree to which they control group dynamics, the type of data they generate, and what they measure.

Focus Groups

Focus groups are also known as an open panel discussion.[4,5] The people who participate are rarely an intact work group, but are individuals who are asked to meet to discuss an issue. The technique is designed to facilitate a group discussion and record the data that emerge from the exchange. During the discussion the participants are asked to focus their attention on their feelings and opinions about a topic, event, or shared experience. The technique measures how strongly people feel about a topic and the degree to which they share the same opinion.

The process was originally designed to do market research, specifically to determine what features and benefits customers found most attractive. It can also be used to gain a deeper understanding about an issue, test out new ideas, and identify barriers to change.

ON-LINE DISCUSSION GROUPS

An association had surveyed its membership to measure their satisfaction with the current list of services and to identify future services. One of the findings of the survey was that members wanted a way to discuss problems, pose questions, and share ideas with other members beyond the annual conference. The solution they came up with was to set up discussion groups through the Web page. Members could sign on, present their questions, or tell their stories. Other members would have access and could either respond or add their own experiences. The feature was added to the Web page. Announcements were sent to members telling them of the new service. It was featured on the website, in publications, and at conferences. However, participation fell way short of what was expected. It was decided to conduct focus groups at the upcoming annual conference to find out why members did and did not use the service. The plan was to pull a random sample of people who registered by a specific date, who had been a member for more than three years, and who had attended two or more conferences in the past. There would be five ninety-minute sessions with fifteen members at different times over the course of the annual conference. Members would be sent an e-mail asking if they would be willing to participate and offered a small token of appreciation. Exhibit 10.5 shows the plan for the session.

Exhibit 10.5. Focus Group Process and Questions

Estimated time: 45 to 55 minutes

1. Which membership services have you used during the past year?
2. Which ones do you use more frequently?
3. What other services do you use?

Exhibit 10.5. (*Continued*)

> Probe if there was no mention of participating in the organization's on-line information exchanges.
>
> 4. Which services are especially effective at helping you obtain information or exchange ideas?
> 5. How has being able to access information over our Web page affected you?
> 6. Have any of you participated in an on-line discussion group through our Web page?
>
> Probe for specifics.
>
> 7. Those of you who have used our on-line services, why have you used them? How do they help you?
> 8. Those of you who have not used them, why not?
>
> Probe for specific expectations.
>
> 9. How might our on-line information exchanges better help you in the future?
> 10. Are there any resources that would help you that we haven't talked about?

At the beginning of the session, people were asked to briefly describe who they were and what they did. The facilitator then confirmed that the purpose of the session was to discuss their experience with the association's services. No mention was made of the on-line services. The facilitator asked what services they used. After most of the people had commented, the facilitator asked what each felt about moving more of the services on-line or to an electronic format. After the group exchanged their experiences and made recommendations, the facilitator asked if any had used the on-line discussion groups and if so what their experience had been. Many offered that they had used the service and found the discussions interesting. They also mentioned that they only "listened in" and did not initiate, offer recommendations, or provide input. They shared that their employers had a policy that participation in on-line discussion groups or chat rooms was forbidden and they may not disclose what their organizations were doing in the subjects being discussed.

In this situation, the process helped the association learn that people wanted access to information but were not allowed to contribute any.

Tool 10.6 contains the rules for designing and conducting a focus group session.

TOOL 10.6. RULES FOR DESIGNING AND CONDUCTING FOCUS GROUPS

Purpose

Focus groups are designed to facilitate discussions about issues. The goal is to gain a better understanding of what the issues are and how strongly people feel about them. The output is a list of items that may warrant further study or possible action. Focus groups were originally designed for market research to identify products and product features that consumers felt were attractive. In the arena of performance improvement, training, and HRD it is used to identify possible barriers to adopting new procedures, to analyze discrepancies in other data, to test a group's reaction to a new idea such as a new delivery format, and to better understand why behaviors or results do or do not materialize.

Process

1. Plan.

   - Define the objective. Ask yourself: "What specifically do I want to find out?"
   - Identify people who either have shared an experience or have a shared interest in the topic you want to learn more about.
   - Identify on what basis people among that group will be selected to participate.
   - Determine how many sessions you want and the size of the groups.
   - Develop the questions you want to use to get people to engage and what questions you might use to focus them on specifics.
   - Practice your questions by saying them aloud; try them out to see whether they focus people's attention as you had intended.

2. Select and invite people. Try to keep the number somewhere between six and twelve.

3. Explain:

   - The purpose of the meeting is to discuss the topic and get a better understanding of their views on it.
   - Why they were selected.
   - The rules for participation, such as let people finish making their comments (no interruptions), that you may ask people to limit what they say so that everyone is given a chance to speak, that if there are any sidebar conversations you will ask them to stop, and that you will ask people directly what they think if they do not share their ideas.
   - How their comments will be captured or recorded.
   - How the results will be used.

4. Start the conversation by asking them to respond one at a time and then pose a question that focuses them on the topic and causes them to share information, for example:

   • What has been your experience with . . .
   • Which programs have you used . . . .

5. Probe or prompt if the conversation fails to bring out specifics. If necessary, prompt until all or most have responded; even ask individuals directly to get their thoughts.

6. Continue prompting until the group responds to each other not just to you.

7. As the conversation continues, probe for specific details, expectations, concerns, and so forth.

8. At the end, thank everyone and follow up with any information that you may have promised to give.

Nominal Group Technique

The Nominal Group Technique (NGT), like the focus group technique, polls the opinions of people who are a group in name only, that is, they need not be an intact work team, but individuals who are asked to meet to generate a set of data, identify requirements, provide input, and so on.[6,7] The technique was designed to control group dynamics, specifically the influence of people of higher status. The technique is especially useful when doing a job or task analysis or when identifying competencies. The technique measures how many variables are relevant to the topic and the degree to which the group agrees on those variables. The results can be used to develop other data-gathering instruments, such as surveys, structured interviews, and observations. They can also be used to design job requirements, performance standards, selection criteria, and curricula.

FUTURE NEEDS

Learning and Development (L&D), a division within HR, wanted to poll the opinions of managers from five different departments to find out what their needs were for the coming year. Learning and Development decided to use a stratified random sample to assure each department was equally represented (see Table 10.1). Eight managers were selected at random from each department.

Table 10.1. Stratified Random Sample for Focus Group Session

Department	1	2	3	4	5
Total # of Employees	111	197	133	287	734
Total # of Managers	15	22	19	35	113
Sample Size	8	8	8	8	8

The data-gathering method they used was the Nominal Group Technique (NGT) to control the group dynamics because of known status issues among the different functions. The plan was to conduct five half-day NGT sessions during which the participants would be asked the same four questions in the same order.

- What will be required of your people in the future if your department is to meet its business goals?
- What do you see as the major challenges your people will have to address in the future?
- What do your people have now that will help them meet these challenges?
- What are they missing, but must have for the department to be successful?

Learning and Development planned to analyze each department's answers to determine what the significant variables were. Then it would compare each department's answers to identify those variables that were common across all groups, shared by some groups, and unique to specific groups. They used the results, along with historic data on its services and the company's projected growth plan, to develop its plan for the coming year.

Tool 10.7 gives rules for designing and using the Nominal Group Technique.

TOOL 10.7. RULES FOR DESIGNING AND USING THE NOMINAL GROUP TECHNIQUE

Purpose

The Nominal Group Technique was developed to improve group decision-making ability. It was specifically designed to reduce the influence of powerful personalities over a group's ability to generate and impartially examine ideas. The process helps groups come to consensus without sacrificing individual ideas. In the arena of performance improvement, training, and HRD, the technique is effective at helping groups identify tasks that make up a job and outputs or accomplishments that distinguish exemplar performance. The results can be used to develop assessment tools, job descriptions, competency statements, and curriculum.

Process

1. Explain the purpose and format of the session.
2. Generate answers to questions.
3. Report out individually.
4. Discuss briefly.
5. Combine and/or eliminate.
6. Select the most important.
7. Rank.
8. Assign values.
9. Accumulate values.
10. Discuss results.

Rules

1. Plan the session.
   - Decide what you want to accomplish.
   - Identify the people who have the information you require to fulfill your goal.
   - Decide how you will select them.
   - Decide how many sessions you want to hold.
   - Limit the number of people per session from six to fifteen.
2. Explain how the session is structured.
   - Tell the participants they will be asked three to four questions.
   - Tell them you will ask one question at a time and they will be asked to answer privately.
   - Then everyone will be asked to share his or her answers one at a time in a round-robin manner until every answer is captured.
   - Ask them to please refrain from asking questions or commenting on each other's responses until all of the responses are captured.
3. Display the first question on a flip chart or pre-made poster.
   - Read the question aloud.

- Tell the group they are to privately and silently come up with a list of six to ten answers (you will accept more). Without the silent generation, people will look to the highest ranking or more powerful person in the group and go along with whatever he or she says. Silence gives everyone an equal voice.

- Ask that they try to state their answers in the active voice and in short phrases.

- Give them a time estimate, perhaps five minutes for this step.

4. Report out individually.

- In a round-robin style, ask each person to read one answer.

- Do *not* ask people to volunteer to go first. Select someone who is not considered a leader. For subsequent questions, start with different people or reverse the order.

- The first person reports his or her first answer, the second person does the same, the third next, and so on until all have reported their first answers.

- Record the answers on flip-chart paper.

- Number each answer.

- Continue in the round-robin style, asking for the second answer from each participant.

5. Combine and/or eliminate.

- After everyone has exhausted his or her list, ask the group to identify any answers they feel could be combined or eliminated because of duplication.

- No answer can be eliminated unless the person who submitted it agrees and confirms the intent is adequately covered in another answer.

6. Select their top choices.

- At this point you may have anywhere from twenty to fifty or more answers. It's time to get the group to agree about which ones have the most merit.

- Ask everyone to privately select and write down the most important answers from all the ones given.

- You may want to hand out cards to participants and ask that they silently make their selections and put one item on each card (four cards apiece for twenty items, six cards for twenty to thirty-five items, eight cards for thirty-five to fifty items).

7. Rank items. Ask each person to rank his or her top choices (four, six, or eight) choices in decreasing order.

8. Assign values. Ask each person to assign values to his or her top answers. The highest value depends on the number of items selected (four, six, or eight points). No fractions or duplicate numbers.

9. Accumulate values. Collect the cards and add up the points given to each item. Show the results on the flip chart.

10. Discuss results.

   • Ask the group to discuss the accumulative values.

   • Look for trends. Often the top three to five answers are easily favored over the others. Sometimes, though, the count is rather flat (that is, many answers have similar totals).

   • Be sure the group has enough time to think about these ideas before continuing with the next question or situation.

GROUP DYNAMICS

There are two data-gathering tools that are useful for evaluating group dynamics and social interactions. They are the sociogram and the Flanders Interaction Analysis (FIA). Both can be used in the beginning to measure the effectiveness of a group's behavior and communication patterns and, after an intervention, to measure changes in the group's behavior. The FIA can be used to identify individual development needs and to measure learning.

Sociograms

Sociograms are graphic representations of the interactions or relationships within a group. They are created from data collected through interviews or surveys to determine opinion leaders, loners, cliques, and popularity.[8] They are best done with groups from twelve to thirty-five people, as it is difficult to draw conclusions with fewer than twelve people and more than thirty-five are hard to record. Figure 10.1 is a graphic representation of a group's communication patterns.

In this example, the circles with letters represent the twelve members of the group. The letters F and E are people outside the group. The arrows show the direction of the choices people made, that is, some people chose specific individuals (C chose F and E), were chosen by others (C by G, L, H, and A), and were mutually chosen by others (C and B). Some people appear to be excluded in that no one chose them (I and L), yet they appear to choose others. When an arrow circles back to the person (A, H, and B), it usually means that person chose himself or herself. The person who is "B" seems to be the center or hub, as more people chose him or her. The people who are "D," "M," and "N" seem to be outside the group yet stay connected through "D."

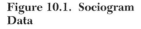

Figure 10.1. Sociogram Data

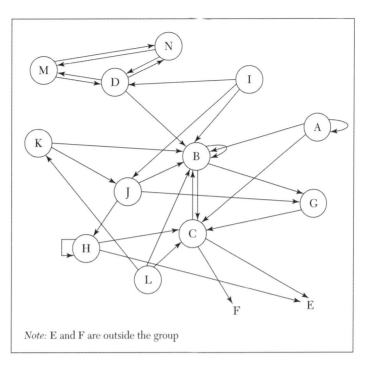

Note: E and F are outside the group

The instrument used to generate sociogram data is easy to construct. You simply ask this question, "Name three people from the X department you would choose to. . . ." What you use to complete the query will determine the nature of the data you will obtain. For example, if you wrote, "Name three people from Sales you think could become vice president of sales if given a chance to prepare for the job," you might find out who the group thinks would be a good leader.

Sociograms must be interpreted in context, as they only tell you *what* is going on—not *why.* Therefore, they are best done in conjunction with other data-gathering methods such as interviews or focus groups to gain a better understanding of why behaviors are the way they appear. Sociograms can quickly give you a snapshot of how a group interacts in any of several ways. They chart popularity, leadership, and cliques; how people work together; on whom each relies for information; and with whom they like to associate. Sociograms are also interventions in themselves because they give groups feedback about how their behavior appears to others. The group can then decide whether or not to modify its behavior.

If you use a sociogram, ensure that people's choices will remain confidential. Support any recommendations you might make with other data, such as from a focus group or interviews.

TEAM BUILDING

A small architectural firm was concerned about the effectiveness of its project teams. The firm went to a team structure on the belief that teams would produce more innovative solutions for clients while reducing the incidence of false starts. The firm had hired a trainer to come in and do "team training." After six months, the firm's partners were not seeing the results they wanted. The firm then hired a consultant who specialized in communications to help the teams be more effective. The consultant interviewed each member separately. During the interviews, she heard complaints like "Some people do all the fun work and the rest of us are left out." As part of the interview, the consultant asked everyone the same questions:

- Who do you rely on when you are stuck on a design issue?

- Who do you go to when you have a technical question about how to execute (graphically display) a concept?

  She then compiled everyone's responses on a worksheet (see Exhibit 10.6).

Exhibit 10.6. Sociogram Worksheet

Chooser	Chose	Times Chosen	Comments
C	C,P,A	/////	
P	C,A,D	/////	
A	A	///	
N	P,Q,C	–	
D	M,B,X_1	///	
Q	Q	///	
B	V,M,D	///	
O	C,P	/	
E	Q	–	
R	X_1,X_2,X_3	/	
G		–	
T	R,D,B	–	
F	M	–	
S	W,U,K	//	
W	S,U,P	//	
U	S,W	//	
K	C	/	
V	P,B	/	
M		///	
H	M,O,H	/	

The consultant then charted their responses as shown in Figure 10.2 and presented the team with a picture of how they worked together. The arrows represent the direction of the communication and with whom each member of the team communicates.

- P = Sue is the team leader
- C = Mary is her best friend
- A = Irene is a close friend of Sue and Mary
- X = Are people outside the group

Figure 10.2. Sociogram of the Group

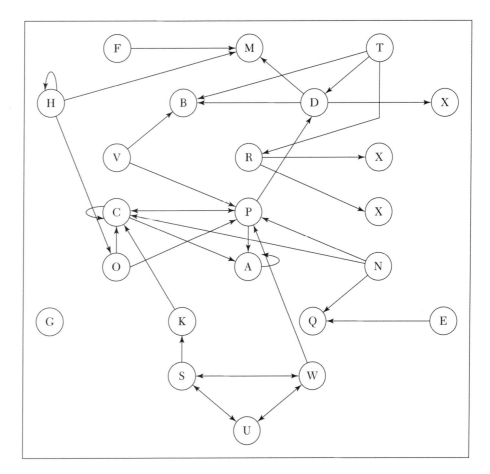

The number of people not chosen on the chart is important information. In our example G didn't choose anyone and was not chosen. F, T, E, H, and N chose others, but no one chose them. This supports the data from the interviews that some people felt left out.

There is no clear choice pattern. (Usually one or two people in a group are chosen by at least half of the group.) This might indicate a lack of leadership or the absence of an opinion leader. There appear to be two cliques (C, P, and A) and (S, W, and U), which further supports the accusation that some people feel left out. Three people chose themselves. This can be an indication of self-confidence or frustration because they don't know anyone else they'd like to choose.

In this situation, the role of measurement was to assess the group's cohesiveness. The technique also served as an intervention, as it provided feedback to the group on how they did and did not include people. The group could then decide if and how it wanted to change the way it operated. The team leader recognized that she needed to encourage the group to rely on others, to purposefully include everyone, and to set up smaller subteams to work on problems that allowed everyone an opportunity to contribute. Six months later, the consultant returned to measure the group's effectiveness. She applied the same measurement technique so the group could compare how it was operating with how it had been operating. This time the technique was used to evaluate how effective the group was in honoring their commitment to be more inclusive.

Tool 10.8 is in two parts. Part A has the rules for designing and using the sociogram technique. Part B has a worksheet that you can modify to record people's responses.

TOOL 10.8A. RULES FOR DESIGNING AND USING THE SOCIOGRAM TECHNIQUE

Purpose

The sociogram was designed to graphically display a group's communication patterns, specifically who they choose for guidance, information, and recognition. The method should be used in combination with other methods, such as interviews, to identify leaders or social cliques and to measure group cohesiveness. It is used with intact work groups.

Process

1. Plan

   • Decide what you want to find out. For example, do you want to identify potential leaders or possible experts or to find out how the group members relate to each other?

   • Develop two to three questions that will ask group members to choose other members of the group.

2. Ask each one the questions. Let people know that their responses will be confidential.

3. Compile responses in a table like the one shown in Part B, placing people's names in Column 1 (chooser) and the names of those they choose in Column 2 (chosen).

4. Tally the number of times each person was chosen by counting the number of times that his or her name appears in Column 2 and put the total in Column 3 (times chosen).

TOOL 10.8B. SAMPLE SOCIOGRAM WORKSHEET

1. Chooser	2. Chosen	3. Times Person Was Chosen	Comments

Process

1. Assign each person a letter.

2. On a large sheet of paper plot each person's profile based on the value in Column 3. Start with the three people chosen most often. Draw circles in the middle of the page for each of these people and label the circles with their initials.

3. Plot these three people by drawing lines from them (the chosen) to the person who was the chooser. Use arrow points to direct the line from chooser to chosen. Draw other circles as required to plot all of the choosers.

4. Add circles and draw arrows until each person has been recorded. Draw isolated circles for those who were not chosen, chose not to choose, or only chose themselves.

5. Review the chart and note the following:
   - Those chosen most often
   - Those never chosen

- Pairs who chose each other
- Pairs or small groups that are not chosen by anyone outside their pair or small group (These will appear as separate from the larger group)

6. Note the number of individuals who exchange information or just give or receive information.
7. Formulate some hypotheses as to why the pattern is at it seems.
8. Consider other data or pursue other data-collection methods to confirm or disprove your hypotheses.

Flanders Interaction Analysis

Flanders Interaction Analysis is another technique for evaluating individual and group behavior. The technique was developed by Ned Flanders to study teachers' interactions with students. His techniques have been modified and expanded to study behavior in the workplace. Unlike the sociogram, which produces a graphic created from interview data, the FIA produces sketches and charts based on data derived from observation. The technique is to chart movements as well as classify and record behaviors against a time grid. The results can be used to determine:

- How people use space, such as how they move within and around their workspace or work area. This information might help determine whether the layout is inefficient or if a person's lack of organizational skills results in repetitive, redundant movements.

- The type of activities people engage in, such as entering data, answering questions, retrieving information, checking work, and so forth. This information can measure what people do, how often they do it, and how much time it requires.

- The type of verbal and non-verbal communication people engage in, such as giving orders, answering, active listening, passive listening, social interaction, and so on. This information can measure the degree to which the job requires interpersonal skills as well as people's ability to coach, lead teams, and do consultative selling.

The technique can be used in the beginning to identify the developmental needs of individuals in the areas of social interaction and communication skills. Later it can be used to measure whether and how well an intervention improved an individual's skills. Depending on what you want to measure, the technique may require you to sketch the floor plan of the area where the behaviors occur. It will require you to pay attention to time and classify and record the number of times behaviors occur; however, you might record the occurrence of behaviors on a sketch or on a worksheet. A sketch might look like the one in Figure 10.3. The numbers indicate where person "A" was at specific time intervals. The worksheet shown in Exhibit 10.7 notes what "A" was doing.

Figure 10.3. Sketch of Office Activities

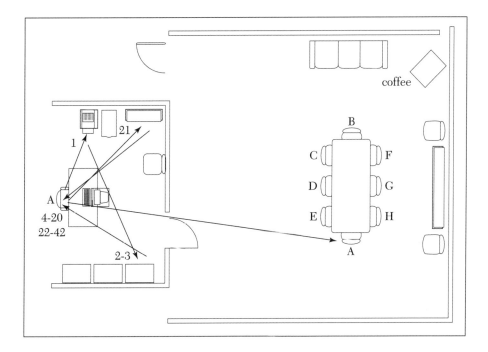

Later, if you wanted to chart A's interactions during a meeting, you might create another sketch; however, the worksheet would include different classifications (see Figure 10.4 and Exhibit 10.8).

One of the challenges of using the FIA to measure communication and interpersonal skills is that the observer must be able to recognize and classify behaviors, even subtle ones, such as:

- clarifying
- coaching
- facilitating
- surfacing feelings

- paraphrasing
- counseling
- giving orders
- overcoming objectives

- probing
- enrolling others
- explaining
- reframing constructs

- listening
- acknowledging
- summarizing
- asking open-ended questions

Exhibit 10.7 Office Activity Worksheet

Category	Time Intervals 15 Seconds															
	1	2	3	4	5	6	7	8	9	10	11	12	13	14	14	16
On phone				X	X	X	X	X	X							
Checking messages										X	X	X	X	X	X	X
At printer	X															
Retrieving book																
Returning to file		X	X													
Socializing																
No activity																

Category	Time Intervals 15 Seconds															
	17	18	19	20	21	22	23	24	25	26	27	28	29	30	31	32
On phone						X	X	X	X	X	X	X	X	X	X	X
Checking messages	X	X	X	X												
At printer																
Retrieving book					X											
Returning to file																
Socializing																
No activity																

Figure 10.4. Sketch of Meeting Room Activities

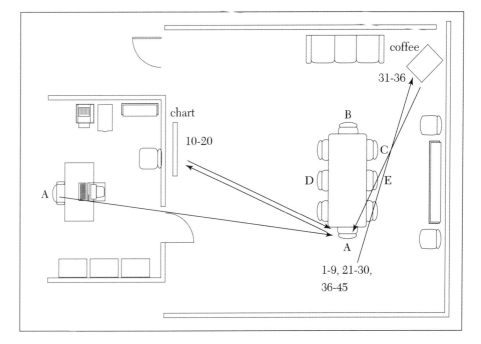

Exhibit 10.8. Meeting Room Activities

Category	Time Intervals 15 Seconds															
	1	2	3	4	5	6	7	8	9	10	11	12	13	14	14	16
Give direction					A	A	A	A								
Give information									B	A	A	A	A	A	A	A
Active listening					BC	BC	BC	BC	AC DE							
Passive listening	CD E	CD E	CD E		DE	DE	DE	DE								
Socializing	AB	AB	AB	ALL												

Exhibit 10.8. (*Continued*)

Category	Time Intervals 15 Seconds															
	17	18	19	20	21	22	23	24	25	26	27	28	29	30	31	32
Give direction																
Give information	A	A	A	A	BC	C	C	C	C	D	D	D	E	E	E	E
Active listening	BC	BC	BC	BC	A	AB	AB	AB	AB	AB	AB	AB	AB	AB	AB	AB
Passive listening	DE	DE	DE	DE	DE	DE	DE	DE	DE	CE	CE	CE	CD	CD	CD	CD
Socializing																

Exhibit 10.9. Activity Log

Activities	1	2	3	4	5	6	7	8	9	10	11	12	13	14	15	16
On phone	10				5											
Advising a manager		7														
Review status reports			5													
Briefing staff				20												
Touring production						25										

Note: Times recorded in minutes

Another challenge is deciding on the time intervals. In intensive one-on-one interactions, the time interval might be every five seconds. If the goal is to identify activities, the time element may or may not be important. Yet, if you want to assign times to activities, instead of putting time intervals at the top of the chart, you could put numbers indicating a change of activity and put the amount of time spent in the column opposite the row for that activity, similar to an activity log (see Exhibit 10.9).

The technique is labor-intensive and, depending on the goal, the observation may require one or more days!

COACHING

One of the required courses in the new supervisory development curricula is "coaching." The course was added to the curriculum because of tense labor relations. A needs assessment showed that supervisors lacked skills or were unwilling to acknowledge people of lower status and were ineffective at coaching. The course focused on communication skills, specifically making distinctions among:

- Giving advice, such as, "The next time make sure you check with Mary first."
- Passing judgment, such as, "You were right on, you were right to take matters into your own hands."
- Paraphrasing, such as, "So a major customer complained about our return policy. Is that right?"
- Clarifying, such as, "Help me understand. What exactly did the customer say and what happened before that?"
- Acknowledging, such as nodding to someone in recognition of his or her presence or greeting someone with a hello.
- Giving credit, such as saying aloud in front of peers, employees, and management the names of the people who did the work, made the suggestions, or whatever.

After the course, supervisors were assigned personal coaches who observed them for two days in staff meetings and in one-on-one exchanges with employees. The observation form used by the coaches is shown in Exhibit 10.10. The coaches would place hash marks in the appropriate columns. At the end of each day, the coaches reported on how many times the supervisors used each of the communication skills. Periodically, the coaches attended staff meetings to observe and report on the presence and absence of the communication behaviors. They used the same form.

Exhibit 10.10. Coaching Worksheet

Category	Opportunities to Coach															
	1	2	3	4	5	6	7	8	9	10	11	12	13	14	14	16
Give advice																
Pass judgment																
Paraphrase																
Clarify																
Acknowledge																
Give credit																
Other																

After the course was introduced, the number of grievances and the ratings on the all-employee survey that asked questions about supervisory effectiveness were tracked and compared to the number of supervisors who completed the program to see whether there was any change.

Tool 10.9 gives the rules for designing and using a Flanders Interaction Analysis.

TOOL 10.9. RULES FOR DESIGNING AND USING A FLANDERS INTERACTION ANALYSIS

Purpose

The Flanders Interaction Analysis is a method of recording observation data that results in a map or chart of activities, movement within a physical space, or communication between individuals.

Process

1. Plan.

   • Decide what you want to accomplish or measure.

   • Select the type of observation that will support your goal (identify tasks, time, communication patterns, use of space, and so forth).

- Identify the person or people you want to observe.
- Prepare the forms you will require.
- If it would be helpful, sketch the area you will be observing in advance.
- Explain to the people the purpose of the observation and what information will be shared with them when it is over.
- Discuss how the person wants to handle exceptions like confidential exchanges.

2. Chart communication. If the purpose is to find out how individuals communicate with each other by observing their interaction, then:
   - Identify communication categories to be tracked (listening, answering, directing, critiquing, and so on).
   - Place yourself so you can see the people you want to observe.
   - In pre-determined time intervals, record who is speaking, the category under which the speech falls, and what the others are doing (listening, socializing, or whatever).
   - At the end of the observation, list the communication categories and the frequency by person.

3. Chart activities and movement. If the purpose is to find out how much time people spend doing various things and the kinds of things they do, then:
   - Develop a form to track activities.
   - At the beginning of each activity, record what the activity is.
   - At the end of the activity, note the time and record the next activity.
   - At the end of the observation, list the activities and time spent on each.

4. Summarize the results.

DIRECT OBSERVATIONS

There are two common types of observations. One is to look at people while they perform a task; the other is to look at documents or work samples. In both cases the purpose is to judge proficiency or adequacy, to identify deficiencies, and to identify patterns.

Observations of People

Observations of people are usually done for the following reasons:

- To see whether someone follows a procedure or protocol
- To find out what activities make up a job

- To understand the work environment and find out if it varies according to location or other factor
- To assess skills and abilities

If you want to watch people at work, you should identify what specifically you want to see happen or not happen. For example, companies hire "secret shoppers" who pretend they are customers and evaluate how well employees follow the company's protocols for dealing with customers. They are trained to observe customer interactions. They have a form they fill out that addresses specific behaviors. They mark the behaviors that were demonstrated and those that were not. The employees have seen the form before, but they don't know when they are likely to be observed. As with all measurement techniques, you should be clear on your purpose and on the criteria to be used to judge performance.

Observations of Work Documents

Observations (reviews) of work products and documents are done for the following reasons:

- To confirm that the product or document meets some criteria
- To assess how much they vary from standard
- To determine how much variance there is in different locations, work shifts, by employee, or other measure

The purpose may be to judge whether or not they comply with standards or to determine whether they possess specific features. As with all measurement, you identify in the beginning what attributes or features you are looking for or want to consider when judging. The process is not about arbitrarily looking for deficiencies. An important consideration is your sampling strategy. You can pull representative, random, or stratified random samples of things just as you can of people; however, you should decide on what basis you are going to select samples to evaluate.

Performance Checklists

Performance checklists are used to support observations of both people and products and open interviews. They can be used to measure whether a person can perform a procedure or a task and whether a piece of work meets a standard. The benefit of a performance checklist is that it contains the criteria for judging proficiency or adequacy so the people who are being evaluated know what is expected.

STATUS REPORTS

The plant manager was concerned that his supervisors lacked the skill to interpret data on the daily status report accurately. To measure their ability, he developed a performance checklist and handed it out. He told each of his supervisors that he would use it to evaluate their ability to interpret the data. He arranged for them to meet with him once a week to go over a daily status report from the previous month. He would give them the status report and ask them to do each of the tasks on the checklist. He used the opportunity to coach them in how to do what he believed was a fundamental part of their job. After they had accurately interpreted six status reports in a row, they would be certified in that task. To assure fairness, the manager selected the status reports at random. Exhibit 10.11 shows the performance checklist used.

Exhibit 10.11. Status Report Checklist

Evaluator: _____   Person: _____

Date Administered: _____

Goals	Yes	No	Comments
The person could accurately determine:			
1. The amount of overtime put in by hourly workers.			
2. Whether the amount of overtime is less than X percent of the total hours worked.			
3. The number of cases per hour averaged over any five working days.			
4. The ratio of temporary workers compared to the permanent work force.			
5. That the temporary workers are signed up and available as needed.			
6. The average inventory shrinkage compared to the average monthly value of total inventory.			
7. If mark-outs are less than X percent.			

Exhibit 10.11. (*Continued*)

8. If merchandise began to move within forty-eight hours and was distributed in the billing cycle.			
9. The percentage of detention and demurrage compared to the average monthly inventory value.			
10. If the put-away report is less than X items.			
11. If the status report conforms to corporate standards.			
12. If the status report was based on current data, less than five days old.			

(The manager filled in the numbers for each status report that was used.)

Manager: _____   Person: _____

Manager: _____   Date: _____

(Signatures signify competence for this section.)

HR AND KNOWING THE BUSINESS

Management continually complained that HR didn't understand the business and that the generalists couldn't talk about business issues. Human resources generalists complained that they were never invited into any meetings but were only called in to clean up employee relations issues that could have been avoided. HR wanted to be a strategic partner with line management. The new vice president of HR decided to create an aggressive development program for the generalists. The program included: individual assignments (learning about the basic principles of the topic), classroom work (practicing applying the principles through case studies), and mentoring (actually doing what was practiced under the guidance of a more experienced person). In the end the generalists were expected to submit a report and give a presentation about the specific topic. The program focused on six topics:

- Knowing the business
- Analyzing processes
- Designing major change strategies

- Developing business cases for programs or acquisitions
- Managing projects
- Making presentations and developing summary reports

The final task was a presentation to a selected group of line managers, who evaluated how well the generalist had mastered the topic. The generalist, his or her mentor, and line managers all had copies of the performance checklist that would be used to judge the generalist's presentation. The checklist for judging a generalist's understanding of the business is shown in Exhibit 10.12.

Exhibit 10.12. Checklist to Analyze HR Generalist

Instructions:

As you listen to the presentation, put a check mark opposite those elements that are present. Do not put a check mark if the element was missing, incomplete, or did not follow the guidelines. Wherever a check is missing, please add a comment explaining why and what has to be done to rectify the deficiency.

Date of the Evaluation: _____

_____
Name of Person Being Evaluated

_____
Name of Person Doing the Evaluation

Element or Activity	Present	Comment
Described: • The customer's goals and business strategy • How the customer is organized • What the customer produces • Who depends on what is produced and why • How what is produced is used and by whom • Who the competition is		
Described: • Where customer is in the supply chain		
Described: • The customer's processes • The activities that make up those processes • How different work groups interface across processes • The roles different work groups play within and across processes		

Exhibit 10.12. (*Continued*)

Element or Activity	Present	Comment
Spent time with work groups Validated information: • Met with finance • Met with representatives from different work groups • Met with people from different levels within the customer organization		
Described what drives costs.		
Described what is expected of an HR generalist.		
Checked HR records and identified any trends in the following: • Turnover • Retention • Patterns of internal promotions • External salary comparisons • Other		
Identified how to apply what was learned about the customer's business and the process of doing the assignment to his or her own job.		
Summarized how HR might better support the customer.		
Conclusions were based on what was learned about the customer.		
Applied the guidelines for organizing the presentation and report.		
Applied the guidelines for delivering the presentation.		
Once you have completed the evaluation, meet with the participant and go over why each element was or was not checked. The signatures below mean that you reviewed the evaluation with the participant.		

_____/_____   _____/_____

Signature of the Evaluator/Date   Signature of the Participant/Date

In this situation the goal was to help HR be better prepared to work with its clients. The checklists were used to guide the generalists' professional development and serve as a tool to judge capability.

BEHAVIORAL INTERVIEWS

Human resources wanted to improve its ability to select capable job candidates. It decided to develop a series of scenarios that would be presented to candidates. The selection scenarios were designed to give candidates an opportunity to demonstrate they possessed one or more of the following attributes:

- *Customer orientation*—seeks to understand customers' concerns

- *Achievement orientation*—organizes efforts and resources to get things done that are worthy of accomplishing and is willing to commit to action by identifying tasks, setting timetables, and defining roles

- *Concern with impact*—thinks through and questions how decisions and actions might impact others (customers, stakeholders, co-workers) now and in the future; looks ahead; searches for hidden implications; and anticipates challenges or objections

- *Initiative*—demonstrates initiative through action versus reticence; assumes authority; doesn't wait to be asked; initiates communication, action, establishing relationships, and so on

Candidates were given one of six scenarios and told they had thirty minutes to read it and either (a) write [not to exceed two pages] a response or (b) prepare an oral presentation [not to exceed ten minutes]. They were told that the response should include:

- How he or she would approach the assignment
- What he or she would do to accomplish the assignment
- On what basis he or she would want his or her performance evaluated upon completion of the assignment

The people who were to either listen to or read the candidates' responses reviewed the checklist(s) and agreed to what they would accept as evidence that a respondent possessed the desired attribute. One of the scenarios read:

"If you are hired, one of your first assignments will be to join a newly formed cross-functional committee to review our current policies related to security and recommend any revisions or additions. The head of the security department asked that HR be represented to make sure the recommendations take into account the needs of employees and the company's relationship with the community.

Exhibit 10.13 shows the checklist to be used for this scenario.

Exhibit 10.13. Scenario Checklist

Make a check mark after each attribute you believe the candidate's response indicated. Do not make a mark if the attribute was absent. Add comments to help you discuss your evaluation with others.

#	Action or Behavior	Yes	Comments
1.	Will initiate questions to the team about how it will work together.		
	Will wait to find out how the team works together, basically watch and see.		
2.	Will ask what exactly is expected from the team or self.		
	Will wait to see if the team thought about finding out what the expectations are.		
3.	Will suggest the team develop a project plan with a timetable.		
	Will wait for someone else to build the agenda.		
4.	Will describe steps the team might take to clarify the issue or request.		
	Assumes has all the information at hand.		
5.	Will propose a way for the team to identify the key stakeholders.		
	Assumes the team knows who the stakeholders are.		
6.	Will propose a way to get greater customer involvement.		
	Assumes the team already has or does not require involvement.		

Exhibit 10.13. (*Continued*)

#	Action or Behavior	Yes	Comments
7.	Will suggest ways for the team to monitor its progress.		
	Will assume progress is being made.		
8.	Will propose how the team might address possible future impact of its recommendations.		
	Assumes once the project is done it's done.		
9.	Will suggest ways for the team to test out their recommendations to identify barriers or unforeseen complications.		
	Will assume that whatever recommendations are made will be accepted and adopted.		
10.	Will suggest the team think through the implementation of its recommendations.		
	Will assume that whatever recommendations are made will be accepted and adopted.		

Name of Candidate: _____ Name of Evaluator: _____

Date of the Evaluation: _____

Tool 10.10 lays out the rules for designing checklists for observations and document reviews.

Tool 10.11 has guidelines for assuring the people who use your checklists are qualified.

TOOL 10.10. RULES FOR DESIGNING CHECKLISTS TO SUPPORT OBSERVATIONS AND DOCUMENT REVIEWS

Purpose

The checklist is a tool for documenting observations and the results from open interviews and for evaluating work products or documents. The checklist helps observers apply the same criteria to each observation. It also communicates to the person being observed what is important and how his or her performance will be judged.

The benefits of checklists are

- People have access to the steps and criteria against which their performance is being compared
- They assure the evaluator is applying the same criteria consistently
- They help the person and evaluator come to agreement on what the criteria mean and what will be accepted as evidence of proficiency
- They allow people to practice using the same criteria the evaluator will use
- They allow people to observe a competent person and identify what and how that person does a task

How a Performance Checklist Works

The items on the checklist are analogous to questions on a test. Normally, the checklist is dichotomous, that is, it has two choices per item. This is because most checklists test for the presence or absence of an action, criteria, attribute, factor, or other item.

Some checklists have scales. When scales are used, it is very important that specific observable criteria be given for each point on the scale. If the scale lacks these specific observable criteria, the evaluator has to apply his or her own criteria, making them less fair. There is a greater possibility of error in judging the performance.

What Goes on a Checklist

A performance checklist has six parts:

1. The headline that identifies the area being evaluated
2. The steps or criteria
3. A yes/no column
4. A comments column
5. A place for the signatures of the evaluator and the person being evaluated
6. The date the evaluation occurred

General Rules

1. Show the people the checklist with the steps or criteria before they are evaluated. If possible people should have used the same checklist to assess their own performance prior to the formal evaluation.
2. Document the evaluation session and the results.
3. Provide the evaluator with a script. This is particularly important if the evaluator is presenting the problem orally.
4. Train the evaluator in how to use the checklist.
5. If the score is considered in personnel decisions, arrange for at least two independent evaluations or other corroborating evidence, such as documents or records of the number of assignments completed, time records, accuracy records, complaints, and so on.

Process

1. If it is a procedure:
   - List the steps the evaluator will look for
   - Note which steps must be done
   - Indicate where the sequence must be followed
2. If it is a performance:
   - List the attributes, criteria, factors, or accomplishment the evaluator will check for
   - Strive for a level of detail that is useful and unambiguous to the evaluator
   - Mark those attributes, criteria, factors, or accomplishment that must be present
   - Start with as few factors as reasonable and add more detail after the pilot and when you know what level of detail the evaluator actually needs
3. If the checklist is used as a self-assessment, each performance item should reference a source for additional information or skill building.
4. Provide a column to check whether or not the performance or attribute was present or absent.
   - Use N/A if "not applicable" is an appropriate response
   - If you use Y only, make it clear what *not* marking it means, for example, "not performed to standard," "not performed at all," or "not observed."
5. Provide a column for comments. Be clear in the directions when comments must be provided.
6. Provide a place for both the evaluator and the person being evaluated to sign and date when the evaluation occurred.

7. Make sure the directions about how to complete the checklist are complete so everyone will use it in the same way. Directions should include:

- When comments are required
- Whether or not time is a factor and if so how much time is allotted
- Whether or not the person can ask for help or reference some resource
- What the person can and cannot be told after the evaluation
- How the results will be used
- What marks in the Y, N, and N/A columns mean
- What not marking a column means

TOOL 10.11. GUIDELINES FOR QUALIFYING REVIEWERS

Purpose

Whenever someone is asked to judge the adequacy of someone else's performance, the person doing the judging should be qualified, that is, he or she should be knowledgeable about what he or she is observing and be able to recognize work products or performances that satisfy requirements or comply with a standard. This tool is to help you decide on what basis people should be qualified to judge the adequacy of others' work.

Rules for Qualifying Reviewers

1. Be clear whether or not there are any requirements for becoming an evaluator such as:
   - Having successfully performed the task to the same criteria
   - Having performed the job previously
   - Being responsible for quality assurance
   - Being a supervisor
   - Having specific credentials, education, or experience
2. Train the evaluators prior to asking them to administer a performance checklist.
   - Have them practice observing and completing the checklist
   - At the same time, have someone who is already qualified do the observation and complete the checklist
   - Review the evaluator's decisions and comments and compare them to the ones from a qualified evaluator

3. Be sure the evaluator is free of any conflict of interest concerning the people he or she is evaluating.

4. Remove any information about the people being evaluated that is not related to the performance being evaluated.

5. Have detailed criteria for selecting evaluators and evaluating the performance.

When more than one evaluator is used, have each evaluator score the performance independently.

MISSTEPS

Here are some of the common mistakes people make:

1. They fail to take advantage of the abilities of people in the organization who are already collecting data that would be useful.

2. They overly rely on one data-gathering method or audience for their information.

3. They apply techniques without fully understanding their purpose, strengths, and tradeoffs.

4. They do not standardize their implementation and, as a result, introduce bias into the data.

5. They fail to pilot-test their methods to confirm they are easy to use or actually capture the data required.

6. They do not decide how to select documents or work samples to review, but arbitrarily pull examples, which makes it difficult to generalize.

TIPS AND TECHNIQUES

Here are some suggestions for how to conduct your data gathering:

1. When doing interviews, remember to explain the purpose of the interview to each respondent. This is especially important if more than one person will be conducting the interviews. It is important that each respondent experience the interview in the same way. Include the "rules" of the interview. The rules should include, at a minimum, statements similar to the following:

   - "Everyone we are interviewing is being asked the same questions, in the same way, and in the same order."

   - If it is a structured interview, add: "The other interviewers and I are not allowed to explain the questions or to add any explanatory statements, but we can repeat the questions."

2. Structured interviews are best done with groups of twenty-six or more. Having fewer people makes it difficult to compare their responses with what other groups said previously.

- Once you have your introduction and forms completed, it is wise to pilot-test your interviews. This gives you an opportunity to practice asking the questions in the same way and classifying answers.

- Practice saying the lead-in statement aloud. What appears natural in writing may come across as stilted when spoken. You want the statement to sound natural.

- Practice classifying answers. One of the hardest parts of this technique is listening to the meaning behind what is said and then finding an expected response to put it under. People can use many different words to mean the same thing.

3. Always pilot-test or practice the method you are using. You will be surprised how people will interpret your questions. Your forms for observation may look simple, but may be unwieldy to use. Your intervals for tracking time and activities may be undoable. You will only find out by testing them.

4. Be aggressive when it comes to finding out who is already measuring performance. Find out who it is and work with that person on how you might use the information for your own work.

5. Create an audit trail. Document what you did, who or what the sources of your data were (interviews, observations, and so on), why and how they were selected, and why you chose the methods you did. Documenting what you did and why will help you be more effective and efficient in future efforts. You may also be able to build on what you learn and the tools you used.

SUMMARY

This chapter was about how to select and use the more common data-gathering methods. It described the processes and tools for conducting interviews, group sessions, and observations to discover whether or not action is warranted and if a change has occurred. To decide what data-gathering methods to use (always use at least two), do the following:

1. Decide on the purpose of your measurement effort. Is it to uncover needs, track progress, or measure change?

2. Identify where the information is. Is it in people's heads or in documents?

3. Identify who else might be collecting the information you could use.

4. Think about how much money and time you have and the people you have access to. How might you gain access to those who have the data you want?

5. Review the possible ways to obtain the data (see Tool 10.1).

6. Select one primary way and one or two secondary ways to corroborate your findings. The more you rely on one method, the greater the burden you put on that method. You can rarely be certain when you base your decisions on one source from one method.

WHERE TO LEARN MORE

Audrey, J. *Finding Out: Conducting and Evaluating Social Research* (New York: Wadsworth, 1989).

Flanders, N. A. *Analyzing Teaching Behavior* (Reading, MA: Addison-Wesley, 1970). Mr. Flanders has written a number of books and articles on the subject of measuring teacher interactions with students. However, it was his development of methods to code verbal and non-verbal exchanges that allows us greater accuracy in evaluating behavior.

Hale, J. *Performance-Based Certification: How to Design a Valid, Defensible, Cost-Effective Program* (San Francisco, CA: Jossey-Bass, 2000). See Chapter 3 on sampling and data-gathering techniques when doing a job or task analysis.

Johann, B. *Redesigning Work Processes* (San Francisco, CA: Jossey-Bass, 1995).

The Memory Jogger and other publications by GOAl/QPC. See www. goalqpc.com

Westgaard, O. "Measuring Performance," *Performance and Instruction,* Fall 1985 (Washington, DC: ISPI).

Westgaard, O. *Tests That Work* (San Francisco, CA: Jossey-Bass, 1998). See the section on how to create surveys.

Any of the publications from Sage on social research.

NOTES

1. Delphi studies are not included because they are designed to forecast needs and trends, not to measure deficiencies or changes. They are effective at gaining consensus about an issue, allow people to rate their confidence and the importance of a variable, are ineffective at measuring change, are excellent at controlling group bias, and can be done on a Web page, but are never live or in real time. It is important to maintain the anonymity of the participants.

2. Affinity diagrams are not included because they are not done for measurement purposes but are used to identify and organize variables. They are good for helping a group surface issues or variables, good for generating a large number of issues or variables and then organizing them, designed to encourage creative thinking and break down communication barriers, not effective for measuring change, and meant to be done live and in-person with everyone in the same room at the same time. Here are the steps: (1) ask a question, for example, "What's wrong in this situation?"; (2) the individual writes as many answers as possible, putting each one on a separate "sticky" note; (3) post all notes on a common surface; (4) have the participants group similar responses together; and (5) discuss the results and how to use them.

3. Flanagan, J. C. The Critical-Incident Technique, *Psychological Bulletin*, 51, July, 1954, pp. 327–58, American Psychological Association, 750 First Street, NE, Washington, DC 20002–4242.

4. Greenbaum, T. L. *The Practical Handbook and Guide to Focus Group Research* (Lexington, MA: Lexington Books/D.C. Heath & Company, 1987).

5. Hayes, T. J. *Focus Group Interviews: A Reader* (2nd ed.) (Chicago, IL: American Management Association, 1989).

6. Delbecq, A. L., and Van de Ven, A. H. *Group Techniques for Program Planning: A Guide to Nominal Group and Delphi Processes* (Glenview, IL: Scott Foresman, 1975). This is the seminal research on these methods. It is also excellent reading.

7. Toseland, R. W., Rivas, R. F., and Chapman, D. "An Evaluation of Decision Making Methods in Task Groups," *Social Work,* July-August, 1984, pp. 339–346 (National Association of Social Workers, Inc.).

8. Horace Mann-Lincoln Institute of School Experimentation, *How to Construct a Sociogram.* New York: Bureau of Publications, Teachers College, Columbia University, 1947. If you want to learn more about sociograms, check out http://maxweber.hunter.cuny.edu/pub/eres/EDSPC715_MCINTYRE/Sociogram.html or http://miavx1.muohio.edu/~edp201/sociometryfiles/SOCIO_INTRODUCTION.HTMLX

Chapter 11

How to Analyze Data Using Descriptive Statistics

The interviews with managers went well, but it wasn't clear how to analyze the data. The survey data was back; now the challenge was how to analyze it. The results from five focus groups were piled up. Making sense of it seemed very time-consuming.

*T*his chapter is about the mechanics of analyzing the data you have obtained when (1) measuring what the current state is, (2) comparing what you learn to some standard or expectation, (3) deciding whether a gap exists that warrants action, and (4) measuring what changed as a result of some intervention. The chapter includes guidelines and tools about the statistical side of measurement; however, the information is designed to make you a smart user of measurement tools, not a statistician. Once you have the data, the next step is to analyze it. Analysis involves manipulation to make sense of the data. How you manipulate the data depends on whether or not it is qualitative or quantitative in form.

QUANTITATIVE AND QUALITATIVE DATA

Quantitative data are counts, times, weights, and rankings. They can be expressed in whole numbers, fractions, decimal points, or percentages.

227

Qualitative data are

- Concepts, ideas, opinions, conclusions, preferences, and so on that are expressed orally or in writing through words, phrases, stories, or narrative passages
- Qualitative attributes such as balance, harmony, line, symmetry, and so forth that are expressed through the visual, graphic, musical, and performing arts

Most of the qualitative data we get in our work comes from open interviews, comment sections of surveys, critical-incident questions, focus group and nominal group sessions, and observations. One of the biggest challenges is what to do with the information obtained when people agree to be interviewed or observed, or to participate in a group discussion. The analysis involves:

- Identifying the major and recurring opinions or concepts by listening for the topics and descriptive words used
- Judging how strongly people feel about the opinion or concept by the amount of energy contained in the oral expression or the adjectives attached to it
- Identifying patterns and frequencies by noting how often a person mentions an opinion or concept and how many other people mention it, whether they use the same language or synonyms

Once you have identified the main themes, topics, points, and so forth, the next step is to make the data quantitative. You do this by

- Converting the data to counts, such as how many times an opinion was mentioned and by how many people and how many different opinions were mentioned
- Converting the data to weights or ranks by asking people to sort, weigh, and rank their own and others' opinions or ideas

Whenever possible, the goal is to convert qualitative data to quantitative data so you can apply statistical analysis techniques.

Tool 11.1 explains how to analyze qualitative data derived from open interviews, focus groups, and other methods.

TOOL 11.1. HOW TO ANALYZE QUALITATIVE DATA

1. Decide in advance what you want to learn. This will help you sort, group, and classify the data later. If the data are from open interviews or focus groups, go back to your plan.

2. Put a team together (preferably the people who helped develop your plan and the questions) to help you classify the data.

3. Examine the responses for each question or subject area from each person or each group, one at a time.

4. As a team, identify the key points, opinions, and preferences that were shared by the first person or group.

5. Note any adjectives that indicate a positive or negative feeling about the opinion or point. Pay particular attention to absolutes, such as "must," "always," or "every time," as this is an indication of how open the individual or group is to differing opinions.

6. Next, identify themes by looking for points that the individual or the group made by repeating, restating, paraphrasing, or using synonyms.

7. The themes might serve as labels under which you can sort or classify the responses from subsequent individuals and groups.

8. If the themes are insufficient, come up with a set of labels under which you can place or classify the key points and themes.

9. Create a table with the labels as headings so you can count how frequently a key point is made. Start by entering those from the first person or group you studied.

10. Repeat Steps 4 through 6 for every individual and group. Classify each subsequent person's or group's answers according to the labels you created on the table. If necessary, add new classifications.

11. Show how frequently the points were made or opinions were expressed by putting hash marks in the column under the appropriate label.

12. The total number of key points or opinions generated is a measure of the scope of the issue and the diversity of opinions.

13. The total number of times a particular point or opinion was mentioned is a measure of how alike or cohesive the people are on an issue.

There are two types of statistical analysis, descriptive and inferential. This chapter focuses on the descriptive techniques shown in Table 11.1.

Descriptive statistics are the most frequently used methods for analyzing data because they are relatively easy to calculate and provide a sufficient level of meaning. Table 11.2 shows the descriptive treatments used to analyze data derived from various data-gathering methods.

Table 11.1. Types of Descriptive Data Analysis

- Frequency counts
- Percentages
- Averages (mean, mode, median)
- Standard deviation
- The weighing or ranking of variables

Table 11.2. Common Statistical Treatment

Data-Gathering Technique	Descriptive Analysis
Data derived from group sessions	
Focus groups	Frequency and weight of a theme
Nominal groups	Mean, standard deviation
Interview methods	
Open	Frequency of a theme
Structured	Mean, standard deviation
Critical-incident	Frequency of a theme
Sociogram	Number and pattern
Questionnaires and surveys	Mean, standard deviation
Observations	
Direct observations	Frequency and time
Flanders Interaction Analysis	Frequency
Document Searches	
Work samples	Frequency, percentage
Pre- and post-production reports	Frequency, mean, standard deviation
Activity logs	Frequency of a theme
Performance checklists	Mean, frequency

Counts, Percentages, and Averages

The most common method is counting and then comparing the total count to a standard, historical number or expectation. For example you (1) determine how many occurrences there are in the beginning and compare that number to some standard to see whether there is a need for action and (2) then count the number of occurrences after you do something and compare that number to the previous one to see if there was a change. Counts are often transformed into percentages and averages. Some examples are

- *Test scores*—320 people took the test, this is 20 percent fewer than last year. 205 or 64 percent passed. Last year 68 percent passed. The overall average score was 78, two points less than last year.

- *Quantity and time*—there were 3,500 work tickets this year. This number has gone up 1,000 percent in the last twelve months. 1,400 or 40 percent of the tickets this year involved painting, and the average time reported to do a paint job was forty-two hours. This time has stayed the same over the last twelve months.

- *Ratings or reactions*—three hundred people completed 360° evaluations on their bosses. This is a 20 percent increase over last year. The 360° evaluations used the same ten-point scale as previous years. 250 people or 83 percent rated their boss at 7.5 or above on honesty, yet the overall average rating for honesty was 6.9. This average has gone down. Last year it was 7.2.

You calculate the *average* by adding up a set of numbers to find the total and then dividing the total by the quantity of numbers in the set. However, averages by themselves don't always give you a complete picture. For example, assume you want to show that as a result of your intervention the time to do a task went down on average 20 percent or is now forty-five minutes, with no loss of accuracy. Precision comes into play in the meaning of forty-five minutes. It could mean people's actual time on average falls somewhere between thirty-five and fifty-five minutes (45 minutes ± 10 minutes), or forty to fifty minutes (45 minutes ± 5 minutes), or forty-three to forty-seven minutes (45 minutes ± 2 minutes). The need to better understand what is or is not within the realm of "average" or the "norm" is one of the reasons why statisticians developed four conventions for interpreting averages:

- *Mean*—the arithmetic average (Statisticians use these symbols to represent the mean: $\bar{x}$ or μ (mu).)

- *Mode*—the most frequent value

- *Median*—the mid-point at which there is an equal number of values above and below

- *Standard deviation*—a number that when added or subtracted from the mean indicates when values are no longer within normal range.[1] Statisticians use the symbol *s* to represent the standard deviation.

Standard Deviation (s) and Weighing and Ranking of Variables

Statisticians learned that there comes a point when a value is different from the norm—or outside of what can be considered average. Statisticians refer to that point as being one standard deviation either above or below the mean. They also were able to prove there are other points at which a value is even more different and they refer to these as two and three standard deviations from the mean. They refer to values that are one or more standard deviations above or below the mean as being statistically significant. What statisticians have proven is that, for normal populations, about 34 percent of all values drawn at random will fall between the mean and one standard deviation above it and another 34 percent will fall between the mean and one standard deviation below it (see Figure 11.1).

Figure 11.1. The Normal Curve

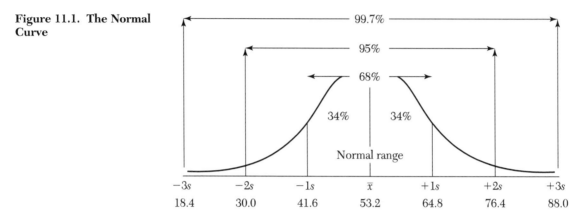

In a normal population, about 68 percent (68.26 percent to be exact) of all values drawn at random are within one standard deviation of the mean or are within normal range. About 95 percent of all values will fall within two standard deviations of the mean and 99.7 percent will fall within three standard deviations. You use a calculator or software to determine the standard deviation for your situation. You then add or subtract the standard deviation to or from the mean to find those values that lie outside of the normal range.

HOW TO USE THE STANDARD DEVIATION TO DETERMINE STATISTICAL SIGNIFICANCE

If the mean is 29.5 and the standard deviation is 9.89, then anything between 39.39 (29.5 + 9.89) and 19.61 (29.5 − 9.89) is considered to be normal or not significantly different. For a value to be considered "different" or significant it would have to be 39.40 or greater or 19.60 or less. In our example:

- 42.98 or greater is two standard deviations above the mean
  (29.5 + 9.89 + 9.89 = 42.98)

- 9.92 or less is two standard deviations below the mean
  (29.5 − 9.89 − 9.89 = 9.92)

- 52.87 or greater is three standard deviations above the mean (29.5 + 9.89 + 9.89 + 9.89 = 52.87)
- .03 or less is three standard deviations below the mean (29.5 − 9.89 − 9.89 − 9.89 = .03)

Here is an example of the process using test scores. You would calculate the mean and standard deviation to determine if any scores were significantly different. In this example, all of the scores are within normal range (see Table 11.3).

Table 11.3. Test Scores

Ninety-one people took this test. Their scores fall as shown below.

Score		Quantity	
100.		0	
99.		0	+1 standard deviation (+12.79 above the mean of 86)
98.	\	1	
97.		0	
96.	\\	2	
95.		0	
94.	\\\	3	
93.	\\	2	
92.	\\\\ \	6	
91.	\\\\	5	
90.	\\\\ \\\	8	
89.	\\\\ \\\\	9	
87.	\\\\ \\\\	9	median (half of the scores are above 87 and half below)
86.	\\\\ \\\\ \\	12	mode (twelve people received the score of 86); mean is 86
85.	\\\\ \	6	
84.	\\\\ \\\	8	
83.	\\\\	5	
82.	\\\	3	
81.	\\\\	4	
80.		0	
79.	\\	2	
78.	\	1	
77.		0	
76.	\	1	
75.		0	
74.		0	
73.		0	
72.		0	
71.		0	−1 standard deviation (−12.79 below the mean of 86)
Total		91	

The median and mode help you determine how well the mean reflects the average. The mean may be the statistical average, but it may not be a true representation of how values cluster or fall along the range of possibilities. You use the standard deviation to identify values that are outside the normal range. Collectively the mean, mode, median, and standard deviation give you a better understanding of the data and help you identify variables that are perhaps worthy of further investigation or a different consideration. Tool 11.2 has rules for analyzing counts that are fundamental to descriptive statistics.

TOOL 11.2. RULES FOR ANALYZING COUNTS

Purpose

The most frequently used methods to analyze data are descriptive statistics, specifically frequency, total, mean, median, mode, standard deviation, percentage, and squaring deviations. These statistics are useful for identifying preferences and significance. They also provide the basis for other inferential treatments.

Steps

1. Count how many numbers or values there are in the set of data you wish to analyze.
2. Add the values of the data in the set to find the total value.
3. Divide the total value (from Step 2) by the count (from Step 1) to find the numerical average or *mean*.
4. Put the numbers or values in some order (highest to lowest, for example) and identify which if any value was selected more often than others. The value that was chosen most often is the *mode*.
5. Identify that value where there are an equal number of values above it and below it. This value is the *median*.
6. Use a statistical calculator or software and calculate the *standard deviation*. Generally, the higher the standard deviation, the less agreement there is on the question or issue you are asking about; therefore, it will be harder to generalize or make definitive statements about the results.
7. Add the standard deviation (from Step 6) to the mean (from Step 3). Values above this number are one standard deviation above the mean and are statistically significant.
8. Subtract the standard deviation (from Step 6) from the mean (from Step 3). Values less than this are one standard deviation below the mean and are statistically significant.
9. To calculate a percentage:
   - Decide on the sub-set of the data you are interested in, for example, only those people who chose a particular response to a specific question or only those who returned a survey.

- Count or identify the value of the sub-set data.
- Identify what makes up the total set, for example, all of the people who responded to the question or all those who were sent the survey.
- Count or identify the value of the total data set.
- Divide the sub-set data value by the total data set value to find the percentage.

10. To square a value, such as a standard deviation, multiply the value by itself (4^2 is 4×4 or 16).

SURVEYS

Surveys are one of the more common data-gathering methods. You analyze the results by determining:

- Percentage of response
- Mean and standard deviation for each question
- Mean and standard deviation for all of the questions

You use the answers to identify significant responses.

MANAGERS' TIME

A forced-choice survey was sent to managers asking them to identify how frequently they performed specific tasks and to rate the importance of those tasks. Table 11.4 is an excerpt from that survey. What follows is a detailed analysis of the data using the mean, median, mode, and standard deviation.

		Frequency	*Importance*	*Total*
		1 = Rarely	1 = Unimportant	Sum of
		2 = Monthly	2 = Of Minor	Frequency
		3 = Weekly	Importance	and
		4 = Daily	3 = Important	Importance
		5 = Hourly	4 = Very	
			Important	
			5 = Crucial	
Number surveyed 89; number returned 47 or 53 percent				
Manager Tasks	*Skill Set*	*Frequency*	*Importance*	*Total*
1. Identify e-mails that need to be forwarded to employees so they are aware of the information.	ADM	4.52	4.37	8.89

Table 11.4. Survey of Managers' Tasks

Table 11.4. (*Continued*)

Manager Tasks	Skill Set	Frequency	Importance	Total
2. Review incoming e-mail to prioritize tasks, appointments, training, and so on.	ADM	4.74	4.09	8.83
3. Check calendar to prioritize daily tasks.	ADM	4.21	4.26	8.47
4. Review attendance (check for phone messages) to account for all employees.	ADM	4.11	4.33	8.44
5. Run management reports to track employee phone statistics and ensure productivity.	ADM	4.15	4.20	8.35
6. Review queries to ensure client requests are completed.	ADM	3.84	4.14	7.98
7. Maintain required records for compliance audits.	ADM	3.54	4.37	7.91
8. Review incentive reports to identify possible missing data and ensure accuracy.	ADM	3.22	4.59	7.80
9. Review Quality Assessment Report to identify training opportunities and team member best practices and provide individual and team results to appropriate people.	ADM	2.79	4.30	7.09
10. Review timesheets on a bi-monthly basis for payroll.	ADM	2.80	4.24	7.04
11. Complete employee action forms for terminations, leaves of absence, promotions, changes to job codes, and salary adjustments.	ADM	2.37	4.54	6.92
12. Update all records related to staffing changes.	ADM	2.65	3.91	6.57
13. Review the team lead report to understand their activity and discover training opportunities.	ADM	2.84	3.72	6.56
14. Respond to e-mails from various sources (for example, employees, peers, other departments) that require a response with information to meet the needs of the sender.	ADM	4.53	4.18	8.71
15. Read e-mails to get updated on things such as local events, requests, new corporate initiatives, and training.	ADM	4.61	3.94	8.54
Totals		54.93	63.15	118.08
Mean of Means (**0**)		3.66	4.21	7.87
Median (Middle Point)		3.84	4.24	7.98
Mode (Most Frequent)		0	4.37	0
Standard Deviation (*s*)		.82	.23	.87

Here is what you can learn by analyzing the survey data shown in the example above:

- Eighty-nine managers (the total population) were sent the survey and forty-seven returned it for a return rate of 53 percent (47 divided by 89 is .528 or 53 percent).

- The tasks appear to have been classified by a skill set. All of the tasks in the sample are classified as administrative tasks (ADM). In the complete survey, other tasks fell under different classifications, for example, some were classified as demonstrating leadership, providing feedback, and so forth.

- By reading the columns labeled Frequency and Importance from top to bottom, you see the forty-seven managers' mean (average) rating of every question.

- Frequency is rated on a five-point scale from 1 = rarely to 5 = hourly.

- Importance is rated on a five-point scale from 1 = unimportant to 5 = crucial.

- At the bottom you see the mean of means (the average of all mean values) for all the questions and the mode, median, or standard deviation.

- By reading left to right you can see the mean value for frequency and importance for each question and sum value of the frequency plus importance for every question.

- By reading the column labeled Frequency from top to bottom, you can:

  - Add up the average rankings in the sample of fifteen questions to get a total, or 54.93

  - Calculate the total mean (average) frequency rating by dividing the total score of 54.93 by 15 (the number of questions in the example) to get the arithmetic average, or 3.66

  - Find the median (mid-point) by putting the scores in sequence from lowest to highest, locating the middle score (or the eighth score in this example), as there are seven scores higher and seven lower than the median of 3.84

  - Determine there is no mode because no two or more questions received the same ranking

  - With the help of a calculator determine standard deviation (.82) to identify which rankings are outside the normal range

- Tasks in questions having a ranking of 4.48 (3.66 + .82 = 4.48) are done more frequently than normal. This means that tasks 1, 2, 14, and 15 (identify e-mails, review e-mail to set priorities, respond to e-mail, and read e-mail to get updates) are done significantly more frequently than the other tasks on the list.

- Tasks with a value of 2.84 (3.66 – .82 = 2.84) are done significantly less frequently, so tasks 9, 10, 11, 12 (review quality assessment reports and timesheets, complete employee action forms, and update records related to staffing changes) are done significantly less often.

- However, the frequency of tasks 3, 4, 5, 6, 7, 8, and 13 is not outside the normal range.

- You use this information to help you decide what tasks might be better supported through job aids because they are done so infrequently.

- If you do the same type of analysis to Importance, you find that:

  - The total is 63.15, the mean is 4.21, the median is 4.24, the mode is 4.37, and the standard deviation is .23

  - The standard deviation (.23) is smaller than that for frequency (.82), which means there is more agreement on what is important compared to what they believe they do more or less frequently

  - The important tasks that are significant (those whose values are greater than 4.21 + .23 or 4.44) are items 8 (review incentive report) and 11 (complete employee action forms)

  - You can use the information to help you decide how to best assure managers are proficient at the important tasks

Assume you want to know what tasks are done frequently and are important, as you think this information will help you decide what interventions are required to support managers. You total the scores for each question and then calculate the overall score for frequency and importance, which is 118.08, and by dividing that number by 15 (the number of questions in the example) you obtain an overall mean of 7.87.

Again, you determine the median score by putting the scores in sequence from lowest to highest, finding the middle score (8 or 7.98), as there are seven scores higher and lower than this value. Again, no two scores are the same, so there is no value that is the mode.

The standard deviation is .87, so tasks with a total value of 8.75 (7.88 + .87) or higher are done significantly more frequently and are more important than the other tasks. In this case these are task 1 (identify e-mails that need to be forwarded) and 2 (review incoming e-mail to prioritize tasks). Those with a value of 7.07 or below are done less frequently and are less important. They are 13, 12, 11, and 10 (review team leader reports, update records of staffing changes, complete employee action forms, and review timesheets).

You use this information to help you decide if support tools or training are appropriate methods of preparing managers to do these tasks.

HR GENERALIST

The corporation wanted to do job analysis to identify the roles, responsibilities, and competencies required of HR generalists. One part of the project was a survey that was sent to generalists and managers. One of the questions was about how the generalists allocated their time. The analysis of one question is shown in Table 11.5.

The overall mean is 14.3 with a standard deviation of 10.2. Next look for those values that are one or more standard deviations above or below the mean, or those whose values are greater than 24.5 (14.3 + 10.2 = 24.5) and less than 4.7 (14.3 − 10.2 = 4.7). Two activities stand out: (1) employee relations is significantly above the average (mean of 33.8) and (2) employee health and safety is significantly below average (3.4). This indicates that overall the generalists spend a lot of time on employee relations issues and less on employee health and safety. Yet, when they compare the average time in employee relations, they see that some generalists spend a lot more time than others. The same is true for recruiting/

Table 11.5. Job Responsibilities— Generalists

Responsibility	Respondents									Total	Mean	Std Dev
	1	2	3	4	5	6	7	8	9			
Organizational Effectiveness	20	5	10	15	–	30	20	10	5	115	14.4	8.6
Employee Relations	40	45	20	50	–	30	30	10	45	270	33.8	13.8
Recruiting/ Staffing	5	20	0	10	15	10	25	70	12	167	18.6	20.7
Compensation	15	15	50	10	20	10	5	3	14	142	15.8	13.9
Training	10	10	10	5	5	5	10	2	17	74	8.2	4.5
Benefits	5	3	10	7	5	10	5	5	5	55	6.1	2.4
Employee Health and Safety	5	1	0	3	10	5	5	0	2	31	3.4	3.2
Other	–	1	–	–	45	–	–	–	–	–	–	
Total											14.3	10.2

staffing and compensation. This variance is reflected in the size of the standard deviation for employee relations (13.8). The standard deviation for staffing and recruiting is even higher (20.7). The variance in how they spend their time might be because some work at corporate and others in remote manufacturing plants. For example, respondent #3 spends 50 percent of his or her time on compensation, while none of the others spend more than 20 percent of their time on this same task. The conclusion was that the jobs, even though they have the same title, were not comparable as currently defined.

The same question was asked of eighteen HR managers. Their responses are shown in Table 11.6. The overall mean was 16.1 with a standard deviation of 10.64. They decided that this meant the managers think HR generalists spend most of their time doing tasks related to employee relations and benefits (values above 16.1 + 10.64 or 26.74) and the least time in health and safety (16.1 – 10.64 or 5.46). It also seemed that the managers were not totally in agreement about where generalists spend their time based on the amount of variance, particularly in the areas of recruiting, organizational effectiveness, and employee relations. The analysis showed that much more information was needed to fully understand what HR generalists do and must be proficient in.

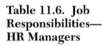

Table 11.6. Job Responsibilities— HR Managers

Resp	*Respondents*																		*Mean*	*Std Dev*
	1	2	3	4	5	6	7	8	9	10	11	12	13	14	15	16	17	18		
OE	10	10	15	20	5	30	20	5	25	20	20	15	10	5	30	0	60	10	17.6	14
ER	35	60	35	20	45	30	20	30	30	50	40	60	50	50	30	20	25	50	37.8	13.3
RS	20	10	20	15	5	10	10	5	20	0	13	5	5	20	10	70	10	5	14	15.3
C	20	10	10	20	5	10	5	10	5	10	10	10	5	10	5	10	25	5	10.7	6
T	10	5	5	15	20	10	25	10	10	5	14	7	10	10	5	0	10	10	10	5.9
B	5	5	5	5	10	5	5	5	5	0	1	2	15	3	15	0	0	15	18	5
HS	8	0	10	5	10	5	5	5	5	0	2	1	5	2	5	0	10	5	4.6	3.3
																		Total	16.1	10.64

Key: OE = organization effectiveness; ER = employee relations; RS = recruiting and staffing; C = compensation; T = training; B = benefits; HS = health and safety

Tool 11.3 has the rules for analyzing survey results.

TOOL 11.3. RULES FOR ANALYZING DATA DERIVED FROM SURVEYS AND QUESTIONNAIRES

Purpose

Surveys and questionnaires are done because they are efficient at reaching a wide audience. They are used to identify opinions, preferences, feeling states, and demographic data such as age, employment role, experience, habits, hobbies, and so forth. The data are analyzed to see whether a hypothesis proved true and to validate the results from other efforts.

How to Analyze the Results

1. If appropriate, group the data according to some characteristic of the people who responded (sales or service, field or corporate, seniority, role, or other). This will allow you to determine whether responses differ based on some characteristic of the group.

2. For each group, count the number of times a response was selected for each question.

3. Calculate the percentage of times a response was chosen (see Tool 11.2).

4. Calculate the mean and standard deviation (see Tool 11.2).

5. Note those responses that are significant.

6. If you want to see whether subgroup (Step 1) responses correlate with each other, apply the Spearman rho treatment (see Tool 12.2 in the next chapter).

7. If you want to find out if the results correlate with or are similar to data derived from other sources, apply the Spearman rho or the chi-square treatments (see Tools 12.2 and 12.3 in the next chapter).

NOMINAL GROUP DATA

Nominal group data is qualitative data that can be converted to quantitative data. The process for analysis consists of calculating the mean and standard deviation of the points assigned to various responses. You can also analyze the responses qualitatively by classifying them by theme.

INTERIOR DESIGN STUDY

An occupational analysis of interior design was done. The study consisted of sixteen nominal group sessions. Fourteen of the sessions were with practitioners, one with academics, and one with employers. In all of the sessions, a representative sample was used. Local leaders nominated the participants. At each nominal group session, participants were asked the same four questions. The response from one group to one question is shown in Table 11.7.

The responses that received points are listed from most to the fewest points. The results were analyzed qualitatively and quantitatively. The first

Table 11.7. Responses to Nominal Group Question

Responses are sorted by order of importance, based on the points awarded; only those responses receiving votes are listed.

#	*What do professional interior designers do that other professionals who contribute to the environment do not typically do?*	Class	PTS
21	Use existing conditions to create a new environment	SD	15
7	Listen	SC	12
9	Add impact to productivity and bottom line	AUP	12
1	More intimate relationship with client	AUO	10
16	Serve as coordinator for large groups of unrelated professionals	ABI	10
25	Concentrate on ergonomics and human dimension issues	KHE	10
11	Interpret the client's personality	SDN	10
12	Psychology of enclosed environment	KPS	9
20	Solve problems created by other professionals	STP	7
24	Deal with individual preferences	AU	7
3	They "give a damn"	AU	5
22	Accept more responsibility for outcomes	AIN	4
28	Relates to space: traffic pattern and spatial perception	KPS	3
29	Ask the right questions	SDN	3
30	Humanize using scale and proportion	KPS	3
33	Can make client succeed or fail	AUP	1
31	Details, details, details	AOD	1
	Mean		7.18
	Standard deviation		4.23
	Total of mean and standard deviation (to identify responses that are statistically significant, that is, exceed this total)		11.41

level of analysis was qualitative. Each response was classified and assigned a code. The first letter indicates whether the response is about knowledge (K), skill (S), or attribute (A). The second and third letters further define the knowledge, skill, or attribute. Table 11.8 is an example of how responses were classified.

Table 11.8. Classification of Qualitative Data

Knowledge	*Skill*	*Attribute*
KH—Knows local and national safety requirements **KHC**—Knows the codes and regulations related to space, layout, and so forth	**SB**—Skilled in business management practices **SBB**—Skilled at working within budget	**AU**—User oriented **AUA**—Acts as an advocate, assures the user's needs are represented

The second level of analysis was to determine the mean and standard deviation for the points assigned to each response. Three responses received more than 11.41 points (7.18 + 4.23), making them statistically significant. Two responses received fewer than 2.95 points (7.18 − 4.23), making them relatively insignificant. According to this group, the main attributes that distinguish interior designers from other professions were that they:

- Use existing conditions to create a new environment
- Listen
- Add impact to productivity and the bottom line

This type of analysis was done for every question and for every group. Then the practitioner's answers were compiled and compared to those of the academics and employers. The results of the nominal group sessions were used to develop a survey that was sent to a random stratified sample of two thousand interior designers and their employers. The results from the nominal group sessions and the survey were used to develop a national certification exam.

Tool 11.4 has the rules for analyzing the results derived from using the Nominal Group Technique.

TOOL 11.4. ANALYZING NOMINAL GROUP DATA

Purpose

The Nominal Group Technique was developed to elicit the opinions and preferences of groups, while controlling bias introduced by strong personalities. The product of the sessions is a list of ideas, attributes, and characteristics, in rank order.

How to Analyze the Results

1. List all of the responses that received points on a worksheet similar to the worksheet at the end of this tool.

2. If you put the numbers into a spreadsheet, you can automatically sort the responses in a descending order beginning with those that received the most points.

3. Total all of the points and compute the mean (arithmetic average) (see Tool 11.2).

4. Determine the standard deviation using a calculator or software.

5. Identify the responses that are one or more standard deviation above the mean. These are the significant responses (see Tool 11.2).

6. You may also want to consider responses above average (higher than the mean).

7. Note on the worksheet the mean, standard deviation, and where those values fall on the list of responses.

8. If you classify the responses, put the classification next to each response (see Tool 11.1).

#	Response	Classification	Points Assigned
1	Description		
2	Description		
3	Etc.		

	Total
	Mean
	Standard Deviation

CRITICAL-INCIDENT QUESTIONS

Critical-incident questions are used in conjunction with surveys and other interview questions. The analysis involves identifying the themes and counting the number of people who mention the same theme. If you interview more than twelve people, you can determine the mean and standard deviation to see if any themes are significant.

INDEPENDENT SALES REPRESENTATIVES

A study was done to find out what was expected of independent sales representatives. The study consisted of phone interviews with facility managers and interior designers. The interview format consisted on open-ended questions and two critical-incident questions. The analysis consisted of

- Grouping the responses by the two different audiences, facility managers and designers
- Listing all of the responses given by everyone in each group
- Combining similar responses

Table 11.9 shows the responses from facility managers. The analysis of the critical-incident questions was similar. These questions asked the facility managers to limit their response to key attributes only. In this case, all of the responses given were included. Table 11.10 shows the responses to the first critical-incident question.

Table 11.9. Responses from Facility Managers

When asked why they use (or would use) the services of an independent sales representative and what using one did for them, the respondents gave the following reasons.

Independent sales reps:

- Represent products in a wider price range (moderate to high) and represent local and national manufacturers.
- Bring a larger perspective on a variety of products; they have access to resources that cross portfolios.
- Are experienced as neutral and open. They know my business and problems; dealers don't. They are less inclined to come in with a predetermined solution. They bring alternatives, alternative solutions.
- Are the only way I have of finding the products that meet my requirements.
- Know more about products than dealers. They know what is new and what will be late.
- Follow through on problems. They are my connection to the manufacturer.

Table 11.10. Responses to the First Critical-Incident Question

The attributes mentioned that make an independent sales representative outstanding are

- Being honest. They do not try to sell just to sell, but suggest viable alternatives; they do what they say they'll do, they are consistent.
- Initiating action. They follow through to see if a problem was corrected.

Table 11.10. (*Continued*)

- Making an extra effort. They place calls to the factory to check on delivery status; they bring ideas to me; they pay attention even when I'm not buying.

- Being responsive. They get back to me right away, check product availability and order status, follow up, are supportive, and don't point blame but focus on finding a solution.

- Knowing the product (what they represent and the competition's) and listening to my needs.

- Knowing me, my business, the industry. Follows through and initiates when there's a need; works well with my people not just with me; bothers to ask a lot of questions to understand my needs; doesn't waste my time; connects enough but not too much.

- Taking the time to understand the business. Finding out what we're about so they can make suggestions and help solve problems in advance.

- Taking the time to build a strong personal relationship. They are involved; they learn your business needs instead of buying you lunch or bringing you presents; they talk in conversational ways, they don't follow a script.

- Bringing furniture whose specs are compatible when you give them a pre-engineered solution.

The analysis consisted of simply reporting the responses on a list. If more people had been interviewed, making the list unwieldy, the analysis might have consisted of a listing of shorter summary headings and notes about how often each one was given.

Tool 11.5 has the rules for analyzing data derived from the critical-incident technique and a template for recording your findings.

TOOL 11.5. ANALYZING CRITICAL-INCIDENT DATA

Purpose

The critical-incident technique was developed to identify characteristics (skills, knowledge, accomplishments) that distinguish high performers from others. It can be used with individuals and with groups.

How to Analyze the Results

The purpose of the analysis is to determine the degree to which (1) the attributes generated by the group cluster around certain themes or fall into similar classes of things and (2) whether the people who were interviewed agree on the attributes.

1. Begin by recording all of the attributes or characteristics given in a listing or a table format such as the sample below. Look for similarities and combine responses as appropriate.

2. Classify and group the attributes by theme.

3. Count how many people mentioned the same attributes or similar characteristics.

4. Count how many different attributes were mentioned.

5. If the list is sufficiently long, calculate the mean (average x attributes mentioned) and the standard deviation. This will tell which attributes the group agrees on (see Tool 11.2)

#	Attributes or Characteristics Mentioned	How Often Mentioned
1	Description	Put counts here
2	Description	Put counts here
3	Etc.	Put counts here
	Total	
	Mean	
	Standard Deviation	

GROUP DYNAMICS

Techniques designed to measure group dynamics are analyzed by classifying the observed behaviors, counting the frequency of the behavior, and totaling the time spent on each behavior. Tool 11.6 has the rules for analyzing data derived from the Flanders Interaction Analysis technique.

TOOL 11.6. HOW TO ANALYZE FLANDERS INTERACTION ANALYSIS DATA

Purpose

The Flanders Interaction Analysis is a method of recording observation data that results in a map or chart of activities and movement within a physical space or communication between groups and individuals.

How to Analyze the Data

1. Count how frequently with each behavior occurred.
2. Determine the average amount of time consumed by each behavior (see Tool 11.2).
3. If appropriate, determine the standard deviation.
4. Identify those activities or times that are significantly different from the rest (see Tool 11.2).
5. Compare the results to a goal, expectation, or standard.

MISSTEPS

Here are some of the common mistakes people make:

1. They manipulate data after it is collected, perhaps by combining data sets to get a larger sample after the data have been collected.
2. They omit data to make the results look stronger, for example, omitting data from those respondents who answer all survey items by marking the middle position. This practice causes respondents who mark the extremes to have a stronger effect on the results.
3. They change the design once data collection has begun, which will invalidate the measurement. Piloting the method or instrument will allow you to make adjustments prior to data collection.
4. They apply techniques that are only appropriate for interval data to ordinal data. Most data used to evaluate training is ordinal, such as scales and forced-choice instruments. A lot of nominal data[2] is also used in the evaluation of training.

TIPS AND TECHNIQUES

Here are some suggestions for how to use descriptive statistics:

1. There are software packages especially designed to analyze survey data. Some of those packages can be used to distribute and analyze surveys on the Web and by e-mail.
2. Many spreadsheet programs will calculate means and standard deviations.
3. For smaller sets of data, use a calculator.
4. If you are going to do open interviews, keep the number low. It is very difficult to analyze great amounts of qualitative data.
5. Develop a plan for how you will analyze the data. Develop the data-collection tools and practice using them.

6. Put together a team to help you classify qualitative data and do the analysis.

7. Remember that meaning comes from comparisons. It is not enough to know costs, test scores, and so on without also knowing what the value was historically or before your intervention. It is by comparing that you can say something went up or down or became better.

SUMMARY

This chapter is about how to analyze data derived from interviews, group sessions, observations, and reviews of document or work samples. These methods produce qualitative and quantitative data that can be analyzed through the application of descriptive statistics. A difficult part of the analysis of qualitative data is classifying the information so it can be counted and compared. It is difficult because people use similar language to represent like and unlike attributes.

Descriptive statistics involve:

- Determining the frequency (how many times) a variable, such as a topic or attribute occurs

- Counting the number of people who mention the same variable, topic, or attribute

- Weighing or ranking the variable, topic, or attribute (if respondents were asked to weigh their or others' responses)

With this information, you can calculate the percentages, means, and standard deviations. The standard deviation is required to identify values that are out of normal range.

WHERE TO LEARN MORE

Blank, S. *Descriptive Statistics* (New York: Appleton-Century-Crofts, 1968).

Hale, J. A. *Performance Consultant's Fieldbook: Tools and Techniques to Improve Organizations and People* (San Francisco, CA: Jossey-Bass/Pfeiffer, 1998). Check out Chapter Three on costs, Chapter Six on the use of the scorecard, Chapter Seven on how to select interventions, and Chapters Eight and Nine on evaluation and measurement. The book has a number of tools for helping you select appropriate measures.

The Memory Jogger and other publications by GOAl/QPC. See http://www.goalqpc.com

NOTES

1. Standard deviation is a measure of the dispersion of a frequency distribution.
2. Nominal data are those where a number or a name is used to classify the data, such as Democrat or Republican; and male or female.

## Chapter 12

How to Analyze Data Using Inferential Statistics

The trainers' merit raises were partially determined by the overall average score they received on students' evaluations, but they didn't know how this data reconciled with student performance on the job. Tests were administered at the end of every course, but the company didn't know whether or not the scores predicted job performance. A question came up whether there was any correlation between the number of people who attended the mandated safety classes and the number of reported safety incidents. The person who did the safety training did not know how to find the answer. A training manager wanted to show the impact of the cross-cultural training curriculum, but did not know what to use for comparison.

*T*he focus of this chapter is on how to determine if there is a relationship between (1) what you did and people's performance; (2) what one group expects and another group expects; and (3) a change in one variable and a change in another variable.

Tool 12.1 is an if/then table for selecting a statistical treatment. It can be used to help you choose a statistical treatment based on what you want to accomplish.

Table 12.1 shows the common statistics used to manipulate data to determine whether a relationship exists.

TOOL 12.1. IF/THEN TABLE FOR DECIDING WHICH TYPE OF ANALYSIS TO USE

If You Want / Then Consider Using	Means, Standard Deviation	Rho Correlations	Chi Square χ^2	t-Test
To evaluate survey and test results	X			
To determine whether two different tests administered to the same group of employees tested the same thing	X			
To compare entry and exit accomplishments, that is, gain or growth in skill or knowledge				X
To compare scores from pre- and post-tests				X
To compare performance pre- and post-intervention				X
To determine how closely two sets of data are related		X		
To compare a set of data to what was expected			X	
To determine whether the results are normal or not	X			
To determine how individuals compare with others or the group as a whole	X			
To determine whether the data are a valid representation of the population	X			
To determine that the difference between groups is real, that is, that a difference exists and how significant that difference is				X
To determine whether a positive or negative relationship exists between two sets of scores		X		

Table 12.1 Types of Inferential Data Analysis

Inferential Statistics
Correlation Coefficient (Spearman Rho) Chi Square Goodness of Fit Two-Tailed *t* Tests

INFERENTIAL STATISTICS

Inferential statistics are analysis methods that allow you to make inferences about (1) data from two groups or (2) two sets of data from the same group. For example, management might complain that new hires are less capable. So you might pull test scores from previous years and compare them to those of recent new hires (data from two groups). Assuming the curriculum is the same, you would compare the scores to determine whether there has or has not been a change significant enough to warrant further analysis. Another example is to compare pre- and post-test scores from the same group of students to measure whether the learning was significant.

Inferential statistics involve formulas and the use of statistical tables to help you determine what the probability is that a value is significantly different or greater than chance. For people who are number challenged, the dilemmas are picking the right formula, applying it, and selecting the correct statistical table to interpret the results. Two of the more frequently used tables are in this chapter. There are some user-friendly references on statistics in the section "Where to Learn More."

Just like descriptive statistics, inferential statistics rely on a set of conventions to determine what values are and are not significant and how confident you can be in your conclusions. The two conventions are (1) degrees of freedom[1] and (2) level of significance (also called criterion levels). The level stands for the potential for error.

Degrees of freedom, shows up as "df" and $(n - 1)$ on statistical tables and means the sample size, less one $(n - 1)$. You subtract 1 from your sample size and then locate values on the table that are opposite that number. So if your sample size is 12, you go down the table to 11 and read across to find numbers relevant to 11. If the sample size is 90, you use the values opposite 89.

Levels of significance or criterion levels shows up on tables as column headings like .20, .10, .05, .01, and .001. The first value is the least certain, as .20 means you can expect to be wrong 20 percent of the time, .10 is 10 percent, .05 is 5 percent, .01 is 1 percent, and .001 is .1 percent. You select values in the column that matches your need for certainty.

Degrees of Freedom

If you want a specific value (like a total or mean), all but one in your sample can assume any value possible. Because once you choose all but one value, the last value is set. Here are two examples:

Example 1. You want to pick two hundred people to interview (a specified total) and you want one hundred to be male and one hundred female (specified totals). If you want fifty from HR and 150 from operations (specified totals), you might build a table like the one below (Table 12.2). In this example, you have two samples (sex and department). So the degree of freedom is 1 or $(n - 1)$.

Table 12.2. Interview Totals by Gender and Department

	50 from HR	150 from Operations	Totals
Males to be interviewed	20	80	100
Females to be interviewed	30	70	100
Total number to be interviewed	50	150	200

Once you pick a value for one of the samples (a gender and a department), all of the other values are decided. For example if you pick *twenty* males from HR, the only way you can get the rest of the distribution to meet your specified totals is to pick thirty females from HR, eighty males from operations, and seventy females from operations. Your greatest freedom was in selecting the first number, because after it was picked the remaining values were dictated. Similarly, if you pick thirty females from operations, all of the other numbers are determined for you as long as you keep the desired totals for gender and department.

Sample 2. If you wanted to interview one hundred people (specified total) and you wanted them to represent five different departments [(1) legal, (2) HR, (3) operations, (4) sales, and (5) customer service], you would have five groups and four degrees of freedom. You are relatively free to pick as many people as you want for any of the four groups, but once you decide on those numbers, the number for the last group will be decided for you to reach the total of one hundred. So in a sample of five you have four degrees of freedom.

Statistical Tables. Inferential statistics makes use of statistical tables that are based on the conventions of *df* and level of significance. The tables lead you to a value against which you compare the number you derived through some calculation. Your number must be higher than the number on the table for your result to be considered significant. Table 12.3 shows how you read a table. First, locate the correct degree of freedom and the appropriate level of significance. In the example, the sample size is nine and the criterion level is .01, that is you are willing to accept being wrong one percent of the time (one in a hundred times). In the column labeled df, you go down to 8 and across to the value in column .01.

Table 12.3. Table of Chi-Square Values

df (n − 1)	Criterion Levels	
	.01	.001
1	6.64	10.83
2	9.21	13.82
3	11.34	16.27
4	13.28	18.46
5	15.09	20.52
6	16.81	22.46
7	18.48	24.32
⑧	⟨20.09⟩	26.12
9	21.67	27.88
10	23.21	29.59

In this example, if the value you derive is less than 20.09, your results are probably not significant or greater than chance.

Because much of the evaluation done by trainers, HRD, and performance improvement specialists is based on small samples, this book only describes three inferential statistical treatments that are especially useful for comparisons of data from small samples:

- *Rho or correlation coefficient*—designed to measure if there is a relationship between two sets of data.[2,3]

- *Chi-square goodness of fit*—designed to measure if data from a small sample are different from a standard or expectation (chi-square is notated as χ^2)

- *Two-tailed t test*—designed to measure whether two sets of data are similar or different

CORRELATIONS

A correlation is a measure of relationship—the degree that one variable is influenced by another. The influence might be *positive,* that is, when a value goes in one direction the other value goes in the same direction. The influence may be *negative,* in that when the first value goes in one direction, the second goes in the opposite direction.

Correlations are particularly useful when it is difficult to prove cause and effect. To prove cause and effect, you have to be able to control other factors that might influence behaviors, results, and so forth. Correlations allow you to see if there is any relationship between training (or any other intervention) and other results, such as customer retention, profits, or faster product launches. For example, you might want to know whether there is any correlation between how well a new hire in customer service scores on a test given at the end of his or her training and

- Retention—how long the person stays with the firm only (captured by HR)
- Average call-handling times (captured by the call center)
- Technical errors (captured by quality assurance)
- The supervisor's level of confidence (to be captured by training using a short survey)

Your assumptions (technically called *hypotheses*) might be that people who score high on tests administered at the conclusion of the new hire training are more likely to stay with the firm longer, do well on other job-related tests, be more productive, make fewer errors, and earn the confidence of their managers faster.

Some other examples would be to measure the correlation between:

- Training of customer service representatives and the cost of service
- Implementation of new product diagnostic tools and product defects
- The amount of sales training and the retention of customers or the cost of sales
- The type of supervisory training and employee retention

Here are two common ways to determine whether or not there is a correlation:

1. Display the two variables on a scatter diagram or graph and see if a pattern emerges.
2. Calculate a Rho or correlation coefficient using a formula.

Scatter Diagram

Assume you want to see whether there is a correlation between end of training test scores and retention. Your hypothesis is that the higher people score on a test, the more likely they are to stay with the firm. First you would find people's test scores and then determine how long they stayed with the company. You would then plot the two variables (test scores and tenure on the job) on a graph (see Figure 12.1). On this graph, it appears that some people score well but leave in about eighteen months and others stay for thirty-six months or more. Two scores that seem to stand out are circled. The chart indicates that test scores are *not* a predictor of retention. The chart will not help you identify whether other variables affect retention and what those might be.

Figure 12.1. Correlation Between Test Scores and Retention

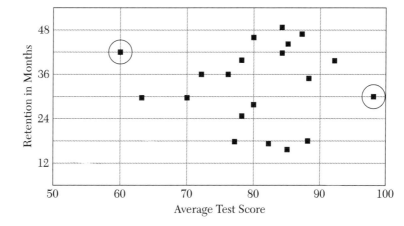

PROFESSIONAL AND MANAGEMENT DEVELOPMENT

Precision Instruments, Inc., implemented a certification program for all employees worldwide. Employees could go on-line to find performance criteria for almost every job in the company. Along with the criteria were assessments employees could use to determine their own readiness and level of proficiency. The assessments even directed them to possible programs they could sign up for to develop their skills. Most of the developmental programs were self-administered on-line. When employees felt they were ready to prove their proficiency, they would contact their boss. The boss would then conduct the formal assessment. Employees had to demonstrate they could apply the skills in the context of the job a minimum of six times to be certified. The program was started because of the belief that if people really knew what was expected, had a way to evaluate their performance, and could easily locate developmental resources, the company's financial performance would improve.

The time came to find out if there was any correlation between the number of people certified and the financial performance of the business. The director of training tracked the level of participation at sites in thirteen countries and correlated that with the cumulative average pre-tax profit of each worker at that site. The director of training plotted the number of people certified on the X (horizontal) axis against the reported average profitability on the Y (vertical) axis to get a picture on a spreadsheet. The program created a graph (see Figure 12.2) that shows how the level of participation compares to the pre-tax profit. Those offices with higher participation in the certification program tended to have higher pre-tax profit.

Figure 12.2. Correlation Between Average Certification Level and Profitability

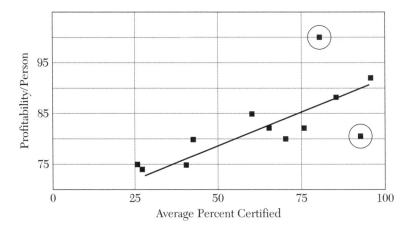

The director of training circled the two countries that had values that seemed too high or too low. He contacted those two sites to see if any other factors might be influencing the results. Profitability is a good measure because the cost of any training to achieve certification is already figured in. Had another variable been selected, such as revenue per person, a different analysis would have been required to see if the increased revenue offset the additional cost of the certification program.

HOW TO CREATE A SCATTER DIAGRAM

1. Determine the two variables you want to compare.

2. Plot one on the Y (vertical) axis and the other variable on the X (horizontal) axis.

3. Pay particular attention to the scale, as the size of the scale can distort the appearance and cause you to misinterpret the results.
4. Look at the results and decide if there appears to be any relationship.
5. If there is a significant correlation, the values cluster, suggesting a line. If the values are widely scattered, there is probably no correlation.

Rho—Correlation Coefficient

The second method to determine correlation is to do a statistical calculation called a Rho. The procedure requires you to put the first set of data in a rank order (highest to lowest, most positive to least positive, or the reverse), then do the same with the second set of data. Both sets of data should have the same quantity, because you are going to compare pairs, one datum from each set. Next, you determine the difference between the rankings. You square the differences and then total the squared differences. Finally, use the formula in Figure 12.3 to obtain a value.

Figure 12.3. Formula for Rho

$$1 - \frac{6\,(\Sigma d^2)}{n(n^2-1)}$$

HOW TO CALCULATE RHO

Key: Σ is the symbol for sum; d^2 is the symbol for differences squared. You square by multiplying a value by itself (4^2 is 16); n is the size of the sample (in a correlation it is the number of pairs); n^2-1 is the square of the pairs minus 1.
   The formula in Figure 12.3 reads as follows:

1. Multiply the sum of the squared differences by 6.
2. Next, square the number of pairs, subtract 1 from that number, and multiply the result by the number of pairs.
3. Next, divide the result from Step 2 into the result from Step 1.
4. Next subtract this new result from 1. You will get a value from somewhere between +1 and −1.

   A correlation of +.6 or −.6 indicates that there *may* be a correlation. A value of +.8 or −.8 says there is a correlation. Again, there are software packages that will calculate the Rho for you.

In the example where a scatter diagram was created to see if there appeared to be a correlation between test scores and retention, you could also analyze the data using Rho (see Table 12.4).

Table 12.4. Test Scores and Retention

Person	Test Score	Rank	Tenure in Months	Rank	d	d^2
1	77	6	10	3.5	2.5	6.25
2	88	17.5	10	3.5	14	196
3	85	14.5	8	1	13.5	182.25
4	78	7.5	16	5	2.5	6.25
5	63	2	20	8	6	36
6	60	1	30	15.5	14.5	210.25
7	72	4	25	11.5	7.5	56.25
8	70	3	20	8	5	25
9	76	5	25	11.5	6.5	42.25
10	80	9.5	18	6	3.5	12.25
11	82	11	9	2	9	81
12	88	17.5	24	10	7.5	56.25
13	98	20	20	8	12	144
14	92	19	28	13.5	5.5	30.25
15	85	14.5	32	17	2.5	6.25
16	87	16	34	19	3	9
17	84	12.5	36	20	7.5	56.25
18	80	9.5	33	18	8.5	72.25
19	78	7.5	28	13.5	6	36
20	84	12.5	30	15.5	3	9

| Total Variance | | | | | | 1273 |

Rho Formula

$$Rho = 1 - \frac{6\,(\Sigma d^2)}{n(n^2 - 1)} \qquad Rho = .043$$

1. $6(\Sigma d^2)$ is 6×1273 or 7638
2. $(n^2 - 1)$ is $20 \times 20 - 1$ or 399
3. $n(n^2 - 1)$ is 20×399 or 7980
4. $7638 \div 7980 = .957$
5. $1 - .957$ is .043

A value of .043 indicates there is no correlation between test scores and retention.

INTERIOR DESIGNERS

A forced-choice survey was sent to a random sample of two thousand interior designers and employers. One of the questions asked designers to indicate if they specialized in commercial or residential design. This allowed the team doing the study to compare the two groups' responses. This particular analysis correlated the commercial designer's responses to the residential designer on eighty-five tasks. Table 12.5 shows only a portion of the survey. The first column indicates the number of the task. The second column shows the rank for commercial designers' responses, and the third column shows what the rank is for residential designers. The fourth column is the difference between the two ranks, and the fifth column is the difference squared.

Table 12.5. Correlation Between Commercial and Residential Designers' Responses

#	Com.	Res.	d	d^2
14	6	5	1	1
15	3	4	1	1
16	17	7	10	100
22	73	70	3	9
23	55	72	17	289
24	8	17	9	81
37	45	2	43	1849
60	78	39	39	1521
61	58	40	18	324
62	61	44	17	289
63	64	51	7	49
64	33	25	8	64
65	16	58	42	1764
66	26	60	34	1156
81	77	79	2	4
82	66	69	3	9
83	85	41	44	1936
84	79	34	45	2025
85	81	27	54	2916
86	76	14	62	3844
98	65	54	11	121
99	83	75	8	64
Rho = .81				$\Sigma d^2 = 30636$

There was a high degree of correlation, *more than 80 percent* agreement, despite serious disagreement on items 37, 60, 65, 66, 69, 83, 84, 85, and 86. Items 84, 85, and 86 were valued significantly less by the residential respondents.

Correlations are very useful for showing how one variable affects another. They are particularly helpful for doing a Kirkpatrick's Level 4 evaluation by showing the relationship between training and something the organization cares about. Whether the performance management and infrastructure are or are not in place, you can correlate the level of participation in an intervention with specific business measures such as the cost of recruitment, rate of retention, customer satisfaction, length of time to proficiency, cost avoidance, and pre-tax profits. Tool 12.2 has the rules for determining correlations. It is in three parts. Part A has the rules; Part B has the formula; and Part C is a worksheet for doing the calculations if you do not have a software package that will do it for you.

TOOL 12.2A. RULES FOR CALCULATING A RANK ORDER CORRELATION COEFFICIENT (SPEARMAN RHO)

Purpose

The Rank Correlation Coefficient is used to discover whether there is a relationship between two sets of rank data. It results in a number that estimates the probability that two sets of data are related. Rho values will range from $-.99$ to $+.99$. The value (positive or negative) describes the nature of the correlation. A positive Rho value means that as one increases or decreases, the other will change similarly. A negative Rho means that as one increases or decreases, the other will do the opposite. The value itself indicates the degree or strength of correlation; the closer the value is to positive 1 or negative 1 the more significant the relationship.

You use the statistical treatment to compare two sets of rank data and to confirm the existence or absence of a relationship and the positive or negative nature of the relationship.

Results

A Rho above $+.60$ suggests there is a positive correlation, but a Rho greater than $+.80$ suggests there is a significant positive correlation. Conversely, a Rho of $-.80$ mean there is a significant negative correlation.

Steps

1. Rank the scores in two sets of data from the same sample or group.
2. If two or more scores are the same, give each of the duplicates the same ranking. The ranking is the average of the rank values they would have used if they had followed one another in rank instead of being identical. For example, if three values are the same but would have been ranked 4, 5, and 6, give all a rank of 5; then start the next ranking with 7.
3. Find the difference in the scores for each individual.
4. Square the differences.

5. Find the sum of the squares of the differences.

6. Use the Rho formula to find the correlation coefficient.

   a. Multiply the sum of the squared differences by 6

   b. Next, square the number of pairs, subtract 1 from that number, and multiply the result by the number of pairs

   c. Next, divide the result from Step b by the result from Step a.

   d. Next subtract this new result from 1. You will obtain a value from somewhere between +1 and −1.

   e. A correlation of +.6 or −.6 indicates that there *may* be a correlation. A value of +.8 or −.8 says there is a correlation. Again, there are software packages that will calculate the Rho for you.

TOOL 12.2B. FORMULA FOR RHO

$$\text{Rho} = 1 - \frac{6(\Sigma d^2)}{n(n^2 - 1)}$$

TOOL 12.2C. WORKSHEET FOR CALCULATING RHO

Rank order of the first set of scores	Rank order of the second set of scores	d—the difference between the two rankings	d^2—the difference squared
Highest score Next highest Etc.	Highest score Next highest Etc.		
			Sum (Σ) of the squared differences d^2

COMPARING RESULTS WITH EXPECTATIONS

Chi-Square Goodness of Fit or χ^2

The second statistical technique is the Chi-Square Goodness of Fit. It is particularly useful for analyzing data derived from structured interviews and surveys completed by one group with a set of expectations from another group, such as management, a regulatory agency, customers, distributors, or field personnel. For example, if you wanted to find out if the opinions held by sales representatives about what their customers expected was different from what customers said they wanted, you could interview each group separately. You could then compare their answers to find out if they were statistically different. The results would tell you if some type of intervention were required to either bring their opinions in alignment or to change one group's views. Later, after a communications program explaining what customers want, you could survey the sales representatives to see if their opinions had changed.

MANAGERS' TIME ALLOCATION

Assume it was believed that managers did not spend enough time coaching employees. A solution was to change the criteria on which managers were evaluated and train them in how to coach and give feedback. Now you are being asked to determine whether or not managers are spending a sufficient amount of time supervising (overseeing, coaching, and so forth) compared to doing administrative tasks or being engaged in activities outside of the department. First, you would need to establish the expected values. These might be known standards, managerial expectations, or industry averages. In this case, the expected times could be based on observations of outstanding managers (master performers). Next, you would measure how much time the managers spent on average in these three categories. The result would be the obtained values (see Table 12.6).

Table 12.6. Managers' Time

% Time Spent	Obtained Value (O)	Expected Value (E)	(O − E)	$\dfrac{(O - E)^2}{E}$
Supervising	35	40	5	.63
Doing paperwork	51	40	11	3.03
Outside duties	14	20	6	1.80
			Total or chi square	5.46
	Value from chi square table at .01 level of significance			9.21
	Value from chi square table at .001 level of significance			13.82

You would calculate chi-square and compare that value with the chi-square table value (see Table 12.7). Since there are three variables in the sample, the df value is 2 (3 minus 1). Given df of 2 and a .001 level of significance (1 in 1,000 that your conclusions are wrong), the chi-square table value is 13.82 and exceeds the obtained value of 5.46. Therefore, your conclusion would be that the managers' use of time is not significantly different from what was expected. If you accepted a greater chance of error, you could use the column .01 (1 chance in 100). The conclusion is the same.

Table 12.7. Excerpt from Table of Chi-Square Values[4]

df $(n-1)$	Criterion Levels	
	.01	.001
1	6.64	10.83
②	⑨.21	⑬.82
3	11.34	16.27
4	13.28	18.46
5	15.09	20.52

Chi-Square Goodness of Fit is not a frequently used statistic; however, when you want to know if one set of results is significantly different from what is expected, it can be very helpful.

Tool 12.3 is in three parts. The first part has the steps for applying the chi-square analysis; the second part has a worksheet that you can use for your specific situation; and the third part has the statistical table you would use to compare your results.

Tool 12.4 has guidelines for analyzing data from structured interviews using chi-square to determine whether the respondents' answers match what is expected as determined by another source, such as management. It is in two parts. Part A has the rules and Part B is a worksheet that you can adapt to your needs.

TOOL 12.3A. RULES FOR APPLYING CHI-SQUARE GOODNESS OF FIT

Purpose

Chi square determines the existence of a significant difference between two sets of data. It does this by comparing obtained frequencies with expected frequencies and then calculating the difference. Chi square can be used with samples as small as six.

Chi square allows you to say that the difference between groups is real. Once the chi square value is calculated, it is compared to values on the chi square table. The relationship between the chi square value and the criterion value tells you whether a difference exists and the significance of that difference.

Steps

1. Create a table to capture obtained and expected values. See Worksheet B.

2. Enter expected values. Expected values reflect some standard, for example, optimal time at task, test scores of master performers, or management expectation.

3. Conduct some measurement activity to find the obtained values (interviews, document checks, observations).

4. Enter obtained values on the worksheet.

5. Find the difference between the obtained and expected values by subtracting the expected from the obtained.

6. Square the results of Step 5 and divide by the expected value. This gives you the variance.

7. Find the sum of the variances. This is the value of chi square.

8. Compare the chi square value with the appropriate value from Table C, Distribution of Chi Square Values. (Note that this table is frequently labeled "Distribution of X^2 in statistics books.)

TOOL 12.3B. WORKSHEET FOR CALCULATING CHI-SQUARE

	Obtained Value	Expected Value	*(O − E)*	$\frac{(O - E)^2}{E}$ Variance*
		Sum of the variance or chi square		
		Value from Chi Square Table at a level of significance		

*Variance is the square of the standard deviation. Variance is the state of being variable, variant, or in disagreement.

TOOL 12.3C. DISTRIBUTION OF CHI-SQUARE VALUES

df (n − 1)	Criterion Levels			
	.10	**.05**	**.01**	**.001**
1	2.71	3.84	6.64	10.83
2	4.61	5.99	9.21	13.82
3	6.25	7.82	11.34	16.27
4	7.78	9.49	13.28	18.46
5	9.24	11.07	15.09	20.52
6	10.65	12.59	16.81	22.46
7	12.02	14.07	18.48	24.32
8	13.36	15.51	20.09	26.12
9	14.68	16.92	21.67	27.88
10	15.99	18.31	23.21	29.59
11	17.28	19.68	24.73	31.26
12	18.55	21.03	26.22	32.91
13	19.81	22.36	23.69	34.53
14	21.06	23.69	29.14	36.12
15	22.31	24.99	30.58	37.70

This table stops at a sample size of ten.

.10 is the percentage of time you might be wrong, or 10 percent, or one in ten.
.05 is the percentage of time you might be wrong, or 5 percent, or one in twenty.
.01 is the percentage of time you might be wrong, or 1 percent, or one in a hundred.
.001 is the percentage of time you might bc wrong, or .1 percent, or one in a thousand.

If you have a larger sample, or can accept a higher percentage of error, consult a statistics book of mathematical tables.

Excerpted from *Statistical Tables for Biological, Agricultural, and Medical Research, 2nd Ed.* by Ronald Fisher and Frank Yates (London: Longman Group Ltd.; previously published by Oliver & Boyd, Edinburgh, 1943), p. 31.

TOOL 12.4A. RULES FOR ANALYZING DATA DERIVED FROM STRUCTURED INTERVIEWS USING CHI-SQUARE OR RHO

Purpose

Structured interviews were developed to take advantage of the strengths of open interviews and forced-choice surveys. They allow for people to respond any way they wish instead of picking a pre-determined response, yet lend themselves to large audiences, statistical treatment of the results, and the ability to compare the results with data from other sources.

How to Analyze the Results

1. Count the number of times a response was given.

2. Determine the mean or average number of responses, and determine the standard deviation. Responses that received points in excess of the mean plus the standard deviation or less than the mean minus standard deviation are considered statistically important.

3. Compare the responses to an "expected" response. You could use a statistic such as a rank correlation coefficient (Rho), which is used to discover whether there is a relationship between two sets of data or the Chi Square Goodness of Fit, which is used to determine whether two groups' answers differ significantly.

4. Compare each response to some attribute of the target audience, such as age, years of experience, completion of training, and so forth, to see if they differ.

TOOL 12.4B. SAMPLE STRUCTURED INTERVIEW FORM

Question goes here

	Mgmt	Respondents A B C D E	
List of expected answers			*n*
Answer #1			
Answer #2			
Answer #3			
Blank			
Blank			
Total or sum Mean Standard deviation			Σ μ S

Notes:

Note: Σ is the symbol for the sum total.   μ is the symbol for the mean or average.   S is the symbol for standard deviation.

PRE- AND POST-COMPARISONS

The *t* test is designed to find out if there is a difference between two sets of data, specifically two means. For example, you might want to know whether error rates went up or down after some intervention, such as making the training self-paced on CD-ROM, adding help screens, or migrating to a new software program. First, you need baseline data, that is, the number of errors prior to the change. Next, you would need to gather error data at some point after the change. Using the before and after values, you would calculate the gain or loss, then sum the gain or loss values for a total. Next, you would square each gain or loss value and sum those values. Next, you apply the *t* value formula to calculate *t* and compare your result to the *t* Table. Table 12.8 shows how the before and after error rates are compared to see if they are significantly different using a *t* test.

Table 12.8. Before and After Error Rates

Person	Errors Before	Errors After	d = Difference Gain or Loss	d^2 Is Difference Squared
1	35	12	23	529
2	43	26	17	289
3	45	31	14	196
4	47	23	24	576
5	44	32	12	144
6	41	22	19	361
7	45	29	16	256
8	47	36	11	111
9	50	47	3	9
10	33	31	2	4
11	29	18	11	121
12	27	21	6	6
Totals			(Σd) 158	(Σd^2) 2642

Formula:

$$t = \frac{\Sigma d}{\sqrt{\dfrac{(n)\Sigma d^2 - (\Sigma d)^2}{n - 1}}}$$

$t = 6.37$

Here is the calculation, starting at the bottom.

$$\frac{(n)\Sigma d^2 - (\Sigma d)^2}{n - 1}$$

Table 12.8 (*Continued*)

1. $12 \times 2642 - 158^2$ becomes $31704 - 24964$ or 6740.
2. Divide 6740 by $12 - 1$ or 11, which is 612.7.
3. To find the square root of 612.7, use a calculator. The answer is 24.8.
4. Divide 158 by 24.8 and the t value is 6.37.

Note: If you don't have access to a calculator and want to use a square root table, here are the steps.

1. Start by rounding 612.7 to 613.
2. Move the decimal point two places to the left to 6.13.
3. Look in a square root table under 6.13, where you find 2.476 and round to 2.48 (2.48 × 2.48 is 6.13).
4. Move the decimal point to the right one space or 24.8 (24.8 × 24.8 is 613).

As you can see in the table, given a df of 11 (12–1) and .001 level of significance, the t table value is 4.437. Since the calculated t value of 6.37 is larger than the t table value, you would conclude that there was a significant increase in errors after the change. Table 12.9 is an excerpt from a t table.

Table 12.9. Distribution of *t* Probability

df	.1	.05	.01	.001
(11)	1.796	2.201	3.106	(4.437)
12	1.782	2.179	3.055	4.318
13	1.771	2.160	3.012	4.221
14	1.761	2.145	2.977	4.140
15	1.753	2.131	2.947	4.073

The analysis methods described in this book are intended for use with small samples with some tolerance for error; however, you should always rely on more than one source of data to increase you level of confidence. Tool 12.5 has the rules for performing t tests. It is in four parts: the rules, a worksheet, the formula, and the statistical table.

TOOL 12.5A. RULES FOR USING A TWO-TAILED *t* TEST

Purpose

The t Test is used to determine whether there was a gain in skills or knowledge. It is used to calculate the difference between two sets of data from the same group. Like chi square, it was specifically developed for small samples.

Use it to judge the adequacy of a training program or implementation of other interventions. A *t* value larger than the value from the *t* table indicates a gain. A *t* value less than the criterion score value from the *t* table would indicate a loss.

Steps

1. Calculate the difference between before and after values for each person or item in the sample.

2. Square each difference.

3. Total the differences or Σd.

4. Total the squared difference values or Σd^2.

5. Use the values from Step 3 and Step 4 with the t-test formula to calculate the *t* value.

6. Start near the bottom of the formula

$$\frac{(n)\Sigma d^2 - (\Sigma d)^2}{n - 1}$$

This formula reads

a. Multiply the total of the squared differences (Step 4 above) by the size of the sample.

b. Now square the sum of the differences (Step 3 above).

c. Now subtract b from a.

d. Take the answer from c and divide by one less than the sample size $(n - 1)$.

e. Take the result of d and find the square root (most calculators and spreadsheets will do this or follow the steps below).

   e1. Round the number to get rid of decimal points.

   e2. The number has to be between 0 and 100. If it greater than 100 (in the example 613 is greater than 100), move the decimal point to the LEFT 2 positions at a time. Keep track of how many times you have to move the decimal point (for 613, it was moved two positions only once and the result is 6.13).

   e3. Look up the number in a table of square roots (in the example, look up 6.13). This result is 2.48. In other words, 2.48 times 2.48 equals 6.13.

   e4. Because you moved the decimal point in Step 2, you have to move it back. You moved it two positions, but only once. Now you move the decimal point the opposite direction (RIGHT) the same number of times, but only one position at a time. From the table you will find that the square root of 6.13 is 2.48, so the square root of 613 is 24.8.

f. Now divide the sum of the squares (from Step 3) by the square root (from Step 5e).

g. The result is the *t* value.

7. Now go to the *t* table. Subtract one from the sample size, go to the column with the criterion level of your choice and find the value (see Table D below)

8. Compare the value on the *t* table with the *t* value you got above.

9. If your *t* value is higher than what is on the *t* table, then the difference in the two sets of data is significant. If the value is lower, there is no significant difference.

Note: In statistics books the table is probably labeled "Distribution of *t* Probability."

TOOL 12.5B. *t* TEST WORKSHEET

Sample Size	Data from Before	Data from After	*d* = Difference (Gain or Loss)	*d²* = Difference Squared
		Totals	Σd (sum of the differences)	Σd^2 (sum of the differences squared)

TOOL 12.5C. FORMULA FOR CALCULATING *t* SCORES

$$t = \frac{\Sigma d}{\sqrt{\dfrac{(n)\Sigma d^2 - (\Sigma d)^2}{n-1}}}$$

TOOL 12.5D. DISTRIBUTION OF *t* PROBABILITY TABLE

df	.1	.05	.01	.001
11	1.796	2.201	3.106	4.437
12	1.782	2.179	3.055	4.318
13	1.771	2.160	3.012	4.221
14	1.761	2.145	2.977	4.140
15	1.753	2.131	2.947	4.073
16	1.746	2.120	2.921	4.015
17	1.740	2.110	2.898	3.965
18	1.734	2.101	2.878	3.922
19	1.729	2.093	2.861	3.883
20	1.725	2.086	2.845	3.850
21	1.721	2.080	2.831	3.819
22	1.717	2.074	2.819	3.792
23	1.714	2.069	2.807	3.767
24	1.711	2.064	2.797	3.745
25	1.708	2.060	2.787	3.725
26	1.706	2.056	2.779	3.707
27	1.703	2.052	2.771	3.690
28	1.701	2.048	2.763	3.674
29	1.699	2.045	2.756	3.659
30	1.697	2.042	2.750	3.646
40	1.684	2.021	2.704	3.551
60	1.671	2.000	2.660	3.460
120	1.658	1.980	2.617	3.373
Infinity	2.645	1.960	2.576	3.291

Excerpted from *Statistical Tables for Biological, Agricultural, and Medical Research, 2nd Ed.* by Ronald Fisher and Frank Yates (London: Longman Group Ltd.; previously published by Oliver & Boyd, Edinburgh, 1943), p. 30.

MISSTEPS

Here are some of the common mistakes people make:

1. They try to prove cause and effect, for example, that sales increased because of a training program or that costs went down because of a training program. It is very difficult to show that one thing caused another thing

to happen unless you can isolate all of the other variables that could have influenced the results. The factors that can influence results are things like the skill of the manager, the economy of the region, the strength of the competition in the territory, and so on.

2. They fail to take advantage of the abilities of others in the organization who have command of software that would help in the analysis of data.

3. They apply analysis techniques without fully understanding their purpose, strengths, and tradeoffs.

TIPS AND TECHNIQUES

Here are some suggestions for how to sample people or things:

1. Many spreadsheet programs will calculate square roots, correlations, and *t* tests.

2. If you are going to do *t* tests, chi-square tests, and correlations and your software does not automatically tell you if your values are significant or not, then find a book of tables and copy just those you will use. Keep them handy.

3. Develop a plan for how you will analyze the data. Develop the data-collection tools and practice using them.

SUMMARY

This chapter is about how to apply three commonly used inferential statistical treatments to measure the significance of a relationship or a difference in results. The inferential statistical methods include:

• Rho or correlation coefficient, designed to determine if there is a relationship between the value of one variable, such as participation in training or test scores, and another variable, such as costs, profits, retention of employees or customers, product quality, or some other factor you suspect is influenced by the first variable.

• Chi-Square Goodness of Fit, designed to compare data derived from interviews or surveys with a second set of data that represents the expected; the analysis shows whether the two sets of data are significantly different.

• The *t* test, designed to measure if there is a difference between what people felt or thought at one point in time compared to what they felt or thought at another point in time.

Both descriptive and inferential statistics will help you to determine whether action is required and to measure the effects of your actions.

WHERE TO LEARN MORE

Levine, D. M., Berenson, M. L., and Stephan, D. *Statistics for Managers Using Microsoft Excel with Disk* (Upper Saddle River, NJ: Prentice Hall, 1999).

Rowntree, D. *Statistics Without Tears: A Primer for Non-Mathematicians* (Boston, MA: Allyn & Bacon, 1981).

The Memory Jogger and other publications by GOAl/QPC. See http://www.goalqpc.com

NOTES

1. Degrees of freedom is the realization that if you want a specific value (like a total or mean), all but one in your sample can assume any value possible, because once the other values are set, the remaining value is decided.

2. Spearman Rho Correlation Coefficient is a statistical treatment to determine the correlation for ordinal data (data that are in rank order from the smallest to the largest, such as means, frequencies).

3. Pearson Product Moment is a statistical treatment to determine correlations for interval data (data that are in equal units of measurement, such as Fahrenheit thermometers).

4. The Distribution of Chi Square (Table 12.7) and the Distribution of *t* Probability Tables (Table 12.9) are excerpted from *Statistical Tables for Biological, Agricultural, and Medical Research, 2nd Ed.* by Ronald Fisher and Frank Yates (London: Longman Group Ltd.; previously published by Oliver & Boyd, Edinburgh, 1943). The work of Fisher and Yates is cited in most, if not all, statistical textbooks. To find the complete tables, consult statistical books still in print.

Index

About the Author

*J*udith Hale has dedicated her career to helping management professionals develop effective, practical ways to improve individual and organizational performance. She has used the techniques, processes, and job aids described in this book in her own consulting work, which has spanned twenty-five years. Judith's clients speak of the practicality of her approach and the proven results it yields. She is able to explain complex ideas so that people understand their relevance and can apply them to their own situations. She is able to help others come to a shared understanding about what to do and how to commit to action.

Her consulting firm, Hale Associates, was founded in 1974 and enjoys long-term relationships with a variety of major corporations. The services her firm provides include consultation on alignment, assessment, certification, evaluation, integration of performance improvement systems, performance management, and strategic planning.

She is the author of *The Performance Consultant's Fieldbook* and *Performance-Based Certification.* Her book *Achieving a Leadership Role for Training* describes how training can apply the standards espoused by the International Standards Organization and Baldrige to its own operation. She was the topic editor for *Designing Work Groups, Jobs, and Work Flow* and for *Designing Cross-Functional Business Processes* and the author of the chapter "The Hierarchy of Interventions" in the *Sourcebook for Performance Improvement.* Judith also wrote *The Training Manager Competencies: The Standards,* as well as *The Training Function Standards* and *Standards for Qualifying Trainers,* and she put together the *Workbook and Job Aids for Good Fair Tests,* and was a contributor to *What Smart Trainers Know,* edited by Lorraine Ukens (2001, Jossey-Bass/Pfeiffer).

Judith is an appointed member of the Illinois Occupational Skills Standard and Credentialing Council. She is a past president of the International Society for Performance Improvement (ISPI) and of the Chicago chapter of the National Society of Performance and Instruction (NSPI) and has served on NSPI's President's Advisory Council. NSPI named her Outstanding Member of the Year in 1987. She has also served as president of the International Board of Standards for Performance and Instruction and president of the Chicago chapter of the Industrial Relations Research Association (IRRA). She was a commercial arbitrator with the American Arbitration Association and has been a member of the American Society for Training and Development (ASTD) for many years. She was nominated for ASTD's Gordon Bliss Award in 1995. She taught graduate courses in management for fourteen years for the Insurance School of Chicago and received the school's Outstanding Educator award in 1986.

Judith speaks regularly at ASTD International, ASTD Technical Skills, the International Society for Performance Improvement, and Lakewood's annual training conferences.

Judith holds a B.A. from Ohio State University (communication), an M.A. from Miami University (theater management), and a Ph.D. from Purdue University (instructional design, with minors in organizational communication and adult education).

How to Use the CD-ROM

SYSTEM REQUIREMENTS

Windows PC

- 486 or Pentium processor-based personal computer
- Microsoft Windows 95 or Windows NT 3.51 or later
- Minimum RAM: 8 MB for Windows 95 and NT
- Available space on hard disk: 8 MB Windows 95 and NT
- 2X speed CD-ROM drive or faster

Netscape 3.0 or higher browser or MS Internet Explorer 3.0 or higher

Macintosh

- Macintosh with a 68020 or higher processor or Power Macintosh
- Apple OS version 7.0 or later
- Minimum RAM: 12 MB for Macintosh
- Available space on hard disk: 6 MB Macintosh
- 2X speed CD-ROM drive or faster

Netscape 3.0 or higher browser or MS Internet Explorer 3.0 or higher

NOTE: This CD requires Netscape 3.0 or MS Internet Explorer 3.0 or higher. You can download these products using the links on the CD-ROM Help Page.

GETTING STARTED

Insert the CD-ROM into your drive. The CD-ROM will usually launch automatically. If it does not, click on the CD-ROM drive on your computer to launch. You will see an opening page. You can click on this page or wait for it to fade to the Copyright Page. After you click to agree to the terms of the Copyright Page, the Home Page will appear.

MOVING AROUND

Use the buttons at the left of each screen or the underlined text at the bottom of each screen to move among the menu pages. To view a document listed on one of the menu pages, simply click on the name of the document. To quit a document at any time, click the box at the upper right-hand corner of the screen.

Use the scrollbar at the right of the screen to scroll up and down each page.

To quit the CD-ROM, you can click the Quit option at the bottom of each menu page, hit Control-Q, or click the box at the upper right-hand corner of the screen.

TO DOWNLOAD DOCUMENTS

Open the document you wish to download. Under the File pulldown menu, choose Save As. Save the document onto your hard drive with a different name. It is important to use a different name, otherwise the document may remain a read-only file.

You can also click on your CD drive in Windows Explorer and select a document to copy it to your hard drive and rename it.

IN CASE OF TROUBLE

If you experience difficulty using this CD-ROM, please follow these steps:

1. Make sure your hardware and systems configurations conform to the systems requirements noted under "Systems Requirements" above.

2. Review the installation procedure for your type of hardware and operating system. It is possible to reinstall the software if necessary.

3. You may call Jossey-Bass/Pfeiffer Customer Service at (800) 956-7739 between the hours of 8 A.M. and 5 P.M. Pacific Time, and ask for Technical Support. It is also possible to contact Technical Support by e-mail at *techsupport@JosseyBass.com*.

Please have the following information available:

- Type of computer and operating system
- Version of Windows or Mac OS being used
- Any error messages displayed
- Complete description of the problem.

(It is best if you are sitting at your computer when making the call.)